My Crazy Speedway

Bert Harkins

London League Publications Ltd

My Crazy Speedway World
Bert Harkins

© Bert Harkins. Foreword © Norman Christie. Introductions © Richard Clark, Mike Hunter and Mark Lewisohn.

The moral right of Bert Harkins to be identified as the author has been asserted.

Cover design © Stephen McCarthy; front cover based on an original design by Norman Christie.

Cover photos: Front: Bert riding for Scotland. Back: top: captain of the Wembley Lions (JSC), bottom: riding for Edinburgh Monarchs (JSC).

All photographs are as credited to the photographer or provider of the photo. No copyright has been intentionally breached; please contact London League Publications Ltd if you believe there has been a breach of copyright.

The photo credits are as follows: JSC: John Somerville Collection, including photos from Wright Wood, Alf Weedon and Mike Patrick, any uncredited photos are from Bert Harkins's private collection.

A CIP catalogue record for this book is available from the British Library.

First published in Great Britain in February 2018 by London League Publications Ltd, PO Box 65784, London NW2 9NS.

ISBN: 978-1-909885-16-5.

Original front cover design by Norman Christie.

Cover graphic design by Stephen McCarthy Graphic Design, 46, Clarence Road, London N15 5BB.

Editing and layout by Peter Lush.

Printed and bound in Great Britain by Ashford Colour Press Ltd, Gosport, Hants PO13 0FW.

This book is dedicated to Edith and to speedway fans everywhere.

Foreword

I was 10 years old when I first saw Bert Harkins, and the vision still remains etched in my mind. I'd been walking near my home in Glasgow when I saw a boy of my own age furiously cycling around a dusty oval. Although the day was hot he was wearing a leather flying jacket, gloves, wellington boots and … a pudding basin crash helmet. At each corner, he put down his left foot and deliberately encouraged the rear wheel of his small bicycle to slide.

When he stopped to catch breath I spoke to him. He was quietly spoken but talked at length about a sport I'd never heard of – speedway. After he left to return to his racing, I realised I'd met a likeable and fearless individual, totally focussed on enjoying himself. In the 65 years since then, he's done nothing to change that opinion.

Later, we became pals and would go out cycling together. He showed me how to slide a bike, how to pull wheelies and how to sit on the handlebars and ride backwards. One cold winter's evening, he suggested joining him to ride on the deep snow. We went to a steep hill within the housing estate and spent an hour pedalling downhill and throwing our bikes into a slide at the point where the hill came to a T-junction at the bottom. After a while, Bert suggested I should sit facing forward on the handlebars of his bike while he pedalled. I should have known what was coming. Balanced in that precarious position, with my heels resting on the front wheel nuts, he set off and as we raced downhill I was aware of a scuffle behind me … it was Bert jumping off. With me perched helplessly on the handlebars, the bike sped to the bottom, continuing straight across the junction, bumping over the kerbstone and onto the pavement where I was thrown forward into a hedge, shaking off the snow. After a moment's silence I could hear the sound of laughter from the top of the hill.

His mischief didn't end when we progressed to motorbikes. Most Wednesday evenings were spent at the Avon Valley Motorcycle Club and the ride from Glasgow to the clubhouse was along dark country roads. Usually, I'd ride pillion on Bert's machine but on odd occasions, he'd sit behind me on my bike … and they were 'odd' occasions. On corners, he'd purposely lean out to 'the opposite side' and when I took corrective action, he'd lean the other way, and so it continued left and right, resulting in numerous wobbles. On the straights, it wasn't unusual to feel his hands on my shoulders, which was a prelude to him standing on the saddle behind me and from that position he'd continue shifting his weight from left to right. He evidently had more faith in my ability to stay in control than I had.

Things didn't get any easier when we progressed to cars. The old Austin Cambridge I owned broke down late one night in the centre of Glasgow, and I walked to Bert's house to ask if he could tow me home. He drove me back to town and fixed a shorter than average rope to the cars, then set off. With my car about six feet behind Bert's, I immediately knew the run was not going to be easy. He drove at great speed through the quiet streets, and just as I was settling into the rhythm, his left indicator began flashing. Was he indicating he was pulling into the roadside? … No …he was heading in the direction of a multi-storey car park, which in the 1960s was free of barriers at the entrance. He sped through the entrance and dragged me up the spiral ramps to the top floor where he did a wide and fast U-turn before heading for the downward ramp to return at excessive speed to the main road. When he eventually pulled over, his car was shaking with laughter.

Around that time, Bert's parents relocated to a house immediately behind my parents' home; an arrangement which made it more convenient for us to meet. However, it also made it easier for Bert to get up to mischief, particularly at times when my folks were on holiday and I was alone in the house. On these occasions, on leaving for work in the mornings, I'd often open the outside door to be struck by assorted pieces of timber, a garden rake and dustbin – objects which Bert had carefully propped up against the backdoor at some stage during the night. At other times, I found it difficult to leave the house due to the presence of a rope he'd tied between the exterior door handle and the fence.

He enjoyed getting up to mischief, but when it came to riding in cycle speedway, Bert was no longer a prankster. From the moment he put on a body colour, he was totally focussed on winning. He was a fierce rider, but was fair and never gave up until the finishing line was crossed.

When he progressed to motorbike speedway, he displayed the same never-say-die approach to racing, often surprising established riders, and himself, by crossing the line first. It took a few seasons before he gained heat leader status and when he did, he never looked back. He moved from his native Scotland to race for English teams and during British winters, spent many seasons collecting trophies from rides in Australia. He also raced in South Africa and Israel and when speedway became popular in North America, Bert Harkins became the first British rider to be signed as a member of a USA speedway team – the Bakersfield Bandits. He became firm friends with world class riders from many countries, including Barry Briggs and Ivan Mauger, and was included in the Briggs/Mauger World Champions series – the only Scot to appear in the line-up. A few years ago, I met Ivan Mauger at his home in Australia and the six times world champion was full of praise for Bert. "We liked to include Haggis Harkins in the series" he said. "He was always value for money and was liked by the crowds for his colourful showmanship. He was a trier and easy to deal with … never troublesome." Ivan obviously had no knowledge of the younger Bert.

For someone like Bert Harkins – who came from a world where he and his pals would normally become tradesmen, shopkeepers or accountants – to end up in a career racing motorbikes, with world champions among his friends, is no mean accomplishment.

This book tells how that young leather-clad 10 year old went on to become a successful speedway rider, travelling the world participating in a sport he loved, while collecting fans and friends along the way.

Norman Christie

Norman Christie, my schooldays friend from Glasgow, survived all the pranks I played on him and went on to design building services installations for projects all over Scotland. He also spent years living and working in Hong Kong, Qatar and Botswana. Now retired, he and his wife Karen live in Glasgow where he writes articles for various publications and lists travelling among his interests. He has now swapped painting tartan on my speedway helmets for painting watercolours. Norman did the original design for the front cover of this book which depicts my coming out of Scotland to travel the speedway world. Thanks Nosko, **Bert**.

Introduction: All about Bert Harkins

We felt that Bert's long and varied career justified three introductions. Richard Clark, editor of the Speedway Star *has known Bert for many years; Mike Hunter is the leading Edinburgh Monarchs speedway historian, while Mark Lewisohn (the acknowledged world authority on The Beatles) first met Bert as a Wembley Lions fan and they are now close friends.*

If there's a more popular, jovial, extensively travelled and well known former speedway star than Bert Harkins then our paths haven't crossed. Or, for that matter, one who has maintained such a huge love affair with the sport all those years. As ambassadors go, speedway couldn't ask for better. Bert and I go so far back that I know virtually all his corny jokes. In fact, we became acquainted in 1970, not that Bert knew that at the time. He was riding for Wembley. I was supporting Wimbledon. And, as anyone who develops a passion for a certain team will know, that's hardly a recipe for a lifelong friendship.

Long before I reached the heady heights of being allowed to talk to these titans of the track, my time was spent cheering on those wearing red and yellow race jackets – and booing anyone who wasn't. The first time I saw Bert ride, in 1970, passed without much incident. A flip through the *Speedway Star* files tells me it was Thursday 18 June, Wimbledon 43 Wembley 34, Bert heading back home with five points to his name.

But, almost 12 months to the day later – 3 June 1971 to be exact – we fell out big time! Yet again, Bert would have been oblivious to this at the time. On the face of it, a 45–33 victory for Wimbledon over Wembley would suggest most Dons fans left Plough Lane that evening fairly happy with how things had gone.

Not me. My numero uno in those days was Ronnie Moore – still a class performer despite being in the twilight of a fabulous career. On this particular June evening, Ronnie won Heats 3, 5 and 9 at a canter. Heading into the final Heat 13, Dons had it comfortably sewn up at 42–30 and, seemingly, Ronnie's maximum was about to follow suit.

He and partner Cyril Maidment faced Bert and team-mate Tony Clarke. At that point, the two Wembley Lions had amassed one point between them, courtesy of a Bert third place. So what does Bert go and do in that Heat 13? Beat Ronnie Moore, that's what!

0, 1, ef, 0, 3. That was Mr Harkins's night's work.

Some 46 years on, I've watched Bert eating pasta in most countries where speedway bikes go left as we've shared countless trips to World Finals, Inter-Continentals, Grands Prix, World Cups and the like. I've also watched Bert being the only one brave enough to risk the pits-side barbecue on some of those trips.

Ever-cheery, ever-enthusiastic, ever-willing to chat with the hundreds of fans who recognise him to this day, all of them anxious to share the fond memories they have of Bert Harkins the speedway rider. He's that rarest of breed. A proven champion who completely understands someone's love of speedway – because he's still fanatical about it himself. Just witness the hours he's prepared to put in furthering the cause of the World Speedway Riders' Association. I've had some absolutely fantastic times with Bert over the years.

Thursday 3 June 1971 is not one of them.

Richard Clark

Bert Harkins is one of the great characters of the Speedway world, and I'm very happy to say that for the first 10 years of his excellent career Bert was an Edinburgh and Coatbridge Monarch.

I know he had been a fan in the 1950s so I suppose he might have started his career in the early 1960s with his local Glasgow team had they been running, but happily for us he made the journey through to Old Meadowbank where Ian Hoskins was running the Monarchs. Then as now, he seemed a good-natured and happy-go-lucky fellow, but while that was true this hid his great determination to make the grade at speedway.

He travelled through every week for a second half ride, and in the early days Bert would go anywhere for a chance to race, something that junior riders of today need to be more willing to do than they seem to be.

It was quite tough to break into a team in the 1960s, even though Bert was winning his second half heats (often wearing a Birmingham race jacket – 'B' for Bert!) He had a couple of matches standing in for injured riders in 1962 and 1963, but it was July 1964 when he really broke through. On 8 August he stepped up from reserve for the Provincial Riders Championship qualifying round to replace Tommy Roper, and scored 10 points, just one less than George Hunter and Charlie Monk. He had a race win over George and Trevor Redmond in his second ride.

That was Bert established in the team but it certainly wasn't the end of the hard work. He was an important member of the team in the early British League days, 1965 to 1967, the final years at Meadowbank before we were forced out by the Commonwealth Games.

We didn't want to have to move to Coatbridge but we had to, and for Bert it was a good move as he became a true heat leader at that stage of his career. He travelled out to Australia and that was an important part of his development. The old Rider Control sent him to Newcastle at one point but thankfully that didn't happen. By 1969 he was averaging almost 8 and he took over as team captain from Doug Templeton who had held the job since 1960. Doug and Ian Hoskins had some sort of disagreement if I recall rightly.

Unfortunately, after 1969 the Monarchs bowed out as presumably Hoskins decided that Coatbridge wasn't a good long-term home for the club, too far from Edinburgh. He sold the licence to the returning Wembley Lions and Bert went too along with Reidar Eide, Wayne Briggs and Brian Collins.

We followed the former Monarchs' riders of course and in Bert's case that was a couple of memorable years at Wembley (maybe the best years of Bert's career), then Sheffield, Wimbledon for a good spell and even Bakersfield Bandits. During this time Bert really became a globetrotting star and rode in the World Pairs Final, and many international events around the world.

Edinburgh Monarchs restarted in 1977 and new promoter Mike Parker turned right away to Bert to captain the side. He was a Monarch for three more years, becoming one of the eight Monarchs' riders who have ridden 10 seasons with the club. He had one final year at Milton Keynes at the age of 40 and then hung up the leathers with the tartan edgings.

Bert was always a proud Scot and promoted his country wherever he went. That has continued into retirement and of course he has been very prominent in the WSRA and at gatherings of former riders everywhere. He comes up to Edinburgh quite regularly, including many Scottish WSRA events, and sponsored the Scottish Open at Armadale one year. He's been the official Scotland team manager and has sponsored many young Scottish riders.

I suppose one other thing to say about Bert is that he has never changed. He hasn't put any weight on, not visibly anyway, and he looks as though he could race next season. I think he is rightly proud of what he has achieved in speedway and he is still one of the friendliest guys around, always a pleasure to meet.

I really hope he gets everything into this book because he has had an incredible speedway life, and more than likely knows more people in the sport than anyone else. I'm very honoured to be asked to contribute to his book on behalf of the Monarchs. Bert Haggis Bertola Harkins, a great life!

Mike Hunter

Pride of the Lions

At the age of 13, Bert Harkins was my Number 1.

Every Saturday afternoon in summer 1971 I'd be outside the pits at Wembley Stadium (the original one, twin towers) getting rider autographs and snapping the black-and-white photos my pocket-money would allow. I have them still: here's Ole Olsen and Christer Lofqvist, here's Brian Collins and Dave Jessup, and here's me with Bert Harkins, when he was Wembley Lions' cherished captain and I was a pre-pubescent lad. Bert's not the tallest of men and I'm chin-high on tiptoes.

Now, in 2018, Bert isn't only that golden memory, he's my pal. Our paths chanced to re-cross a few years back and I found that he lives two miles down the road. Our wives get along just fine too, and a comfortable friendship has developed. When I first went to his home, Bert hung his Lions race jacket on the door outside, so I'd know which house was his. I roared, appropriately enough.

Wembley Lions were my reservoir of passion for a sport new to me in 1970 to 1971. The revival of league racing at our national stadium, 14 years after it ended, gave Londoners a refreshed Saturday-night out – and for legions of cinder fans of the 1930s to 1950s, speedway was suddenly back in their weekly lives. Wembley's return gave the sport a surge in profile and attendances and everything seemed up-up-up. In the Lions' comeback season, Bert was a strong heat-leader and huge crowd favourite, worthy of it. In season two, 1971, he was our Number One and captain. That Haggis nickname, those St Andrews leathers, the white boots ... he was the proud Scotsman we Sassenachs loved.

I remember 1971 as Bert's best season in the sport, and how we all shared his agony when a broken collarbone decimated his chances of qualifying for the World Final. What rotten luck. Worse yet, the Lions were forced to fold after those two memorable years, our closure accentuating a decline in British speedway which seems, so miserably, to have no end.

In 1974, when Bert was riding for Wimbledon [shudder], he seriously injured his back in a horrible crash at Plough Lane. *Speedway Star* said he was recovering in Stanmore Orthopaedic Hospital, so, all of 17, I went along to see him and chat about those two Lions seasons. Flat on his back, not yet sure he'd walk again, he was still the same friendly soul with a quip and a laugh. Bert always talks to people and people always talk to Bert, which is why he's been popular with speedway supporters all these decades.

Bert's written words always made a good impression too. His column in the monthly *Speedway Express* was, to my mind, the sport's most entertaining and humorous read. So all's well that publisher Peter Lush (bravo) has encouraged Bert to write this autobiography. I look forward to reading of a young Harkins hurtling round those hard-fenced old Scottish stadia on the track spare, and of his racing in Australia, America and South Africa, and of course I want to read about his years at Wimbledon [shudder] and ... Wembley.

Here again will be the ever-polished Bertola, Captain Harkins striding out to Fučík's *Entry of the Gladiators* – that stirring music, his white boots glinting in Wembley's bright lights. Ah, those memories of our opening night in 1971 when he scored a 12-point maximum to the delight of us thousands of Lions supporters in the magnificent old stadium. You could, I swear, hear the roar in Hendon.

Mark Lewisohn

Publisher's note

One nice thing about running a sports publishing company is that occasionally I get to meet my heroes. In rugby league I have met many of the sport's great players through publishing their books. But in many cases I never saw them play because I only started watching the sport in 1980. Interviewing the Hendon Football Club stars from the 1960s and 1970s – my childhood heroes – was a delight when I was working on the Hendon FC club history.

As with Mark Lewisohn, speedway came into my life in 1970, when a friend took me to Wembley. It went from being something to do on a Saturday night to a major interest. My parents were horrified that I was spending even more time involved in sport, but did agree I could go to Newport in April 1971 to watch Wembley's 'home' meeting with Belle Vue.

Sometimes, though fortunately rarely for me, your heroes let you down. That has never been the case with Bert, who is one of my speedway heroes. He agreed to write the Foreword to *When the Lions Roared*, where I worked with John Chaplin on the post-war history of speedway's most famous league team. I then suggested that we publish this book. I expected to have to 'ghost write' it, but this is all Bert's own work, ably supported and encouraged by Edith.

It is encouraging to see more speedway books being published, recording the history of this remarkable sport. Through Bert's connections with the Williams family, I got an agreement with them to work on a biography of Freddie Williams, another Wembley legend, which will be published within the next year. More books about the Lions former stars are planned for the future. The Wembley Lions will probably never ride again, but the team will live on in history, its achievements recorded in print.

Peter Lush

London League Publications Ltd would like to thank everyone who has helped with this book, Norman Christie, Richard Clark, Mike Hunter and Mark Lewisohn through writing pieces for it, John Somerville by supplying photos, Steve McCarthy with Norman Christie for designing the cover and the staff at Ashford Colour Press for printing it. Any errors are our responsibility!

Preface

From a very tender age I was involved in crazy situations. I mean, have you ever heard of a Fire Station catching fire? Or anyone going to bed wearing a crash helmet? Or a kid almost hanging himself on a washing clothes line? Oh yes, all these things and many more happened to me in my early formative years so perhaps that is why I rode speedway for the thrills and danger and the sheer enjoyment of the sport.

I was the young boy scout of the 49th Troop of Glasgow who, on his first ever camping expedition in the Scottish Highlands, accidently tripped over the pot of beans that were sizzling on the campfire. Needless to say that it was our last tin of beans and a certain Scout Harkins of the Buffalo Patrol wished that one of those American beasts would come along and put him out of his misery and save him from the wrath of his fellow scouts.

I was the skinny schoolboy who preferred bicycles to football boots and in a school football match booted the ball hopefully in the direction of the goal, but hit his teacher square in the face. My career as a budding Scotland international footballer was over before it began. I was one of a minority of Glasgow kids who did not support Rangers or Celtic or want to be a footballer. My heroes rode speedway bikes and didn't run around chasing a leather ball.

I was – well, read on and I will try to give you an insight into 'The Life and (Hard) Times of Robert Pearson Harkins' who grew up from a clumsy bespectacled Glasgow schoolboy into an international professional speedway rider – A clumsy, bespectacled one of course.

I rode speedway in many countries around the globe all across Europe, Australia, New Zealand, USA, Israel, South Africa and even Scotland and I enjoyed them all. Most of my trips were done the hard way, as a freelance rider arranging my contracts wherever I could, a 'Have bike will travel' type of speedway rider. However, I did ride, officially, as a British Lion in Australia and was the lone Scot in the Ivan Mauger and Barry Briggs World Champions Troupe, as well as for Melbourne Demons, McGrath Monarchs and Liverpool Lions in Australia and Bakersfield Bandits in California in the USA.

In Britain I was connected with Edinburgh, Cowdenbeath, Coatbridge, Wembley, Sheffield, Wimbledon and Milton Keynes, depending on the 'requests' from Rider Control. A sort of two-legged chess piece getting moved around the country. I even fielded a couple of teams of my own for open meetings, such as the Bert Harkins Globetrotters, who raced against Coatbridge. That team was made up from riders I had raced with in various parts of the speedway world. And then there was the illustrious, Bert Harkins Haggis-Bashers, a septet of kilt-wearing Scotsmen who struck fear into the hearts of the Wimbledon team – and supporters – when they presented each Don with a real Scottish haggis. Plough Lane was never the same again.

Apart from racing, I have always enjoyed writing about the sport and have had articles published in speedway magazines and programmes in the UK, Australia, New Zealand and America and now this is where the difficult part come in. Writing a book without a 'ghost writer' is a long, hard process. I decided to go ahead and write it myself. My wife, Edith would give me a 'friendly' prod every time my typing finger got tired of bashing the keys. So sit back and relax and in these pages, I will try to let you into my Crazy Speedway World.

Bert Harkins

Contents

Racing at Kembla Grange in Australia, December 1970.

The Mansewood Lions Cycle Speedway team, proudly wearing the race jackets
that Wembley Stadium had donated to them.

1. A speedway dream is born

New Year's Eve in Govan Fire Station in the south side of Glasgow and the fire alarm bells pierce the cold night air. Firemen slide down the Fireman's Pole into the Engine Room from their 'bothy' upstairs, others came running down the stairs, pulling on their heavy tunic jackets as they ran.

As they rushed to jump on the bright red 'TL', (Telescopic Ladder) fire engine, the station officer ran over shouting "Get down from there and get up the stairs fast, it's the Harkins' house that's on fire."

Yes, it was our house on fire. My dad was a Glasgow fireman, or 'firefighter', as they are now known and we lived in a flat inside Govan Fire Station. In an unfortunate incident, a careless Hogmanay guest had dropped a cigarette end down the side of a chair and when everyone had gone next door to visit the neighbours to 'See in the New Year' the chair had burst into flames. Not a good thing for a professional firefighter to do. Fortunately, the other firemen got there quickly and the flames were soon dowsed. I was only a babe in arms at the time, so could not be blamed. This was the start of my crazy and exciting life.

Govan Fire Station was my home until I was 12 years old. Growing up in a fire station certainly was exciting for the young boys and girls living there and, for me, Govan Fire Station was the start of my love affair with speedway.

The station was in Orkney Place, only a 10 minute walk from Glasgow White City Stadium where the Glasgow Tigers raced. Every Wednesday, in the days before speedway machines had to have silencers, the roar of the unsilenced JAP speedway bikes filled the air, echoing down from the stadium in Paisley Road West.

In the late 1940s and early 1950s, people went to speedway in their thousands. My father took me along to join the crowd and to soak up the atmosphere, mingling with the red and white scarves, wooden rattles and the "2-4-6-8-Who Do We Appreciate" chants, not to mention that great aroma of burning Castrol 'R' racing oil. Heady stuff for a wee lad in short trousers and so began my love for speedway and my ambition to become a speedway rider.

My dad George took me along and perched me on his shoulders to watch the action. Some of the firemen were speedway fans, so if my dad was on a night shift, one or two of the off duty firemen would take me to White City. I was hooked right from the start.

Many is the Thursday morning, after attending speedway the night before, when I went to Copeland Road Primary School in Govan hoarse from cheering my local heroes such as Blantyre born Ken McKinlay, Australian Junior Bainbridge and another Blantyre star, Tommy Miller. I was even caught once or twice by my teachers while trying to read the programme under the lid of my desk when I should have been doing my schoolwork.

Schooldays in Govan consisted of the usual lessons sandwiched between the Wednesday night speedway matches at White City and the inevitable waiting for autographs outside the pits and in the car park. Alf MacIntosh, a local lad and one of the Tigers' second strings came a purler one night and after the meeting I saw him limping out to his van in the car park. I joined in the rush to get his autograph and when I got there, he was propped up against the side of his van, obviously in pain, but patiently signing autographs for all the kids. Next morning the newspapers carried the story that Alf had broken his ankle in the crash. The previous evening, he had been signing books and programmes for loads of young fans when he could have been excused for pushing them out of the way and heading for the dressing room for treatment. After retiring from speedway, Alf became a school teacher in the Oxford area. He must have had the same patience with his school pupils as he did with his young speedway fans back in his White City days.

'Atomic' Tommy Miller, as Glasgow promoter Ian Hoskins so aptly named him, was the Scottish equivalent of Ivan Mauger. Lightning fast from the gate with an armchair style, he made speedway racing look easy. Tommy was unbeatable around the big White City track with its long straights and tight corners. He continued his winning habits when he moved south to Coventry following a short spell at Motherwell in 1954.

Ian Hoskins was ever the showman. As well as Tommy, he gave his riders various nick-names, so we had 'Hurri-Ken' McKinlay, Junior 'The Flash' Bainbridge, Alf 'The Tartan Terror' MacIntosh, Gordon 'The Tash' McGregor and 'Cowboy' Bob Sharpe in the team – all great names for the fans to remember.

Glasgow White City ran speedway from 1946 through to 1953 continuously and then in the spring of 1954 for only three matches. Tommy Miller had been transferred to Motherwell in the close season of 1953–54 and then in 1954, Ken McKinlay was transferred to Leicester and Junior Bainbridge and Bob Sharpe to Ipswich. Junior stayed there until the end of the 1956 season before going home to Melbourne for good.

That summer, Ipswich gave trials to a few Scottish riders including Jim Blythe, Larry Lazarus and Douglas Templeton, but none actually made the grade at Foxhall Heath. Dougie, nevertheless, did make a major impact in Scottish speedway when it returned to Edinburgh a few years later.

I continued to follow the various former Tigers riders' progress through the pages of the speedway magazines and I recall, with some embarrassment, one such case of hero-worship. When I heard that Ken McKinlay was due to ride in Edinburgh with his new club, Leicester, I made the long – at that time – trip by train from Glasgow to Edinburgh to watch Mac race. I had sent him a red scarf with white 'Good Luck' horseshoes on it to him c/o Meadowbank Speedway Office. It was appropriate for Leicester; they were 'The Hunters' at that time and their body colour had a horseshoe as their logo. I was very disappointed at not seeing the scarf flying from Hurri-Ken's neck and thought that it must have been lost in the post. Later, in my own racing days, I was too embarrassed to ask Ken if he had ever received a scarf from a kid in Glasgow and if he was not going to wear it, could he please give it back to me.

Kiwi Peter Dykes, who also rode for Glasgow Tigers, later became a champion midget car and production car champion and also a drag racer Down Under. He was also a top speedboat racer until he almost drowned while doing that sport. Years later, in the 1970s when I had realised my boyhood ambitions and was racing in Australia, I stayed with Peter and his charming wife, Audrey, in their Brisbane home. Peter was a real character and one day he loaned me his big Holden car to do some sightseeing. It had been reversed into the garage with the bonnet and driver's door sticking out into the yard. I climbed in full of excitement that one of my boyhood heroes would lend me his car. I turned on the ignition, fired up the big V8 engine which let out a healthy growl as I pressed the accelerator, selected first gear and slowly let out the clutch. The car revved, but didn't go anywhere. Next time I tried more revs and went from first to second gear, but all that happened was that the engine revved even harder. It was then that I noticed Peter and Audrey at the side of the garage doubled up with laughter. As I climbed out and looked at the back of the car, I found out that it was jacked up on some wooden blocks and the wheels were not touching the ground. Ah yes, that Australian and Kiwi sense of humour followed me around on my trips Down Under.

As Tommy Miller won most of his races from the gate and was rarely headed, he made it look all too easy, so my favourite Glasgow Tigers riders were Ken McKinlay and Ron 'Junior' Bainbridge. Ken always looked immaculate with his chrome plated JAP, highly-polished black leathers and white socks over the top of his shiny black boots. On his way from the pits to the starting gate, Ken had the habit of taking his hands off of the handlebars and pulling on his gloves, just a habit or perhaps showmanship, but something the local supporters looked forward to in his every race.

Hard to believe that in those days, 'Hurri-Ken' was often so slow from the gate that it looked as if he had invented handicap racing. He was the world's worst gater, but he was a master of the White City track and it was great to watch him weave his way from last to first; speedway racing at its best. Perhaps Ian Hoskins was paying Ken a little bit extra just to miss the gate and give the crowd some thrills? Later in his Leicester, West Ham and Coventry British League years, to watch McKinlay sit motionless at the tapes was a study of complete concentration, not for him the gamesmanship of rolling back and forward into the tapes to unsettle his rivals, just complete concentration on the job in hand.

As someone who had raced in Australia every winter, Ken was the ideal mentor for his fellow Scot, Jim McMillan, when Jimmy Mac was later selected to ride with Ken in the British Lions tour of Australia. Ken passed on tips on the mechanical side of what was required for the big Australian tracks and how to cope with being away from home for Christmas and the Scottish New Year celebrations.

Meanwhile, back in Ken's White City days, Junior Bainbridge also provided great entertainment for the fans. He was prone to intersperse his flamboyant riding with equally colourful shows of temper and language. Junior was the team captain and a very useful point scorer, but when he had bike trouble during a race, no one dared go near the little Australian.

I remember seeing my hero riding what appeared to be a brand new chrome plated JAP and, when leading the race by the proverbial country mile, the engine suddenly cut out dead. Junior threw his bike to the ground, jumped up and down on his new machine, ripped off his open face helmet and gas goggles and kicked them almost the length of the straight, not a recommended way of caring for your crash helmet. When Ian Hoskins tried to pacify the fiery Aussie, Junior grabbed the promoter's trilby hat and did a war dance on top of it too. He was a colourful character whose antics brought roars of encouragement from the White City crowd.

Even the novices who rode in the second halves had nicknames such as, Jack 'Red' Monteith, so called because of his red hair. Had he been an Australian, I guess he would have been called, 'Bluey'. There was also a novice called 'Whaler Joe' Ferguson. Apparently 'Whaler Joe' was so-called because he would go to sea in whaling ships, save his wages and when he returned to shore, buy a speedway bike and have a few outings in the novice races at

White City. The story – from Ian Hoskins, of course – must have been true because Joe would disappear for a few months then return to the track with a gleaming new JAP. Unfortunately, his enthusiasm did not reflect his ability so he gave up the two wheeled sport and returned to the sea. There was also a novice called 'Leap' Primrose. I don't know if that was his real name or if Ian Hoskins named him that after seeing his favourite flower growing quickly.

As many a Scottish speedway fan will testify, Ian Hoskins was a true showman, just like his father, Johnnie, who brought the sport of dirt track racing to the United Kingdom from his home in Australia in the 1920s. Quite an undertaking considering the distance involved and the long boat journeys across the ocean, something I experienced many years later.

At Glasgow White City, Ian staged stunts such as a diver jumping from a high platform on the centre green into a wet sponge. Well, that's what it looked like from where I was, but it was only a small tub of water that he dived into. Brave man. Not just for diving from such a height, but for stripping down to his swimming costume on such a chilly Glasgow evening.

On another occasion, Hoskins had an Indian 'Yogi' meditating on the centre green while lying on a bed of nails – the Yogi, not Ian – during the meeting to try to 'will' the Tigers to beat First Division Birmingham in a cup match. Unfortunately, it didn't work and the Brummies were too strong for the home team. Although the Tigers narrowly beat the visitors 56–52 at White City, they had lost 74–38 at Birmingham and were beaten on aggregate.

The Speedway Control Board had allowed Birmingham to use a new young Swedish rider against the Second Division Glasgow side. That Swede was Dan Forsberg who went on to be one of the top Swedish riders in Britain.

Ian Hoskins would always have an 'Interval Attraction' to entertain the crowd and on that evening of the Birmingham match, to demonstrate his powers, the Yogi lay on his bed of nails, have a concrete slab placed over his body and have a rider, in this case it was the Tigers' Don Wilkinson, aided by Bob Sharpe wield a sledgehammer and break the concrete slab. It looked very scary and Don looked nervous too, but all went well. The concrete slab broke in two when Don swung the hammer down. The Yogi seemed to have escaped unscathed, but it was reported that he was later seen drinking in the bar after the meeting and the beer was coming out of holes on his chest.

Around that time, one of my friends had been given the present of an old 'Pudding Basin' motorcycle crash helmet, something I had never seen close up before. I gathered up all my toys – no laptops or IPads in those days – and swapped then for this tatty old former Army helmet. I was so pleased with my new 'toy', and here is the embarrassing bit, that on the first night, I wore it to bed and fell asleep with the light on, still wearing it while reading the *Speedway Star*.

My mother thought this was quite amusing – and strange too – as I was sitting propped upright in bed and fast asleep still clutching my copy of *Speedway Star*. Fortunately, there were no camera phones in those days to record this embarrassing scene. However, my mum wrote about it to the big Glasgow newspaper, the *Evening Times*. They published the letter, but fortunately not my name and address otherwise my school classmates would have ribbed me without mercy. So, as Michael Caine may have said, "Not a lot of people know that".

The sequel to this story is that a Glasgow speedway fan saw this in the paper and sent it to *Speedway Star* so they also printed the tale of the kid wearing a crash helmet in bed, so that was the first time I appeared in *Speedway Star*, but luckily it was anonymously. Many years later, my name would be in *Speedway Star* officially in the match reports and in the articles I wrote from around the speedway world, but that was all to come.

Sweet Dreams

"Nice little 'plug' for *Speedway Star* appeared in the *Sunday Mail* (Scottish edition) recently. It was spotted by reader Richard Miller of Auchinlea, Cleland, by Motherwell, who sent it because he thought 'it takes the biscuit'. Headed 'Sweet Dreams', it reads: 'My life is also plagued with a sports maniac. The only hobby of my son, aged 14, is speedway motorcycling, and when we were papering his bed-room we had to have the doors painted red with curtains and wallpaper toning (his speedway team colour is red and white). The other night, he put on his crash helmet, and while reading the *Speedway Star*, fell asleep with it on. I had quite a job getting it unblocked." Dirt Track Mother, Glasgow."

Being a schoolboy growing up in Glasgow taught me a lot about sport, running in particular and also how to be tactful with a view to self-preservation. Scotland had a long ancient history of wars against England, but in cities like Glasgow, there was still a lot of religious rivalry when I was growing up. Protestants and Catholics were like the cowboy and Indian movies I used to watch at the popular Saturday Morning Children's Club at the local Plaza cinema in Govan, always at war with one another, just like the city's football teams, Rangers and Celtic. The Catholic school was only a few streets away from the Protestant school I attended at Copeland Road and occasionally, on my way home, I would be confronted by a couple of tough-looking kids. They asked the inevitable loaded question, "Ur you a Cathie or a Proddie?" ("Are you Catholic or Protestant?"). Unsure of what the correct answer would be in a case like that, I used to reply "The same as you" and run like mad up the street to the safety of the Fire Station – Fort Apache comes to mind.

Like many kids at the time, I had a tricycle which I often rode on two wheels and it was later 'upgraded' to an 18 inch Hercules bicycle. As the small street, Orkney Place, outside of Govan Fire Station lay between the station and a play park, I soon laid out the shape of a track on the smooth surface. I coerced the other kids into playing at speedway riders and racing around the jerseys I had put down to mark the corners. This may have been a very early cycle speedway track, but it came with a big problem. Every time we heard the fire alarm bells going off in the station, we had to rush to clear the street as our 'track' was just outside the doors of the engine room, where the fire engines came rushing out, bells ringing, on their way to tackle yet another blaze.

At that young age, adults would always ask "What do you want to be when you grow up?" Most of all, I wanted to be a speedway rider, but maybe a fireman or cowboy. I did eventually fulfil all of three of those ambitions because I became a speedway rider who set fire to his garage and I also did some 'cowboying' on a ranch on my trips to the USA.

I remember seeing an article and centre page spread photos in, I think, *Picture Post* magazine, of a very small boy riding a very small motorcycle around a makeshift speedway track in his back yard. I studied the photographs of the mini speedway bike, looked back at my own wee pedal cycle and wished I could ride a bike like the one in the photographs. There was even a *Pathe News* film in the cinemas of a very young three year old, Howard Cole ('Kid Bodie') riding the 98cc mini speedway bike that his father, George had built for him. Little was I to know that some 20 years later, our paths would cross and I would be riding against Howard in British speedway and also at Liverpool Raceway in Australia. Howard eventually emigrated there and now lives in Australia where, after retiring from speedway he had worked as a teacher at Edgecliff Prep School in Sydney.

In my schoolboy days, I was a big Roy Rogers fan and watched all his cowboy western movies at the ABC Minors Club at the local cinema. I was a member of the Roy Rogers Fan Club. It was with great excitement that I heard that he was due to visit Glasgow on a publicity trip to the UK and visit some children's hospitals, including the one I was in at the time. Imagine my disappointment when I was told that I was being released from Mearnskirk Hospital the day before he was due to arrive. I was never a keen fan of hospitals, although I admire their work, but on that occasion, I would gladly have stayed on and taken my daily dose of the foul-tasting Children's Castor Oil just to see 'The Singing Cowboy' close at hand.

I managed to delay my departure until 'R.R. Day' and after being told that I could go home, I persuaded my parents to hang around with me in the cold outside of the hospital until Roy showed up. Our patience was rewarded when he came walking down the driveway leading his famous horse, 'Trigger' and accompanied by his wife, Dale Evans and a whole group of important-looking people. I got Roy's autograph and in took pride of place alongside my other heroes, Junior Bainbridge and Ken McKinlay. Another ambition fulfilled.

Later, on my speedway travels in the USA, I visited the Roy Rogers Museum in Victorville, in the High Desert in California on the old Route 66. Among all the Hollywood Western mem-orabilia, there were photos of Roy's travels around the world including one of him arriving in Glasgow so that brought back some memories. The Museum had opened in 1967 but by 2003, with both Roy and Dale having passed on and visitor numbers declining, the Museum was sold and the items auctioned off, so I was lucky to see it when I did.

As a wee boy, speedway was still my main love. I remember my mother having a discus-sion with one of the fire station officers about me rushing around on a bicycle playing at being a speedway rider. He reassured her by saying "Don't worry, he'll soon grow out of this speedway craze." That officer may have been right, but it certainly hasn't happened yet.

Govan Fire Station was always busy, so we were frequently interrupted in 'mid-race'. Glasgow was probably the most dangerous city for fires at that time, with the Govan ship-yards nearby and tenement blocks where the Glasgow diet of fish and chips caused many a chip pan fire.

It could be dangerous too, as one evening my dad was brought back to the house wrapped in blankets and dripping wet. He and three of his fellow firemen had been fighting a fire on board a cargo ship on the river Clyde when the platform they were on gave way and they all fell into the ship's hold. Fortunately, the hold was full of water at the time, so that broke their fall, but they almost drowned as their heavy tunics soaked up the water like a sponge. They were rescued by their colleagues and brought back to the station instead of hospital. No time for long recuperation or compensation and after a day's rest, they were all back on duty the following day.

Govan Fair parade with Andy McNeil on his 10 feet tall bicycle. Bert is on his bike on far left in the parade, his dad George is standing by the wall, both pointed out with an arrow.

To live inside a fire station was fascinating for a young child, surrounded by gleaming red fire engines and clanging fire bells, but perhaps I didn't appreciate it and just accepted it as an everyday facet of life. I was much more interested in the fire station's old American Indian motorcycle with the long box sidecar all painted in red. It was used for carrying out repairs to the fire alarms and water hydrants around the city. The fireman in charge of this motorcycle combination, Alex Garden, a Canadian from Calgary, got into a lot of trouble because of me. I kept asking him for a ride on the motorcycle. One day, he gave us kids a ride around the station yard, all sitting on top of the box sidecar. This must have kindled my love for motorcycles. However, he was caught by the station officer, told off and given other duties.

Another benefit of living in Govan Fire Station was that when the annual Govan Fair procession came around, the station would allocate one of their fire engines to the parade through the local streets. As a special treat, us station kids would be allowed to ride on the platform of the Telescopic Ladder machine, something which Health & Safety would not allow these days. We took turns at ringing the bell as loudly and as often as possible.

Eventually I graduated to riding my little 18 inch Hercules bicycle in the parade following local cycle shop owner, Andy McNeil who would lead us kids like *The Pied Piper of Hamlin* along the Govan streets riding his special 10 foot tall bicycle. Andy's cycle shop was in Govan Road, one of four in Govan. The others belonged to Andy's brother, John McNeil, Neil McCulloch and Robertson's Cycles. Andy was famous for making special cycle frames and his racing bikes under the 'Andy McNeil' name. Many Scottish racing cyclists used his frames.

Although I left Govan at a young age, it is still a special place for me. At the end of my speedway career I was invited to become a member of The Govan Weavers, a charity dating back to 1756 when weaving was a major industry along the River Clyde. It was formed to help their members who fell on hard times. Funds were raised by annual subscription and by the proceeds of the 'Swear Box'. If they had a swear box on television these days they could raise a lot of money. When heavy industry and ship building arrived on the Clyde, the weaving trade died out, but the Govan Weavers kept up their charity work by helping local people who were in financial trouble. The Weavers were instrumental in resurrecting The Govan Fair, that same procession that I had been part of in my schooldays, yes, it certainly is a small world. In modern times, the Weavers raise money by holding dinners and Burns Suppers in Glasgow and it is nice to attend them and go back to my roots. Or should that be, 'Hoots'?

In the early days, Glasgow White City was the only track I was able to visit regularly and it was always a special occasion if my dad took me to an 'away' meeting. Scotland boasted four tracks at the time, two in Glasgow, (White City and Ashfield which were north and south of the River Clyde), Motherwell just outside the city and Old Meadowbank in Edinburgh, some 50 miles away. Later I travelled to Motherwell and my first visit to the Lanarkshire stadium was a painful one. Motherwell was about 12 miles outside of Glasgow as the pre Sat Nav crow flies and we had to rely on public transport because my dad didn't have a car. It was with great excitement that my father and I set off on that train journey from Glasgow Central Station to the home of the Motherwell Eagles. As we got off the train at Milton Street station, someone kindly closed the carriage door behind us, a helpful gesture, but one that I would have appreciated more if my fingers had not been in the way. By the time the door was reopened and my crushed fingers released, I felt rather poorly, but as I was having my injuries treated, I could hear the bikes warming up in the Motherwell pits and felt fine again.

One day, we even managed the long trip through to Edinburgh, 50 miles away. I felt that I was travelling to the ends of the earth – perhaps I was. I was a red hot Glasgow Tigers fan at the time and the Edinburgh Monarchs were the dreaded opposition. Funny how times change because when I eventually rode speedway, I was a true-blue Edinburgh Monarch and Glasgow were the opposition. Fortunately, in my racing days, fans from both tracks treated me well. A Glaswegian riding for Edinburgh; later the Tigers had an Edinburgh-based rider, Brian Collins, riding for Glasgow. Perhaps we should have swopped places and cut down on our travelling?

Glasgow Ashfield, on the north side of the city, was a long journey by tram and as my dad was frequently on fire duty on a Tuesday evening, I only got there once or twice. However, it was a memorable meeting when an American team came to Scotland to take on Johnnie Hoskins's Ashfield Giants in 1951. Although I was still a wee bairn (a small child) at the time, I remember some of the exotic names. There was wonderfully named Manuel Trujillo, who sounded like a Mexican bandit from the cowboy movies I used to watch. Manuel was, I believe, the only Mexican rider at the time. Then there was Johnnie Roccio, brother of the late Ernie Roccio, who later rode for Wimbledon. Don Hawley was a famous flat track racer who turned to speedway. He left an indelible impression on me many years later when he rode over me at Costa Mesa and left tyre marks across my back, but that's another story. Also in the American touring party was Nick Nicolaides, who returned to speedway in the boom years of Californian speedway in the late 1960s and early 1970s.

I was still dreaming about being a speedway rider when I grew up, and many years later, American speedway and California played a large part in my international speedway career, but I wasn't ready for that yet.

2. Cycle speedway days

By the late 1950s there was no speedway left in Scotland, Glasgow White City, Glasgow Ashfield, Motherwell and Edinburgh had all seen their last race for the time being. The boom times for Scottish speedway had gone and supporters had to find other sports to follow.

Fortunately for my friends and me, we got our kicks not through drink, drugs, smoking or kicking a football around, but through cycle speedway. In the early 1950s, my parents and I moved out of Govan Fire Station and had a new house in a new housing estate called Eastwood, on the south side of the city.

Eastwood was still being built when we moved in and some of the roads had yet to be surfaced, so I enjoyed myself sliding round the dirt corners on my bicycle. It was on one of those occasions that I met up with other youngsters like the Christie brothers, Peter, Norman and Ronnie who lived on the other side of our back garden fence and became life-long friends. Peter and Ronnie went on to be singers and guitarists performing in clubs and theatres throughout Scotland until Ronnie moved to Brisbane in Australia and carved a new musical career there.

Norman Christie stayed in Glasgow, but was also involved in show business, writing gags and sketches for many of the Scottish comedians. He also appeared on stage from time-to-time. In later years, Norman painted my Bell speedway helmets tartan before the start of each season. Now some of those helmets are on display in the World Speedway Riders' Association National Speedway Museum in Paradise Wildlife Park in Hertfordshire.

In Eastwood all the roads had Scottish names. The Christie brothers lived in Scarba Drive and I was in number 34 Fyvie Avenue or, as we called it, "3, 4, 5Y". We built a cycle speedway track in the woods on the big hill behind the local Eastwood Parish Church. We called the hill 'The Kirkie' because it was behind the Church, i.e. the Kirk.

In summer, we used The Kirkie for cycle speedway and in the winter, we careered down that steep slope on our sledges. On the track we tried to emulate our speedway heroes on our cycle speedway bikes playing games such as 'Who is this?' and you would slide into the corner with your right elbow up and left elbow down. That was 'Mirac', Ronnie Moore. Riding with both elbows up was meant to be Ken McKinlay or Barry Briggs, but we never mastered the art of the leg-trailing style used by old time dirt track riders and Odsal's Oliver Hart.

Cycle speedway was very popular throughout the United Kingdom at that time and bicycle manufacturer Phillips even made a cycle specifically for the sport. It was called the *Phillips Speedtrack* with a sloping top frame tube, wide handlebars, chrome 'outriders' on the forks and special Avon 'Gripster' tyres. As the KTM motorcycle adverts later said: "Ready to race".

One day, as we were all larking about on the track, another youngster with glasses turned up on a brand new gold Phillips Speedtrack bike. This was long before Ivan Mauger had his gold plated speedway bike. We were all very curious because we hadn't seen a gold coloured cycle speedway bike before and thought that the owner must be very rich.

The new 'Skid kid' turned out to be Dick Barrie, who later went on to be my 'Fuel and oil monkey' when I started speedway. Dick specialised in putting the fuel in the oil tank and the oil in the fuel tank. Later he became the announcer at various Scottish speedway tracks and a regular contributor to magazines and programmes across the speedway world.

Unfortunately, that first meeting ended in tears because I had been playing around riding the wrong way around the track and we collided head-on. That was the first time I 'bumped into' Dick Barrie. He left the track with bruises and tears and with his damaged new bike over his shoulder.

We found out that there was a Glasgow cycle speedway league and were invited to join. Our original team was called the Eastwood Mercuries, mainly because the National Benzoil petrol stations were handing out free stickers with their logo, Mercury, the 'God of Speed'. We collected the decals and stuck them on the front of our home made body colours and called ourselves, the 'Eastwood Mercuries'. Other teams in the Glasgow League included Craigton Eagles, Redhill Rockets, Mansewood Lions, Linthouse Lightnings, Camphill Kiwis, Busby Gulls and Knightswood Toffs, whose riders wore bow ties when they were racing.

One of our gang, Peter Christie, had the bright idea of writing to various speedway teams to ask if we could have their body colours for our cycle speedway team. Some clubs replied to say that either they kept the body colours or the riders kept them as souvenirs, but the one club that did reply with a great offer was the famous Wembley Lions. To our amazement and delight, Wembley sent us a full set of Lions' body colours and suddenly our Mansewood Lions team with the skinny hand painted lion on the front, became the most professionally turned out team in the Glasgow Cycle Speedway League.

Little did I know that, as captain of the Mansewood Lions in the Glasgow Cycle Speedway League, I would one day become captain of the famous Wembley Lions speedway team at the Empire Stadium in London. A long way for a wee laddie from Govan and I guess that is one record no-one can beat.

In our cycle speedway days, we even had our own 'newspaper', aptly named *The Kirkie Kronicle* which carried match reports, point scorers and stories. Newspaper? In those pre-computer times, the *Kirkie Kronicle* was just a notebook with hand written match reports which was passed around the team, so we were hardly at the cutting edge of social media.

Cycle speedway became very popular in Glasgow and on 28 March 1960, we were invited, as a 'minority sport' to put on some demonstration races at *The Schoolboys & Schoolgirls Exhibition* in the main arena of the prestigious Kelvin Hall. We were all issued with a 'Performer's ticket' which gave the riders free entry, not only to the arena, but to all the attractions in the main hall.

A programme had been devised where the performers in one sport would fill a 20 minute slot quickly followed by those from the next sport or activity. Other sports included basketball, five-a-side football, gymnastics, and even pogo stick jumping. Now that is a minority sport.

The programme was strictly adhered to so riders had to be present and ready to race on time. The managers on the night were often sweating right until the last moment waiting for some of the riders who had wandered off and were enjoying the dodgem cars and other attractions in Kelvin Hall. The surface used for racing was smooth concrete and proved tricky especially after one session which followed the gymnastics. Chalk dust and hair from the matting used by the gymnasts made the concrete surface very slippery and quite a few of us went home with bruised hips, knees and left hands. Fortunately there were no head injuries because we didn't wear helmets in cycle speedway at that time.

Spectators in the arena enjoyed the rough and tumble racing but some, when later wandering around the other exhibits in the main hall, must have been amazed to see some of the cycle speedway riders taking cycle proficiency tests in the road safety exhibition.

Kelvin Hall was on the west side of Glasgow and to get back home to the south side, we had to put our bikes onto the little Govan ferry which puffed its way across the River Clyde. We also used that little ferry on our away trips to race against the Knightswood Toffs. On the return journeys, one of the Craigton riders, Pete Bell, used to tie a rope onto his bike, put it overboard and let the River Clyde wash off all the cycle speedway dirt. The Clyde was not the cleanest of rivers so when the bike was hauled back on board, it was usually dirtier than when it went in.

On that homeward journey from Kelvin Hall, on 28 March 1960, we saw large clouds of thick black smoke and bright blue flames coming down the river and lighting up the night sky. It looked very ominous. One of our cycle team, Brian Gilliland's father was a fireman like my dad, so it was an anxious time for us. When we got home, we found out that this was Glasgow's biggest fire, the Whisky Bond warehouse in Cheapside Street and fire engines were called out from all possible stations across the city and beyond.

Initially, three appliances (fire engines) and the St Mungo Fireboat on the River Clyde fought the blaze but as it got worse, more firemen and another eight fire engines were called in. Then the wooden casks holding over one million gallons of whisky and rum exploded, blowing the walls and roof of the warehouse out into the surrounding streets tragically killing 19 firefighters. It was the worst disaster to befall the Glasgow Fire Service and at the time, Britain's worst peacetime fire accident. At the height of the blaze, 30 fire engines and 450 firemen were fighting the blaze. Even off duty firemen were called in to help, but it still took a week to completely extinguish the flames. Fortunately, Brian's dad and mine returned home safely, but they lost some of their close friends and colleagues that sad night.

The firemen who died had been buried in the rubble in the explosion that blew the walls out. Their bodies were later recovered and laid to rest in the Fire Service Tomb in Glasgow's Necropolis Cemetery.

My memories of that sad night, apart from seeing the flames from the Govan Ferry, was in the following morning's newspaper. There was a photo of a poor local 'Down and Out' scooping whisky from the gutter as it flooded down the street. A sad image of the tragedy and for Glasgow.

From its humble beginnings, our track at The Kirkie eventually hosted many top events such as Scotland versus England internationals, Glasgow versus Bradford and Glasgow versus Edinburgh test matches, the prestigious Glasgow Individual Championship – which I won – and the Glasgow Grand Prix – which I also won. Many cycle speedway stars who visited Glasgow went on to greater things. Ian Thomas rode in the Glasgow versus Bradford test matches home and away and later had some second half rides at the old Belle Vue track at Hyde Road. Ian went on to become one of speedway's shrewdest promoters and was also a magician on stage and in the clubs. He stayed with us when the Bradford cycle speedway team came to Glasgow and I stayed with Ian and his parents for the return in Yorkshire.

Stan Stevens and Sandy McGillivary both rode for England against Scotland in cycle speedway and later moved onto the shale sport. England team manager, Dave Stevens, went on to be an official with the British Speedway Promoters Association (BSPA) and also a respected journalist. The list of riders who went from pedal pushing to 'proper' speedway is a long one dating back to when young kids would carve out a track on an old bombsite after the Second World War. The sport is still flourishing today, but in a more professional manner. There is a board naming the many riders who moved from pedals to engines in the WSRA National Speedway Museum.

In addition to riding in the Glasgow Cycle Speedway League, International and Inter City matches, there were also World Championships to contest. I was Glasgow Champion and Scottish Champion and qualified for two World Finals, one at Garrett Park in Tooting in south London and one at Harrison Park in Edinburgh. In the latter I finished as top Scot in fourth place and beat Manchester's Derek Garnett who was favourite for the title. Derek had won the English Championship that season and was the hot favourite to add the World title to his list of achievements, but I spoiled his chances of glory. I wonder if that was why Derek took me off of his Christmas card list? The winner and World Champion was Mike Parkins, son of Norwich promoter, Ted Parkins. Edinburgh's Johnny Murphy, who rode in that World Final, was still riding cycle speedway some 50 years later, just like Glasgow's Chick Mackie. They breed them tough in Scotland and John and Chick are now true cycle speedway legends.

One unusual item from the Edinburgh final was that the trophies that day were presented by Edinburgh Monarchs' promoter, Ian Hoskins. I ended with a unique record which is unlikely to be broken. I rode in the cycle speedway World Final on the Saturday afternoon, and then the novices' race in the second half at Old Meadowbank Speedway on the Saturday evening. From the top of the cycle speedway tree to the bottom rung of the motorcycle speedway ladder. All in a day's work.

This was the second World Cycle Speedway Final I had qualified for, the earlier 1960 World Final at Garrett Park in London had turned out to be a bit of a disaster for my fellow qualifier from Glasgow, Johnnie Speirs and me. We were the only two Scottish riders in the Final, but our journey south turned into a full blown disappointment.

Neither John nor I had a car driving licence at the time, so I borrowed my friend's old Triumph motorcycle and box sidecar to make the long trip down to London but more of that later. We had never tackled such a long journey before, other than taking the overnight bus from Glasgow to London to attend the World Finals at Wembley, so it was a bit of a 'shot-in-the-dark' in more ways than one.

Those long trips to the Wembley World Final were really special to see stars such as Peter Craven, Ronnie Moore and our Scottish hero, Ken McKinlay all chasing that huge Sunday Dispatch World Final trophy. The Wembley World Final nights were magical and well worth the long uncomfortable sleepless overnight bus journey from Glasgow. My first impressions of Wembley have stayed with me ever since, memories such as walking down Wembley Way among thousands of supporters eager to see who would be crowned World Champion that night and the sheer noise and excitement. At a one-off World Final, the World Champion would be crowned on the night. One bad race, fall or engine failure and the rider's chances had disappeared for another year so the pressure on the riders was immense.

Leading the way for the Mansewood Lions in the Glasgow Cycle Speedway League.
Jackie Pinkerton is on the outside.

Scotland Cycle Speedway team versus England in Manchester, June 1959.
Norrie Allan (Craigton), Joe Letts (Craigton), Robert Bond (Arden), Jim Cobain (Knightswood),
Hamish Orr (captain, with bike, Craigton), Bert Harkins (Mansewood),
Pete Christie (Mansewood), John Speirs (Mansewood).

This was what the fans had come to see – the sudden death contest of who would become World Champion on that evening. Today, the modern Grand Prix system is much fairer as the best, most consistent rider over the whole season will be crowned World Champion. They can recover from a bad race or even a bad meeting and still come out on top.

The atmosphere at those one-off World Finals was electric. Sixteen riders in highly polished shiny black leathers on their chrome plated Jap speedway bikes with chrome handlebars, frames, wheels and rear mudguards sparkling under the Wembley floodlights, but there was more to come. Following the introductions and rider parade, four riders rolled up to the starting gate and the crowd held its collective breath. When heat one started, all the stadium lights went out, including the centre green, so the stadium was dark except for the floodlit narrow ribbon of track. The chrome speedway bikes sparkled under the lights and gave the meeting a unique atmosphere which also made the whole show look much more spectacular. As the winner crossed the finishing line in heat one there was a huge explosion. I thought 'What a shame, his bike has blown up as he won the race.' In fact, it was not an engine 'blow-up', but the famous Wembley cannon which was fired at the end of every race.

That noise even fooled me many years later when I was riding for Wembley and the cannon went off as I crossed the line and thought my engine had blown up. I had forgotten about that end-of-race ceremony.

That Wembley World Final was the first time I saw the great Peter Craven in action. From my viewpoint up in the stands on the third bend, the riders came straight towards you and as Peter threw his Jap into the pits corner, all I could see was a pair of hands on the handlebars. "He's off", the crowd yelled, but no, it was the spectacular 'Wizard of Balance' riding a bucking bronco Jap the same way that as modern riders do on their lay-down, lower-centre-of-gravity four-valve rocket ships. Amazing balance and very spectacular to watch. Unfortunately, Peter lost his life on 20 September 1963 in a track crash at Old Meadowbank when George Hunter's bike seized and the Scot fell in front of him. A huge tragedy for British Speedway, Belle Vue and Peter's friends and family. George Hunter was also deeply affected by the accident and I am certain that his own riding suffered for a long time afterwards.

Had this accident happened in the new millennium, Peter's chances of survival would have been much greater. Air fences and better technology with helmets and body armour instead of solid wooden 'safety' fences and 'Pudding Basin' helmets have made the sport much safer, although serious accidents can and do still happen.

But back to our cycle speedway trip to 'The Big Smoke'. With our *Phillips Speedtrack* cycle speedway bikes safely secured in the box sidecar, we headed south intending to stop overnight at my cousin's house in Hayes Middlesex. However, as our famous Scottish poet, Rabbie Burns wrote: "The best laid schemes o' mice and men gang aft agley" which roughly means that even if you plan well, things can go wrong. Well, my planning was not so good because London was a long way from Glasgow by motorcycle and we were plagued with rear wheel punctures and, not having a spare tube, my trusty puncture repair outfit was put to good use. Rear wheel off, fix puncture, rear wheel on and continue heading south, this became the pattern of our journey.

When we eventually crossed the border into England, the weather was unusually hot and the mixture of the hot tarmac and Johnnie's weight on the pillion meant that the patches on

14

the inner tube kept lifting and the tyre slowly deflated. So all along the way we had to make 'pit stops' regularly down the A1 to carry out running repairs.

We didn't make it to Hayes that day and made an overnight stop at a Truckers' B & B en route, but were wakened before 6am with lorry drivers clomping down the stairs and firing up their trucks. We eventually did get to Hayes and set off for London and Garrett Park, but got lost in the traffic until a friendly motorcycle despatch rider led us through the city. However, he was on a solo motorcycle and we had a sidecar attached so we had a few problems keeping up with him.

Eventually, we did reach Tooting and Garrett Park but, to our utter disappointment, the World Championship Final had started and we were not allowed to race. I guess I should have been more assertive, but in those days, you just accepted things. Johnnie and I turned around and headed back to Hayes for an overnight stop at my cousin's house. Then the next morning we started the 400 mile trek back to Glasgow. Somehow I can't see this happening these days. We had no comfortable high speed cars or vans to transport our bikes. We covered all that distance on an old Triumph Speed Twin & box sidecar and returned home without turning a cycle speedway wheel in anger. A disappointing end to a long journey.

The match programme issued by *Amateur Cycle Speedway* magazine.
The inside was a score chart for the teams to complete.

Speedway trial at Motherwell in 1958. Former Scotland speedway star Tommy Miller with the flag, Bill Landels on far left, Bert Harkins on right on a Triumph Tiger Cub, complete with L Plates.

On holiday in the Isle of Man.
(Photo: Norman Christie)

3. From pedals to throttles

Scotland had been a speedway wilderness for some time, but in 1958 Ian Hoskins brought back the Lanarkshire Eagles in Motherwell, just outside of Glasgow and raced against junior versions of the English National League teams such as Belle Vue, Coventry, Bradford, Leicester and Ipswich.

The Motherwell team included Doug and Willie Templeton and George Hunter, who were all from the Scottish grass track scene; Freddie Greenwell, Jimmy Tannock, Gordon Mitchell and Red Monteith. Most of them made up the basis of the Edinburgh Monarchs when they returned to league racing in 1960.

Prior to Motherwell reopening, Ian Hoskins had put an advert in the Scottish newspapers asking for anyone with a motorcycle to come and have a run around the track. I don't know if he was looking for riders for his new Eagles team or perhaps introducing 'Speedway on road bikes' but quite a few riders turned up at the Lanarkshire track.

At that time, with no speedway in Scotland, I was unable to fulfil my early ambition of leaving school at 16 and becoming a speedway rider. I was working as an apprentice motorcycle mechanic at the biggest motorcycle shop in Glasgow, JR Alexander Ltd. I had a second hand 200cc Triumph Tiger Cub motorcycle.

Motorcycling was very popular then and because cars were still very expensive most youngsters and men rode motorcycles. JR Alexander's was on the west side of Glasgow on the Great Western Road, with a large motorcycle showroom, spares department and workshop, a motorcycle accessory department, cycle shop and car workshop. The Great Western Road was the main highway towards Loch Lomond and The Highlands so it was always busy, especially on a Saturday when riders headed for a run 'Up the Lochside'.

There were plenty of motorcycle shops all in the same long Great Western Road, J.R. Alexander, Weddell & Devine, Valente Brothers and around the corner, Bell Brothers. On a Saturday, the area was jammed with motorcyclists collecting spares or just drooling over the new bikes in the showrooms. Jimmy Valente had been a pre-war dirt track rider. He made his debut on an AJS at Glasgow's Celtic Park in 1928 before he bought a dirt track Douglas and had great success at Edinburgh's Marine Gardens and 'Down South' at Crystal Palace where he beat top American, Sprouts Elder, in a match race championship.

I was excited to read that Ian Hoskins was going to run trials at Motherwell and he had former Glasgow and Scotland number one, Tommy Miller, come along to advise these new riders. Although I didn't have a speedway bike or even a grass track bike, I went along to see what was happening. I got quite a surprise when I was allowed onto the speedway track on my little 200cc Triumph Tiger Cub road bike with lights, gears, brakes, very narrow tyres, and 'L' plates. Other hopeful riders had turned up on grass track bikes and motocross bikes, but I was the odd one out on a road bike.

I must have looked very odd, on my road bike with an open face helmet, motorcycle waterproof over-trousers, spectacles and a former Second World War leather flying jacket complete with fur collar. My motorcycle even had a road tax disc. I don't think that anyone could ever have looked less like a speedway rider than I did that day at Motherwell.

I was waved onto the track, I didn't need a push-start like the other track bikes as the wee Tiger Cub had a kick-start. I thought that I was circulating quite steadily at what seemed a fast pace as the safety fence passed by in a blur, then whoosh! I was overtaken at speed by a flying Bill Landels who almost knocked me off my bike as he flew past on his 500cc grass track machine.

I didn't get a chance to speak to Bill that day, but this scenario was repeated in years to come on speedway tracks both here in the United Kingdom and in Australia when Bill and I were team mates in Edinburgh and opponents in the individual championships in Australia.

In Scotland, motorcycle road racing and 'Scrambles', now called motocross, were very popular. Scottish road racers, Bob McIntyre and Alistair King, were the local TT heroes for all young lads on two wheels. I remember Bob Mac coming along to give a talk at our Motorcycle Club, the Avon Valley MCC in Strathaven (pronounced, 'Strayven') just outside Glasgow. The clubroom was packed that night. Sadly, Bob McIntyre died in 1962 aged 33, after a track accident in Cheshire at the Oulton Park circuit.

One of my fellow apprentices at JR Alexander's, Denis Gallagher, was competing in road racing at the weekends, so I used to go along to 'help' him in the pits. He modelled his riding style on Bob McIntyre with his straight elbows. Denis had a lot of success mainly on the Isle of Man and in the Irish road races.

It was Denis who had first taught me to ride a motorcycle by the unusual way of him sitting on the pillion shouting instructions to me. If I made a mistake, he would hammer his fists down on my shoulders. I soon learned to ride correctly to avoid any more bruises.

Denis was doing quite well at circuits in Scotland, Ireland and the Isle of Man and wanted to upgrade to faster machinery. He had been riding a 250cc Velocette special, built by Scottish Champion, Charlie Bruce, but wanted to purchase a German NSU Supermax. So, with no speedway in Scotland, I sold my little Triumph and raised some cash to buy the 250cc Velo. It had a very unusual square-tubed frame, hand made by Charlie and it handled very well.

As luck would have it, when I started road racing in 1960, the Edinburgh Monarchs reopened at Old Meadowbank so once again, I was in the wrong place at the wrong time. Obviously, speedway was still my first love, but I was committed to road racing for that season. I raced mostly at the Scottish circuits, including Errol Aerodrome, Charterhall and Kirkaldy. My road racing debut was at Errol on a very wet Sunday. In my first race, riders were riding wide in one corner to avoid a wet patch on the inside so, after a few laps, I thought I would dive under the other riders, through the wet patch and overtake them. No such luck. The wet patch turned out to be a very deep puddle. The bike just aquaplaned and I went sliding down the road on my backside tearing the seat out of my borrowed leathers. The other riders obviously knew much more about racing in the wet than I did.

I even rode on the Isle of Man when Denis Gallagher and I went over to race in the Southern 100 races in the south of the island but even that ended in tears. I had qualified around 14th in practice, about halfway through the field and was looking forward to the race the following day. However, on my way to the start line on race day the gearbox seized and I was left desolate sitting on a stone wall watching all the other riders blast past my stricken motorcycle and me.

Participating in the Southern 100 race on the Isle of Man in 1960.

Taking a bend on the Isle of Man.

Next day, on the way back to Scotland from the Isle of Man ferry at Liverpool, riding in the dark with my friend Denis who also had his road racing machine on a sidecar, we were somewhere on the A6 heading north when all the lights blew on my Triumph motorcycle and sidecar and I came to a sudden halt. We tried in vain to fix the fault, but the 'God of Darkness' had struck my lighting system and the lights were no more. Undeterred, we decided to press on in the pitch darkness with Denis leading the way and me riding as close as possible to his rear wheel trying to see which way the road went.

We covered many miles with this 'freight-train' method until our luck ran out as we were spotted by a passing police car. With blue lights flashing, he flagged us down then proceeded to walk all around the two sidecar outfits. "OK", the officer said, "Where's the tow rope?" We had been riding so close together that he thought that Denis had been towing me.

The friendly policeman took pity on us and didn't give us a ticket, but told us not to ride any further until daylight or he would have to book us. Fortunately, there was a petrol station nearby. It was closed, but had cars parked on the forecourt and a couple of them were unlocked, so we piled in and slept in our motorcycle gear to wait for the dawn. Then we headed north again.

I continued road racing for the rest of that season but when the season ended, I was determined to realise my boyhood ambition and race speedway.

4. Speedway at last

Speedway had really taken off at Edinburgh's Old Meadowbank stadium and I was among the crowds flocking there on Saturday nights to watch riders such as the Fife farmers Doug and Willie Templeton, New Zealander Dick Campbell, 'The Buckskin Boy – Jimmy Cox, who rode with a jacket with tassels on the sleeves, long before riders such as Dougie Wyer and John Louis wore theirs. They took on the might of the teams from south of the border as Edinburgh was still the only track in Scotland.

Grass tracker Bill Landels, who had performed at that practice session at Motherwell was also in the team, England's Freddie Greenwell and former Motherwell Eagle, Gordon Mitchell plus someone who was heading for the top level of speedway, a young George Hunter, 'The Ladybank Express'.

George quickly became the fans' favourite at Old Meadowbank. The track café even sold 'George Hunter Specials' which were bread rolls filled with Spam (the tinned meat, not the internet spam). We Scots knew how to live.

Ian Hoskins even brought back the legendary Ron Johnson, but the former New Cross star was, by then, past his best and suffering from the aftereffects of injuries sustained in speedway. Ron was still lightning fast from the gate, but would tire quickly and was soon overtaken by the other riders. It was sad to see a former world-class rider in the twilight of his great career, but there were still see flashes of that old brilliance before his arms and wrists grew tired of hanging onto the handlebars of his hard-to-ride Jap. Another Scottish rider with the Monarchs was the aptly-named, Jackie Fortune. However, Jackie found out that the only way to make a small fortune out of speedway was to start with a large one.

Now that speedway had returned to Scotland, I had a chance of realising my ambition to ride speedway and make the grade. However, another 20 or 30 other novices all had the same idea.

First of all, I needed a bike, so I approached fellow Glaswegian Jimmy Tannock who was riding for the Monarchs. He had a little motorcycle workshop on the north side of Glasgow. Workshop? It was actually the kitchen of a Maryhill tenement. Jimmy repaired motorcycles there and promised to find a speedway bike for me.

Jimmy was a reliable team man, never a big star in his racing days with Ashfield Giants, Motherwell Eagles and Edinburgh Monarchs, but a solid second string and a true legend when his racing days were over. He was voted in as president of the World Speedway Riders' Association in 2004 and was also the long-time chairman of the Scottish Branch of the WSRA.

Jimmy was popular with everyone, even although they often had trouble understanding his thick Glaswegian accent. However, the height of his popularity came decades later when he was handing out the free 'Rusty Nails' pre-dinner drinks in 'The Scottish Suite' to all the guests at the annual WSRA Dinner Dance in the Leicester Marriott hotel. A mixture of Scotch whisky and Drambuie, the Rusty Nails ceremony was one of the highlights of the evening.

One year former double World Champion, Freddie Williams had so many 'Rusty Nails' that he was slurring his speech, so the following year, his wife, Pat, put a sign around his neck saying 'No drink from the Scots'. We still managed to sneak a few wee drams to Freddie.

Although living in Glasgow in his racing days, Jimmy 'Titanic' Tannock, as Edinburgh promoter, Ian Hoskins called him, had a wee 'But 'n' Ben' stone cottage up in the Highlands at Glen Orchy. He was later to be known throughout the speedway world as 'The Laird of Glen Orchy' an unofficial title I bestowed on him. To reach the cottage, we had to stop beside the River Orchy and blow the car horn and Jimmy would come out to unlock the gate of the old swing bridge over the river. We crossed this old bridge carefully then walked through some trees to a clearing with the stone cottage in the clearing. There were huge boulders tied with rope hanging over the roof of the cottage at either side. "What is that for?" I asked on one of my visits, "Och", said Jimmy, "It's tae keep the roof on when the wind is blawing". The cottage had no electricity, but he had a generator; no television, but Jimmy kept his guests entertained by playing the piano and singing Scottish songs. He had also connected a water supply from the burn (stream) running through his property, so he was quite self-sufficient. He often caught fish in the River Orchy and even poached the occasional deer for his supper. Jim kept his own bees and also had a vegetable garden for fresh produce. There was a St Andrew's Cross flag, the Saltire, flying from a flag pole which was reputed to have come from Sir Walter Scott's home in Edinburgh.

It was a beautiful picture postcard setting but, in the early evening, 'Scotland's greatest secret', the midgies, would swarm down and bite any piece of skin that wasn't covered so there was no chance of an outdoor barbeque when the sun went down.

On one occasion in my early racing days, I called at Jimmy's Glasgow workshop. He had just returned from the Highlands. Jimmy asked me to go to the kitchen and put on the kettle for a cup of tea, but when I went in, there was a huge stag hanging out of the sink, antlers and all. Jimmy had been poaching the night before. After that shock, I never ate venison for many years to come.

The speedway bike Jimmy sold me was an old Five Stud Long Stroke Jap. He reckoned that the frame had belonged to the legendary Ken Le Breton of Ashfield Giants, 'The White Ghost', who was killed in a track accident in Australia in January 1951. That shows how old the machine was. The bike was going to cost me £50, a tidy sum in those days but, as I hardly had two pennies to rub together, Jimmy took pity on me, an impoverished would-be novice and knocked £5 off of the asking price.

That £5 discount was a standing joke of Jimmy's in the many years ahead because, when I eventually got into the Edinburgh team, he wanted his £5 back and would remind me every time we met.

And so, after my time riding cycle speedway, road racing and touring, I had a speedway bike at last. Speedway was flourishing at Old Meadowbank in Scotland's capital city, so I wanted to get in on the action there.

By mid-1961 I had the bike, but the next question was "How do I get it to Edinburgh and how do I get a ride at old Meadowbank?" The first question was answered by being reunited with that old motorcycle and sidecar which had been used to transport our cycle speedway bikes on our ill-fated trip from Glasgow to London for the Cycle Speedway World Final. The Jap fitted into the box sidecar and I chugged along the old A8 carriageway for the 40 odd miles from Glasgow to Edinburgh.

I also occasionally resorted to putting the bike on the train at Glasgow to Waverley Station in Edinburgh, then hopefully getting a lift to Old Meadowbank. Anything to try to get a ride on the only track in Scotland.

Compared to today's riders, and even novices, I must have looked as if I came from another world, no fancy made-to-measure kevlars, no expensive helmet and boots and certainly no spare bikes or engines, just the basics. And old second hand – or foot – pair of DR (Dispatch Rider) Army boots, baggy leathers and a lot of enthusiasm and Scottish determination. I wore the leather jacket I had used on my road motorcycle and bought a cheap pair of jodhpur-style leather jeans. It was not a pretty sight. Now, in modern speedway, even the rawest novice has new kevlars, a smart laydown bike or two, a multi-storey toolbox and a nice sign-written van with his name on the side. Changed days.

Breaking into speedway in Scotland was far from easy. There were no training schools and about 30 to 40 novices were all trying to get into the Edinburgh Monarchs team or even to qualify for a second half ride in the programme. Speedway racing at Old Meadowbank had really taken off with big crowds, good racing and lots of young novices wanting to break into the sport. Ian Hoskins always put on a great show for the fans. His rapport with the Canadian announcer, Don Cummings, added to the atmosphere of off-track fun and on-track thrills.

Following the normal league match, there would be a second half with individual races for the team riders culminating in a Grand Trophy Final which usually featured the four top heat leaders. Prior to the Trophy Final, there would be a 'reserves' race and also a novice race. For the beginners like me who were not in the programme there was a chance to get in a few laps at the end of the meeting before the track lights went out. Sometimes I was lucky and got to ride for four laps, but on other occasions, there were too many hopefuls and most of us got turned away to try again the following Saturday.

On one memorable occasion, when I did manage to get a few after-the-meeting laps, the meeting had run late. The stadium caretaker, Sandy Sanford, wanted to go home so he just switched off the floodlights when we were on the third lap. Luckily I had gone to night school and could see in the dark.

These after-the-meeting wobbles continued week after week with little progress and little chance of even getting into the novice race in the meeting. Most of my fellow novices eventually got disheartened with the lack of opportunities to progress and pulled out of the sport. But I kept plugging away until eventually I got into the novice race in the second half.

These were very important races for the riders involved. Although we were racing against fellow inexperienced novices such as Eric Hanlon, Norrie Allan (the Glasgow cycle speedway star and not the same Norrie who was manager/right hand man for World Champions such as Ivan Mauger and Mark Loram) and Willie Meikle, who was Jimmy Tannock's nephew, there was the great opportunity of progressing to the reserves race and competing against the team's reserves. Sometimes there would be a 'vultures' race' where the top novices would compete against the team reserve and the winner would ride in the reserve spot the following week. So there was a lot at stake for the team reserves and the novices. These 'vultures' races' were the juniors' equivalent of the Grand Prix Grand Final. The amount of effort, enthusiasm and handlebar bashing that went on just to get that reserve place, would have done credit to a World Final run-off.

Practicing as a novice at Edinburgh.

1962 group of Edinburgh novices: Willie Meikle, Willie Edwards (Scottish motocross champion), Norrie Allan on bike and Bert. The identity of the other two riders is not known.

Bert working on his first bike in 1961 at his lockup in Glasgow.

1963 pre-season practice at Edinburgh with Ian Hart in the wet.

Bert looks longingly at the Scottish Open Championship Trophy in 1963.

Bert with Edinburgh captain Doug Templeton in July 1964.

On parade before the 1964 Provincial League Riders Championship Edinburgh Qualifying Round. Bert's 10 point score was an important breakthrough for him. Right to left: Bluey Scott, Kevin Torpie, Ron Bagley, Trevor Redmond, Alf Wells (in background), Jimmy Tannock, Willie Templeton.

Bert (on right) with (from left) Jimmy Tannock, Doug Templeton, Willie Templeton and Kevin Torpie, having been presented with tyres in the early 1960s.

Ian Hoskins also gave second half trials to Scottish scrambles (motocross) champion Willie Edwards, but Willie found it tough to get used to these skinny bikes with no brakes, so went back to his first love, scrambling. Subsequently, his son Billy was involved in motocross and speedway when he began making Bill Brown's Wulfsport clothing. It was used in speedway and long track by stars such as Barry Briggs and the late, great Simon Wigg.

American Ian Hart, who had organised the students' charity meetings at Old Meadowbank, became a regular in the novice and junior races, but did not make it into the team and faded out of the sport for many years. Now, at the age of 70 plus, Ian is still sliding. He has purchased a bike again and gets his speedway kicks at training schools up and down the country.

Second halves are no more, but I always believed that the paying public enjoyed them. They could see the star riders competing against each other and also the reserves and novices and follow the progress of a novice getting into the team as reserve then hopefully move up into the team proper as he improved.

According to Edinburgh Monarchs' historian, Mike Hunter, my first winning programmed race in the junior race in the second half was on 7 April 1961 which I won in 74.4 seconds, a mere (!) eight seconds outside the track record. I think the timekeeper had to use a calendar instead of a stopwatch.

Back then I wore a Birmingham Brummies body colour, not because I ever rode at Birmingham (it was a body colour I somehow collected in my schoolboy days) but because I could use the large red letter 'B' on the yellow front and write 'ertola' alongside to get the name 'Bertola', a nickname my mum had called me after seeing a Spanish Sherry of that name in a Glasgow supermarket. The name has stuck.

Progress was painfully slow. In September 1962 I had a couple of scoreless rides for Edinburgh at Middlesbrough in a 54–24 defeat. In July 1963, I rode in the Edinburgh team for a few meetings due to injuries to some of the team members. I should have raced at Cradley, but it was rained off then I was sent on the Monarchs' 'Southern tour' to Exeter and St Austell and scored a couple of points on the trip.

I returned to Scotland believing that I now had a reserve place in the team but no, the following Saturday, injured New Zealander Alf Wells was fit again and I was dropped back to the second half. I have a sneaky feeling that my Kiwi friend just did not fancy that long round trip from Scotland to the south of England, but I was happy to get a ride anywhere, so I did not mind the long hours on the road just as long as I could race.

I also got a booking for the Edinburgh Best Pairs Championship and my partner, Wayne Briggs scored a fine 14 points. I only scored a single point, but we still finished third overall. After such a poor performance from me, I was surprised that Wayne still spoke to me.

Ian Hoskins had a talent for bringing over Australians, Kiwis and later Scandinavian riders to fill his team, so it was difficult for any of the many young Scottish juniors to break into the Edinburgh side. The imported riders usually had their fare paid so the promotion had to use them to try to get their money back. Hoskins even brought over the Austrian Champion, Alfred Sitzwohl who was promptly nicknamed 'Alfred Six Volt'. Having always ridden on the larger tracks in Germany and Austria, poor Alfred could not get the hang of the tighter British tracks and soon headed back home to the land of the Lederhosen.

Getting rides in Scotland was becoming harder and by this time I needed to get more laps to gain experience in the sport. I was working as a mechanic in the Glasgow Parks Department – we had the fastest lawnmowers and tractors in the country.

The workshops were in Rouken Glen Park, home of the Craigton Eagles cycle speedway team. I was now the owner of a second hand Morris 1000 van. Now that I had four-wheeled transport, I wrote to various tracks in England to ask if I could get a second half ride. The only successful reply I received was from Ronnie Greene, the promoter at Wimbledon. He said that they did not usually have novice races in the second half, but he would get some local juniors together and I could have a couple of rides at Plough Lane. Wow!

I gathered up another of my Glasgow cycle speedway friends, Brian Gilliland, we loaded my Jap into the little Morris van and headed south to London. Once again, as in my cycle speedway days, the 400 mile journey was a long one, especially as the Morris 1000 van would only do about 45 to 50mph with the speedway Jap in the back, and that was downhill. By the time we reached the outskirts of London, it was pitch dark and we were pretty tired. We pulled off the road into what looked like a quiet field and pitched up for the night. We had to take the Jap out of the van so that we had room to sleep in the back so we just leaned the bike against the side and settled down to sleep.

We were awakened the following morning with the sound of traffic outside and, on wiping the condensation from the windows, saw a huge traffic jam alongside our van and drivers peering at us with question marks above their heads. It wasn't until later that I discovered that we had stopped on a grass verge on the North Circular Road and this was the morning rush hour. Luckily mobile camera phones had yet to be invented otherwise I think that the scene would have gone viral: two 'gypsies' sleeping in a van on the grass verge with a speedway motorcycle propped against the side.

This time there were no punctures and we arrived at the Wimbledon Stadium in Plough Lane in the afternoon. I was tinkering with the bike outside of the Wimbledon workshops when this slim blond figure came walking across the car park with his hands in his pockets and struck up a conversation with us. It was Ove Fundin. He had flown in from Sweden and was due to ride for Norwich at Plough Lane that evening, so he wandered over for a chat.

I had read all about Ove, Ronnie Moore and all the top stars in the speedway magazines at home in Scotland, and was interested in trying to find out some of his secrets. I asked him "What make of clutch do you use, Ove, Norton or Burman?" to which he replied, "Oh, I don't know, my mechanic, Les [Mullins] does all that for me" and with that wandered off towards the grandstand saying that he was going to find somewhere to sleep before the meeting. That was my first encounter with the great Ove Fundin, but a few years later we became team mates at Wembley when the Lions returned to big time league speedway. We also rode together on the Briggs–Mauger World Champions Troupe around the world. We formed a firm friendship which later saw us riding a 2,000 mile round trip from Ove's home in the South of France to Spain in pouring rain on our motorcycles. Ove was on his BMW, I was on my KTM 990cc. We visited the former England and Wembley star, Split Waterman, at his home in Nerja.

The results of my second half races at Wimbledon that night – I think I rode twice – are lost in the mists of time, but I appreciated the fact that Ronnie Greene had programmed a couple of junior races just for this wandering young Scotsman from Glasgow. It was great experience, even if I didn't find out what type of clutch Ove Fundin used.

It was almost a year before I got the opportunity to ride in the Edinburgh team again, in 1964, and this time, I wanted to stay. It had been a long hard road to try to gain enough experience to make any progress, but once I began getting extra rides in the Monarchs team, I started to improve at last. I surprised everyone, including myself, by scoring 10 points and beating star men George Hunter and Trevor Redmond in the Provincial Riders Championship round at Edinburgh.

I was still trying to hold down a full-time job with the Glasgow Parks Department. I was driving hundreds of miles home to Glasgow overnight after away meetings in England, then heading to work after a few hours sleep, but that soon came to an end. I was told by my manager to make a choice, have promotion and a secure future in my job, or to settle for an uncertain future as a speedway rider. Obviously, I opted for the latter because, had I stayed in a 'normal' job, I would always have wondered if I could have made the grade in speedway.

Scotland versus New Zealand, second test at Edinburgh 25 April 1964.
Bert with New Zealand captain Ivan Mauger. Scotland won 65–42.

Bert leading for Edinburgh against Cradley Heath in 1964.

Left: Bert presented with the Portobello Trophy for a second-half win in July 1964.
Right: Bert in the early 1960s.

5. Becoming a Monarch

At last I was making some progress, but I still had a long way to go to be able reach heat leader standard, but that wasn't for the lack of trying. An article in the February 1965 edition of *Speedway Post*, was headed 'Star Potential' with a photo of me sitting on my Jap proudly wearing the St Andrews Cross of Scotland and my favourite tartan scarf. The story went on to say that: "Although the Monarchs did not set the world alight in the previous season due to various team members being injured, this gave Bert Harkins the opportunity to move from second half races into the team where he steadily improved in stature".

It also went on to say that I caused a minor sensation when, from the reserve slot, I scored 10 points in the Provincial League Riders' Championship, beating Trevor Redmond in the process. Needless to say, that 10 point return surprised me too.

Kiwi 'TR' as he was known, was a top man in the Provincial League, having ridden for the famous Wembley Lions a decade earlier and been a World Finalist at Wembley in 1954. He went on to promote speedway at various venues, including Glasgow White City along with Ian Hoskins. At White City at various times, sometimes in the same meeting, he was promoter, rider, announcer and even track grader during his time with the Tigers. He also assisted Edinburgh's Alex Hughson in promoting speedway in Zimbabwe, or Rhodesia as it was then known. "In Rhodesia, I learned a lot from Trevor" said Edinburgh born Hughson, and that experience helped the Scot when he went on to promote further meetings in Rhodesia and later in South Africa. I had a closer relationship with Trevor Redmond when he and Bernard Cottrell resurrected the Wembley Lions in 1970, but that is another story.

The Edinburgh Speedway Supporters Clubs were always among the most generous in speedway. They raised money in the winter with their dinner dances and in summer with their raffles. The riders were often presented with new tyres and other spares and one year, each team member got a brand new engine. I missed out on getting an engine because I wasn't in the team on a regular basis, but I did benefit later when the supporters bought each rider a new Maury Mattingley frame. The Mattingley frame, which was hand-made by the Glasgow Tigers' captain in his Southampton workshops, was reckoned to be one of the best on the market so that also helped my progress in the sport.

I even made my debut for Scotland, albeit at reserve. I had two rides against England in an international at Newcastle on 24 August 1964, but unfortunately I failed to score (again). England won 56– 52.

In May 1965, Ian and his father Johnnie Hoskins opened a speedway track at Cowdenbeath, a small coal-mining town in Fife, some 18 miles north of Edinburgh. They ran a series of open meetings, hoping to establish speedway in the Kingdom of Fife. Cowdenbeath even staged a preliminary round of the World Championship in May, the start of the long haul of qualifying rounds to the World Final at Wembley in September.

The intention of the Hoskins Clan was to develop riders for their Glasgow and Edinburgh teams. The Forth Road Bridge had opened the previous autumn, which made travelling north over the Firth of Forth from Edinburgh much easier. No longer was the 30 mile detour via the Kincardine Bridge necessary, so there was great potential for that circuit. The track, at

Central Stadium, was 380 yards around the Cowdenbeath Football Club's pitch. The team was made up mostly from riders already in Scotland riding for Glasgow Tigers or Edinburgh Monarchs, and so the Fife Lions were born.

It was an ideal opportunity for the Scottish riders including myself and our colonial cousins to get some extra rides and experience. Riders such as Willie Templeton, Bill McMillan (elder brother of Jimmy Mac who were nephews of Doug and Willie Templeton), Bill Landels, Bruce Ovenden, Joe Hicks, Alex Hughson, Bluey Scott, Jimmy Tannock, Red Monteith, Eric Hanlon and many more all turned out for the Fife Lions. The opening meeting drew a crowd of around 5,000. However, the crowds dropped to 2,500, pretty good by today's standards but it was difficult to attract riders from south of the border to drive up to Fife, the UK's most northerly speedway track. The Hoskins promotion found it very hard going and after eight meetings, the Fife Lions were no more.

Cowdenbeath was still used as a training track during the winter of 1965–66. I well remember one freezing cold winter's day when I came out of the pits, raced down the back straight and then hit a patch of ice on the third bend. I came off in a plume of ice and snow. That taught me that I should always look carefully at a track before trying any heroics.

We were pretty tough in those days, practicing in the dead of winter in Scotland, but most of all, it gave us valuable track time to learn our sport. One of the things I did learn in those winter sessions was to make sure that all of my equipment was in perfect order. In one race against one of my fellow hopefuls, Lex Milloy, I came out of the gate with the front wheel in the air and when it landed, Lex's clutch lever went straight into the pocket of my leathers where the zip had broken. We careered down the straight and into the wooden fence, not a good way to start the day. Lexie went on to become a movie stuntman and appeared in some of the James Bond films. I guess those early experiences in his speedway days must have helped his future career.

I had eventually made it into the Edinburgh team, sometimes at reserve and sometimes as a second string and was still making progress gradually. Ian Hoskins had put together a quite useful team for 1965 with Scots Doug Templeton, George Hunter, Bill Landels and myself being joined by Scandinavians Preben Andreason, Bernie Persson and Henry Harrfeldt, brother of West Ham's Sverre.

My season was interrupted when I broke my left ankle at Poole in a collision with the Pirates' Pete Smith. The track doctor checked me out after the crash and gave me the all clear. However, during the night, in my one star bed & breakfast guest house in Poole, my leg was really painful, so much so that even the weight of the blankets on my leg became a painful problem.

I tried to solve that by inventing a 'medical breakthrough'. I used a large cardboard box to keep the blankets off of my leg and tried to sleep with my leg inside the box. Scottish ingenuity at its best – or worst.

Next morning, still in agony, I managed to get to Poole Hospital and, as I was hobbling along the corridor propped up against the wall, I met someone else hobbling in the opposite direction, it was Poole Pirates' Ross Gilbertson who had also crashed at Wimborne Road the previous evening.

Left: Fixing the chain in 1965.

Below: Loading the bike onto the back of the car.

1965 Scotland team that beat England at Edinburgh: Ian Hoskins (team manager), Dougie Templeton, George Hunter, Charlie Monk, Ken McKinlay (capt – on bike), Bert, Willie Templeton, Colin McKee, Bill Landels.

Glasgow Tigers versus Edinburgh Monarchs in April 1965 at White City, Glasgow
– Bert on the outside of Charlie Monk.

On parade before the Scottish Open at Edinburgh, 2 October 1965: George Hunter, Doug Templeton,
Willie Templeton, Ken McKinlay waving to the crowd and Bert.

Cowdenbeath practice in January 1966:

Left: In the pits, with fellow novice Lachie Kennedy and Dick Barrie leaning on the fence.

Middle: Racing against Bill Landels (on left).

Bottom: Coming out of the bend.

X-rays showed that despite what the track doctor had said, I had broken my ankle so my leg was quickly put in plaster. I was handed some crutches and shown the exit door. I was discharged, but there was one small problem – how to get back home to Glasgow. My schooldays and cycle speedway friend, Peter Christie, had travelled down from Scotland with me, but he didn't have a driving licence. Somehow we managed to drive back to Hayes in Middlesex where my long-suffering cousin, Jessie, put us up for a week's recuperation before we attempted the 400 mile drive to Glasgow. We eventually made it all the way back to Scotland with Peter steering and me changing gear. The original meaning of 'dual control".

I had made steady progress that year and was pleased when one of the main Glasgow newspapers telephoned and asked if they could send a reporter and photographer round to my parent's house in Eastwood to interview me for their sports pages. Thinking that this was a good opportunity to publicise both myself and speedway, I gladly accepted.

The reporter and photographer duly arrived and, over a cup of my mum's Scottish tea and cake, a long interview was conducted as the photographer took photos both off and on my speedway bike. I eagerly awaited the publication of this *Hello*-style interview and dashed off to the newsagent to pick up a copy or 10. My hopes of stardom were somewhat dented when I read the short article which began with something like: "Up and coming Glasgow-born speedway rider Bert Harkins, peers out of his thick glasses like a beaky-nosed Bustard looking over the long grass." I was a bit taken aback by this and had to look up the meaning of 'Beaky-nosed Bustard' to make sure that the reporter was not swearing at me. The Bustard turned out to be an unusual bird which was hunted to extinction in Britain in 1832. I wonder what that journalist was trying to tell me.

The broken leg had come at a bad time during my speedway progress, but when getting an injury, there is never a good time. I was out of action for about six weeks and didn't manage to get back into the Monarchs team until September. I had to work my way back up from the second half reserve and junior races again and then managed to finish the season more or less in one piece.

I was also capped as reserve for Scotland against Russia at Old Meadowbank. I even managed to score two points – paid three – in my one and only ride. The Russians came out winners 57–51 in a closely fought meeting. The Russian tourists were a great attraction on British tracks with their new Czech-built Eso bikes with strange 'clip-on' handlebars and long 'banana' seats. The riders too looked strange, with their black and brown leathers, large facemasks and goggles under their open face helmets and motorcycle gauntlets, a far cry from what British riders were wearing at the time.

The Russians were excellent visitors and gave the home fans a taste of the secret world behind the Iron Curtain. They looked very different from Western riders, but now in modern times, it is difficult to tell one nationality from another with all riders wearing colourful Kevlar suits and no big gauntlets and face masks to be seen.

I may not have scored many points in the test match, but at the interval, Ian Hoskins had one of his crowd-pleasing stunts in front of the starting gate grandstand. He persuaded Igor Plechanov – probably the best ever Russian speedway rider – and me to perform an impromptu Highland Fling in front of the huge crowd. Igor must have wondered what these crazy Scots were playing at and full credit to him, he joined in the fun. I am sure when he walked away afterwards, shaking his head he was thinking, "These Scots are Crazeee!"

At the end of the 1965 season, the Monarchs, or rather an Edinburgh Select, made a six match tour of Poland. Unfortunately I didn't make the grade for that trip which I am sure would have helped me to gain some much-needed overseas experience. The Poles would have been too strong for the Monarchs on their home tracks so Ian Hoskins brought in Ray Wilson and Norman Storer from Long Eaton, Jon Erskine from Newport and Geoff Penniket to join Monarchs Doug Templeton, George Hunter, Bernie Persson, Henry Harrfeldt and Colin McKee. The Monarchs lost all six matches, but the riders must have learned a lot on that trip when Poland was still a closed and virtually unknown speedway country.

In 1966, Henry was soon on the injured list with a badly broken thigh, an injury which ended his speedway career. Ian Hoskins then brought in Sweden's Runo Wedin, but Runo had a short stay in Scotland as the Speedway Riders' Association (the riders' trade union) put a ban on all new Swedish riders coming into the country. He was replaced briefly by Knut Syrrist and then more permanently by Reidar Eide.

During his short stay in Scotland, Runo had to fly back to Sweden to compete in World Championship round, so he left his car, a left-hand drive Volvo with me for 'safe-keeping'. By the time he returned, there were about another 500km on the clock.

My friends and I could not resist the temptation to have a drive in this Volvo. There were not many, or perhaps any, left hand drive Volvos with Swedish number plates in Glasgow. Pulling into a petrol station to fill up, my friend, Norman Christie began speaking to the attendant in pigeon English with a fake Swedish accent. Hearing this garbled conversation going on, another motorist came over to ask if he could help in translating and then began speaking to Norman in Swedish. Needless to say, we could not understand a word he was saying and beat a hasty retreat out of that petrol station as fast as we could.

By the end of the season, my fellow Monarchs, Doug Templeton and Jimmy Tannock headed for New Zealand to combine some winter sun with some speedway. It was another one of my ambitions to race 'Down Under' after following old black and white photographs of Australian racing in the winter editions of *Speedway Star*. I was too late – and too broke – to join Jimmy and Doug on their trip to New Zealand, but the seed had been planted and I was determined to make that trip Down Under for the winter season one way or another.

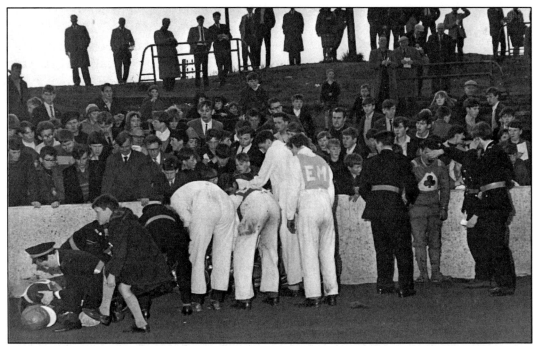

Edinburgh versus Belle Vue June 1966: After a crash, Bert is on the ground on the left, Belle Vue's Gordon McGregor is standing on the right.

Bert with Jack Biggs and (Newport) and Edinburgh team mate Bluey Scott.

Edinburgh versus Long Eaton August 1966 – from left: Kevin Torpie, Ray Wilson, Bengt Jansson, Doug Templeton and Bert judging the Miss Edinburgh Speedway contest.

Edinburgh versus Cradley Heath 8 October 1966, the last meeting of the season: (from left): Jimmy Tannock, Doug Templeton, Brian Collins, Dudley McKean, Bert, George Hunter and Bill Landels.

On parade before Edinburgh versus Coventry in June 1966: from left: Doug Templeton, Jimmy Tannock, Charlie Monk and Bert.

Edinburgh Monarchs 1967 team: Back: from left Bernt Persson, Oyvind Berg, Bill Landels, George Hunter; Front: Bert, Doug Templeton, Reidar Eide.

6. Have bike will travel

My progress in speedway continued slowly as I upped my points average steadily, a word not always associated with my on-track riding. However, I was yet to learn how to ride some of the away tracks.

With most away tracks involving many hours of road travel, the Scottish-based riders tended to 'double-up' with team mates, resulting in the whole team plus team manager, Tommy Hughson and team mechanic, Arty Fisher and the track spare machine, all travelling in two cars with trailers, loaded to the rafters.

Alex Hughson and I usually travelled with George Hunter and with three bikes on the trailer, his car only had a top speed of around 60 to 65mph on the motorways, but where George gained time was that he maintained that speed through the towns as well. The 'Ladybank Express' was fast on the track and off the track even when it came to making a quick 'pit stop' to grab something to eat on our way south. We had our team work organised to perfection. George would come roaring in to the petrol station on the motorway services and pull up at the petrol pumps. Alex and I would jump out and sprint over to the restaurant, order three meals and be sitting down eating by the time George arrived. George would finish his meal while we were still eating and would stand up, head for the door and say "Are ye cu-cu-coming?" George had a bit of a stutter when he was nervous and excited, so Alex and I knew that it was time to go.

At the time, we thought nothing of all the long hours on the road driving to and from Scotland, and we enjoyed the travelling. However, later I realised that we definitely had it tougher than riders who were based in England. The hours we spent on the road could have been put to better use. While we were on the road, southern-based riders could still be in the workshop or even relaxing at home before an evening meeting. The riders based north of the border had put in many hours driving and still had to be fresh, fit and ready to race by the early evening. In speedway, as in any other evening sport, we had to be at our sharpest when other people have done a day's work and are winding down.

In many respects, if top Scots such as George Hunter and Jim McMillan had moved their bases south earlier in their careers, then I think that they would have achieved even greater success than they did. Scottish based riders did not get too many open bookings on English tracks. Why should a promoter pay travelling expenses to bring a rider down from Scotland when he could get an equally talented rider based a couple of hours drive from his track? And that is why, in the mid-1970s, George and myself shared a house in Rugby in the Midlands. It was ideally situated for the motorways and had many tracks within a small radius. Jimmy Mac also moved to Rugby so we had our own 'Scots' corner'.

On my first trip to race at Bradford in a Northern League meeting at the old Greenfield Stadium in May 1962, I was heading south with Doug and Willie Templeton, with our captain, Doug at the wheel of his Ford. Not having been there before and not even knowing the size or shape of the Bradford track and which gear ratio to pull, I asked Willie Templeton "How big is the track at Bradford, Willie?" I was expecting an answer such as "350 yards or 400 yards", but then Willie said "Och, it's aboot twa' Acres". Two acres? I had forgotten that Doug and Willie were farmers from Fife and spoke a different language to me.

I don't remember much about that meeting other than, after riding the super smooth track at Old Meadowbank, Bradford was like a motocross track and so bumpy that on the wavy straight, my handlebars came up and hit me in the face, not very nice when you are wearing an open face helmet.

Improvement was coming slowly. In May 1967 I travelled down to Southampton to buy a new Eso/Jawa from Barry Briggs at his Terminus Terrace emporium underneath the railway arches. Compared to my old Jap, the Jawa was much easier to ride and the Czech machine proved much more reliable than my English Jap. The initials did not mean it was a Japanese motorcycle, only that it was built in London by engine maker, JA Prestwich. My first meeting on the Jawa was the World Championship qualifying round at Edinburgh and I notched up 12 points from five rides, which boded well for my future progress.

The Edinburgh Monarchs 1967 team was a strong one. Swedish star Bengt Jansson had moved down to London where he become a firm favourite at Hackney. His fellow countryman, Bernie Persson, rejoined the Monarchs after a brief spell with us in 1965. Oyvind Berg became our second Norwegian alongside Reidar Eide. We also had home-grown Scots Bill Landels, George Hunter, myself and our skipper, Doug Templeton, not a bad line-up. Unfortunately, we didn't win the league, but I think that we provided some good racing and entertainment along the way.

Ian Hoskins always had something extra for the fans to keep them amused during the interval whether it was Scottish pipe bands, cycle speedway or 'The world's greatest goalie' where Ian came out dressed as a goalkeeper with outsize gloves and tried to save 'penalties' taken by various team members. A lot of fun for the fans and the riders too.

Throughout the season, Ian Hoskins had been running a Miss Edinburgh Speedway competition during the interval. It was judged by the riders who happily gave up their interval cup of tea to survey the beauties on parade. There was a mad scramble for that job. By the end of the competition, the winner was crowned. Miss Edinburgh Speedway and the winner, Liz Mason, went on to become Mrs Liz Landels. That was not officially one of the prizes, but Big Bill certainly had a keen eye for talent and went on to marry the winner.

Bill and Liz were due to get married in Edinburgh at the end of the season and then emigrate to start a new life in Australia. However, on their honeymoon on board ship, they had an addition to their overseas luggage – me!

The 1967 Edinburgh Monarchs: Bert, Oyvind Berg, Reidar Eide, Ian Hoskins (promoter), Jimmy Tannock, Tommy Hughson (team manager), Doug Templeton (Capt – on bike), Bernt Persson, George Hunter, Bill Landels.

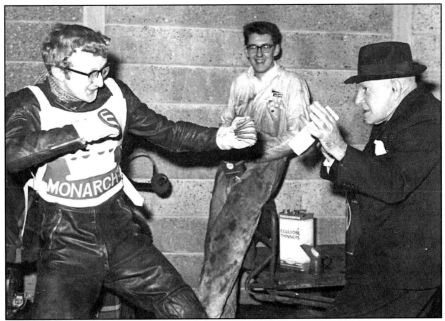

Resolving an issue with Johnnie Hoskins, with Dick Barrie in the background as referee (probably at West Ham).

Left: Bert in the pits in 1967.
Above: The Edinburgh Monarchs badge.
Below: After Bert's first maximum in 1967. A young Norrie Allan in the foreground. Norrie later worked with Ivan Mauger and Mark Loram

7. Australia here I come

Edinburgh's Old Meadowbank stadium was earmarked as one of the sites for the 1970 Commonwealth Games which were to be held in Scotland's capital city. So that grand old stadium was due to be demolished to make way for the new sports facilities.

Unfortunately, despite the healthy attendances at Old Meadowbank for speedway and well supported petitions from Monarchs fans, there would be no room for speedway at this new venue, so Ian Hoskins had to find the team a new home.

During the 1967 speedway season with Edinburgh, I had started planning for my first ever trip 'Down Under'. When I say 'planning', that is a bit of an exaggeration because I had no contacts in Australia, no idea of what the tracks were like and not really any idea of how I could get there.

Edinburgh and Glasgow were always happy hunting grounds for riders from Australia and New Zealand. My Australian team mate, Kevin Torpie, came up with the idea that if I came out to Melbourne, I could stay with him and his wife, Chris, so that was one part of my epic journey organised.

Kevin gave me the address of the Melbourne promoters and I wrote an airmail letter to Earl Vieney and Ez Haken, the promoters at Brooklyn Speedway in the State of Victoria – no emails in those days – to ask for rides there.

Unlike other more experienced riders from Britain, I was unknown in Australia and did not have a contract to get my fare paid. I had to raid my piggy bank and sell whatever I had: record player, records and so on to raise money for my fare. I would hopefully take whatever rides I could get.

At that time, in November 1967, flying to Australia was just too expensive. I also had to take my bike and gear with me, so flying was out of the question and out of reach of my short arms and not-too-deep pockets. This was also at the time when Australia was advertising for British families to emigrate to their country for only £10, with under-19s going free, the 'Ten Pound Poms'. I was neither emigrating nor was I aged under-19, so I had to pay the fare on my own.

I booked my passage to sail to Australia on the Sitmar Line passenger ship, the 13,000 tons MS *Fairsea* along with Bill and Liz who were moving to Sydney. I booked for Melbourne to meet up with Kev Torpie and hopefully get rides at Brooklyn Raceway.

Due to the sailing schedule, Bill and I had to miss the final meeting at Old Meadowbank which was a Best Pairs won by Kiwi Wayne Briggs and Norwegian Oyvind Berg. Edinburgh junior Brian Collins won the Scottish Junior Championship in the second half. Brian later became a star with Edinburgh, Wembley, Poole and Glasgow, so that early second half championship gave him a good foundation to improve.

The final Edinburgh meeting for Bill and myself was the British League match against Sheffield just three days before we were due to sail. I collected my first ever 12 point maximum. A great way to end the British season before heading off down under.

Our Edinburgh team mate, Jimmy Tannock, offered to drive us to Southampton to catch the ship, so we loaded our bike crates onto his trailer and got ready for our big adventure.

Going on board ship with Bill and Liz Landels.

Bill and Liz had just got married, but as we had a very early start in the morning and to save time, I slept outside their bedroom door in Edinburgh, probably not the quiet romantic honeymoon they had anticipated.

Next day, Jimmy drove us from Edinburgh to Southampton where we checked into a small hotel for the night. The manager who checked us in from behind his desk, also became the waiter in the restaurant that evening and when we went for a nightcap, he was also the barman. Needless to say, at breakfast the next morning, the same gentleman was our breakfast waiter and also the front desk receptionist when we checked out. A one-man-band hotel which deserved to succeed.

At the Southampton docks we saw the ship that was to be our home for the next six weeks. It was a small ship and not as fast or luxurious as the big P&O liners, but it was an exciting time. The only other ship I had been on, apart from sailing to the Isle of Man, was the Govan Ferry, a wee 'tug boat' that crossed the River Clyde in Glasgow.

The *Fairsea* had seen a lot of action. It had served in the American Navy, then the Royal Navy as a troop ship during the war, then on convoy duties in the North Atlantic and even caught fire off Panama. It then had a refit which turned it into a passenger ship so it carried the 'Ten Pound Poms' from Europe to Australia.

I shared the cheapest four-berth cabin in the bowels of the ship with three young guys who were emigrating to make a new life in Australia. Despite us having paid the lowest fare, we were still well fed during the voyage. Being so far below decks, we were kept awake at night with the throbbing of the propellers and noises from the engine room, but we soon got used to that and the noises eventually lulled us to sleep.

The journey was new experience for me. When we cast off from Southampton on a cold, wet, October day, the ship's officers were all wrapped up in their dark, heavy coats and the weather was very dull. However, as we sailed further south, the air got warmer, the sun came out and the officers changed into their summer 'whites', crisp white short sleeved shirts with matching white trousers. Suddenly they became a magnet for all the girls and women on board, but I guess that being Italian also helped.

Six weeks on a ship is a long time when we were heading into the 'unknown', but we make new friends en route and got a true impression of just how far away Australia is from Europe. This is not always appreciated when people fly on that journey.

We also saw other countries with their strange customs and ways of life. The *Fairsea* docked at Las Palmas and then went onto South Africa where sailing into Cape Town with Table Mountain in the background was an unforgettable sight. There was a day excursion to a Zulu village where the villagers, with their straw 'kilts', fancy headdresses and spears came out of their Rondavel mud huts and performed some native war dances for us tourists. They beat their animal skin shields with clubs and spears, very scary. It all looked very authentic and I thought that these people must be very poor and just live off the land, but that was until I noticed that the Zulu chief was wearing an expensive looking watch. I realised that this must just be show business and the locals only turn up from their homes when a cruise ship arrives.

From South Africa it was a long drag across the Indian Ocean with nothing to see except sea, sea and more sea until we eventually reached the coast of Western Australia and docked at the Perth port of Fremantle. Everyone went ashore, but had trouble finding our 'land legs' after such a long time rocking around in the sea.

Sailing into Fremantle was quite exciting with 80 degree heat and clear blue skies and a large 'Welcome to Western Australia' sign on the roof of the observation balcony where hundreds of people lined the quay to welcome their relatives and friends to Australia. Flags and banners with signs such as 'Welcome to Granddad Kelly' and 'G' Day from Western Australia' were being waved, but none said 'Welcome Haggis!"

Among the crowd of relatives and friends waiting for the *Fairsea* to dock were former West Ham and Norwich star Aub Lawson, Chum Taylor, the local West Australian who was almost unbeatable around the big Claremont track and former Edinburgh novice, Duncan Mitchell with former Edinburgh Monarch, 'Cuddly Dudley' McKean and his Scottish wife, Barbara who came from Leith. Aub and Chum were promoting at Claremont Speedway in Perth and had come down to the docks with some newspaper reporters to see if there were any speedway riders on board.

Bill Landels already had a contract to race in Sydney, so he could not sign up to ride in Perth, but I was heading to Australia to freelance and get rides wherever I could. Aub and Chum came on board and offered me a deal to race in Claremont for the season with guaranteed money each week and a job in the local Coca Cola factory. It sounded too good to be true, especially as I had not been offered a regular ride in Melbourne. I decided that I would take the plunge and race in Western Australia instead.

Unfortunately, the crate with my bike and equipment was in the part of the ship's hold marked 'Melbourne' and underneath the freight going to Adelaide, so it was not possible to have it unloaded in Perth. So I had to turn down Aub and Chum's offer and sail on to Melbourne. I thought that if it didn't work out for me in Melbourne, I could always come back to race in Perth. It was not such an easy task as the two cities were over 2,000 miles apart, just a wee bit further than my usual trips from Glasgow to Edinburgh.

In Perth I picked up an Australian speedway magazine covering cars, sidecars and solos (that's speedway) with an article about the British Lions and other riders coming to Australia that year. Of me, the journalist wrote: "Scotsman Bert Harkins of Edinburgh Monarchs is one of the few riders to wear spectacles when racing and cannot be a rider of any great distinction". "Wow!" I thought; "I'll show them."

About 200 passengers had disembarked at Fremantle so the ship was a bit quieter en route to Melbourne. Having survived the Bay of Biscay in the Atlantic and got our 'sea-legs', I thought that our days of being sea-sick had ended, but no-one had told me about the Great Australian Bight. This wild stretch of angry ocean sent the little *Fairsea* bobbing up and down all over again with cups, plates, chairs and passengers flying everywhere. Looking at the portholes we saw blue sky and then sea as the poor ship rocked and rolled its way across the ocean. Most people stayed in their cabins or just hung over the side of the ship, so it was a great relief when the *Fairsea* eventually docked in Melbourne in smoother waters.

Hanging over the ship's rail as we came in to dock, I scanned the waiting crowd on the quayside to see if I could spot my 'host', Kevin Torpie, but there was no sign of him. When I disembarked I discovered that he and Chris had moved to Queensland. But he had arranged for his friends, Tony and Louisa Melrose, to meet me and look after this Wandering Haggis.

8. Sunshine speedway

Tony and Louisa Melrose had a nice home in the Melbourne suburb of Seaford, just a short walk to the local beach which was at the bottom of the street, but I was more interested in getting onto the track and riding some speedway. Tony was one of the top 'B' grade riders at Melbourne, so I was able to ask him lots of questions about the track at Brooklyn Raceway.

As I unpacked the wooden crate with my speedway equipment and all my worldly goods at Tony's house, I found a selection of ladies underwear, bras, panties, a couple of bottles of 'Irn Bru' – Scotland's favourite non-alcoholic drink – and a gift-wrapped haggis which had 'gone off' in the Australian heat. My 'friends' in Glasgow had helped to pack the crate when I was not looking.

One addition when the crate was packed in Glasgow, was a young Tigers fan we had nicknamed 'Jimmy the Fan' – also known as James McGregor, who is now a speedway referee – who had been unceremoniously bundled into the crate and the lid nailed down. Luckily we let him out before the crate was shipped.

Still without any contract when I arrived in Australia. I phoned the promoters Earle Vienet and Ez Haken to let them know that I had arrived in Melbourne and asked if I could ride in Saturday night's meeting. They took one look at this skinny bespectacled Scotsman with red hair and I was told that because the coming Saturday was a very important interstate test match between the local Victorian side and South Australia. It was too important an event to risk putting an unknown rider like me into the programme. They said "You can have a ride after the meeting is over and we will see how you go in front of a big crowd and under the track lights."

I thought to myself 'Do they think that we don't have any electricity in Scotland and that we don't get good crowds and floodlights at Edinburgh?' This was a good case of déjà vu, just like returning to my novice days at Old Meadowbank when I and the other juniors rode a few laps on track after the league meeting was finished, if we were lucky.

Come the Saturday night I was in the pits at Brooklyn Speedway, all changed and ready to race but without a ride on the programme. As luck would have it, one of the Victorian riders was involved in a car crash en route to the track and had to pull out of the meeting. The promoters anxiously scanned the pits to see who could ride as a replacement. I put my hand up like a keen schoolboy answering the teacher's question and said: "I am ready". I felt like Oliver Twist asking for more, but with my pale Scottish complexion, ginger hair, slight build and glasses, no one took me for a speedway rider, so once again I was passed by.

"No," the promoters said. "This test match is too important, this track is bit different from Britain, it is fast and bumpy, but you can have a ride after the meeting."

In the end, there was no-one they could use so they reluctantly put me straight into heat one without any practice laps and the anxious instructions: "This Interstate Championship is very important to us, so do your best."

I hopped out of the start, passed South Australian skipper, John Boulger and won the race, breaking the one lap and three lap track records along the way. Scratch races were over three laps and the handicap races over four. I went on to win all my races, with a few more track records, and Victoria won the Interstate Championship. All was well with the world and I was welcomed with open arms.

What I did not realise was that the faster I was going in the scratch races, the bigger the handicap I would have in the second half six-rider handicap events. In my handicap heat, I was off 220 yards behind the gate. I won that race and added the four lap track record to my collection.

In the handicap final, I had worked my way up to third when I had a puncture, but managed to finish the race with the tyre almost coming off and scraped into the points money. After all that Earle Vienet and Ez Haken realised that I could ride a speedway bike a wee bit, even under the floodlights in Melbourne. They asked me to stay for the season and not return to Perth. I was offered a minimum guarantee of $40 [about £19] per meeting, which at that time was quite good money, along with my fare paid to return the following season. I was also offered other meetings at Mildura, Myrtleford, Kembla Grange and interstate in Adelaide and Sydney, along with entry into the Victorian and New South Wales Championships, so all was well with my new world.

A nice touch was that many of the friends I had made on that six week voyage on the *Fairsea* came along to watch the speedway and have a reunion barbeque. Travelling by ship was much slower than flying, but I certainly made friends in board and saw different countries, so the motto should be: "Become a speedway rider and see the world".

This 'Sunshine speedway' proved to be a great way to spend the European winter, especially when I got airmail letters from Scotland telling me all about the cold, wet and wintry weather back home in 'Dear Old Glasgow Town'.

Australian speedway was a world away from what I knew back home. Their 'speedway' was a mixture of cars, sidecars, midgets, saloons and solo motorcycles – that's us – and the racing in each class was very spectacular. When the solos were finished, I watched the other forms of Australian speedway sport.

The sidecar races, with their big Vincent, Triumph and Kawasaki engines, raced the opposite way round to the solos. The passengers hung over the rear wheel like rag dolls while the drivers wrestled with the handlebars and the other competitors. Exciting stuff! The midgets were equally spectacular with the drivers sliding their open-wheeled cars like speedway bikes and, like the sidecars, were often involved in big crashes on the fast Australian tracks.

Race meetings often ran onto about midnight, followed by a barbeque when the weather had cooled down to around 80° Fahrenheit. That was something we could not do on a chilly Caledonian evening.

In the solo scene, the meetings I had 'up country' in Mildura and Myrtleford were usually held in the afternoon with temperatures around 80° to 90° Fahrenheit. Trying to race in those conditions was a million miles away from the cold, damp end-of-season meetings in Britain where we had to put our gloves on top of the engine just to keep them warm.

This was long before riders began to use lightweight Kevlar suits, so it was even a struggle to pull on our one-piece leathers in the heat. Sometimes it was so hot that riders stood under the spray of the water cart to cool down

Australian summers can get pretty hot and there was a story in the newspapers at that time of the Moss family, who arrived from England by ship on a Wednesday, docking on the hottest day for 30 years, 110.8°F. They got such a shock that on the next day, Thursday, they promptly hopped on a London-bound plane and flew home to the cooler temperatures of a British winter.

The local newspapers and television stations begun to hear about this wee Scottish guy with glasses who was beating the locals in Melbourne, and wanted some photos and interviews. There had been weird stories in the papers saying things like, "Melbourne's new Scotsman, Bert Harkins lifts his front wheel going into a corner to gain more speed." Mmm, here is the original story from that Melbourne newspaper:

"If the race had been for travelling straight up he would have won it easily. Unfortunately the riders were supposed to be travelling forward. Scottish speedway star Bert Harkins was one of the leaders for about two yards. Then his machine flew into the air and ... crunch. Luckily he wasn't hurt. And luckily it was only practice.

Bert, one of a number of international speedway stars now in Melbourne, owes a lot of his fame to his ability to ride a speedway motorcycle at high speed with the front wheel in the air. He's one of the few riders to master the trick. And he uses it to advantage in just about every race.

At a start or going into a corner he will flip his machine upwards and ride for perhaps 20 yards balanced on only the back wheel. The manoeuvre is particularly helpful for cutting down the drag involved in cornering. It saves him about two seconds a lap at the most. But against the class competition Bert faces even a fraction of a second saved can win a race. He was showing how it's done out at Brooklyn yesterday. And as this series shows even this expert in haste finds his trick sometimes means less speed."

So there it is, whoever wrote this article had never ridden a speedway bike.

The England team were also in Australia at that time. They won the test series 3–2. Halfway through the series it was agreed that in the tests each team could have two reserves instead of one. I thought that because I was doing so well on Australian tracks, I may be called up as replacement in the touring team, but that was not to be so I continued my solo career as a freelance rider. 'Have bike, will travel'.

Nigel Boocock's England team did come to Melbourne in an unofficial Lions versus Demons 'test' match. The local newspapers, radio and television stations were anxious to see the victorious Englishmen. We were all invited to be at the Brooklyn Raceway at 11am the next morning for publicity photos. Unfortunately, I was only told about this at 11pm the previous evening and, because my bike was in bits and my leathers were away for repair – crashing again – I was struggling to be ready in time. However, I was able to bolt a bike together for the action shots and borrowed a set of black leathers from a road racing friend.

All went well with lots of racing footage of the English riders for the television, but the reporters were struggling with Nigel's Yorkshire accent, especially when he kept asking if they had seen his friend, Edgar Jessup, in the crowd. Now 'Edgar' was a fictitious friend who followed Nigel around and Booey frequently bamboozled everyone from airline staff to speedway promoters when asking about Edgar's whereabouts.

Above and right: Demonstrating wheelies.

One of the national newspaper reporters came along with his photographer and asked me to do some wheelies, "Just like you do when going into the corners", he said. Little did he know that the wheelies I was doing away from the starting gate, not into the corners as reported, during my races were not quite intentional, but I was always able to control them.

The opposite was true when I was asked to perform for the cameras and I succeeded in looping my bike, not once, but twice during the photo session. The following day there was a double page spread in the *Melbourne Sun*, with me rolling around the Melbourne track after my failed wheelie. I hoped that my road racing friend did not see what I was doing to his nice leathers that I had borrowed, but the story had a happy ending. Earl Vienet gave me an extra $20 for helping to promote Melbourne Speedway.

A bumper crowd turned up for our Lions versus Demons international, possibly coming to see if I could fall off again, but really they were coming to see the visiting English riders and how the local stars would fare against them. The Demons ran out winners 32–22. Nigel Boocock was top scorer for the Melbourne Demons and I was top for the Lions. Somehow I think we were in the wrong teams as Nigel was captain of the British Lions on that tour and I was the 'home' rider at Melbourne, but Australian speedway sometimes works in mysterious ways. I think that they just mixed up the riders to even up the teams, The local newspaper said that "The Victorian team will be strengthened by the inclusion of visiting English rider, Bert Harness." Just one of the many different names I have had over the years but they don't usually get my nationality wrong.

It may have been a different type of speedway life for me with sun, sea and barbeques, but on track, the racing was pretty tough. Riders who were unheard of in Britain turned out to be superstars on their home tracks, so even the British Lions touring team did not find it easy. Englishmen Cyril and David Crane, came out to Australia for a holiday, but fancied a ride at Melbourne. In his very first ride in Australia, one of the locals slid off and Cyril clipped his rear wheel and hit the safety fence hard. He lost some teeth and injured his neck, so that was the end of his Australian speedway career. Later on he took charge of the Boston Barracudas in the UK, and found that promoting was not quite as dangerous an occupation.

At Brooklyn Speedway, apart from local stars Johnny Dewhurst, Peter Moore and others, we also had John Boulger and Garry Middleton, the self-styled 'Cassius Clay' of speedway. If there had been a World Championship for talking, then Garry would have been champion many times over. He was a very good rider, but liked to wind himself and his opponents up before, during and after the meeting. He often claimed to be the Melbourne track record holder, but that the timekeeper had cheated him and given him a slower time on purpose.

Starting procedures in Australia were a bit different to what I was used to. Quite often 'Cas' would sit back from the tapes, then drop the clutch and be doing about 20mph as the tapes went up. I soon cottoned on and had to use similar tactics so there were some fearsome battles on the track.

Garry even tried to buy points from me one night saying that he had 'got a deal' from BP Fuels and needed to win races to keep the sponsorship, so he would pay me for first place if I finished behind him. He was such a fast rider that he did not need to buy points from me or anyone else. I was trying to build a reputation of my own in Australia so there was no way I was ever going to throw a race, end of story. I then went out in our race and tried to put as much distance between us as possible, so that he would know that I wouldn't 'play ball'.

To show a typical schedule in Australia, here is the story of one eventful weekend of speedway. After our Saturday night meetings in Melbourne, riders were often booked to race in Mildura the following evening, travelling in two cars with trailers. Mildura was around 340 miles from Melbourne in the Sunraysia area of Victoria. We often drove there overnight, not because of the distance or the traffic, but to try to avoid the heat of the day. Of course there was no air-conditioning in the cars.

By the time our Saturday late night meeting had finished and we had had a shower and something to eat, it was around 1.30am before we got on the road. We usually pulled into Mildura by late morning, checked into a local motel, then found the swimming pool to keep cool in the 100° heat before crashing out in the air-conditioned chalets.

By the evening it had cooled down to around 85° Fahrenheit, so we headed for the track where the local television station was already interviewing Garry Middleton. To open the meeting, Johnny Dewhurst, John Boulger, Garry and I all had separate cracks at breaking the track record. I am not sure who came out on top of the record attempt, or if any of us broke the track record, but the four of us were due to meet in the following individual meeting. I had won my first race and then, next time out, finished second to John Boulger and ahead of Johnny Dewhurst and Garry and that is when the 'fun' started. After the race, 'Cas' complained that there should be a rerun because John Boulger had started from the wrong gate position. However, he had only complained after the race had finished and he ran a last. Garry argued that he wanted a rerun or to be paid for first place. No wonder we called him 'Cas the Gas'. The meeting was held up as the referee, riders, start marshal and other officials had a long discussion about Garry's protest. I didn't want a rerun after doing four laps in the physically draining temperature of 85°, but after much heated argument, it was decided to rerun the race. At that point, Garry withdrew his protest so the race would not be rerun after all and the meeting carried on.

Garry's 'fun and games' had not finished because we met again in the handicap final. I was right on his exhaust pipe when he dropped the bike going into the fast first turn on the second lap. I missed hitting Garry – something I may have come to regret later – but clipped his back wheel and did a 'Flying Scotsman' act as I flew over the handlebars. Local hero Johnny Dewhurst hit my bike in the carnage and then hit the wooden fence, dislocating his shoulder. Both Johnny and I were lying on the track with a couple of bent-up Eso machines on top of us and Garry did not even come up to say 'Thanks for missing me, fellas'. The meeting was held up for about 20 minutes while the track staff untangled us from the bikes and cleared the debris. The ambulance took Johnny to the local hospital.

When I eventually got back to the pits, there was commotion everywhere. 'Cas' was sitting on his bike waiting for the rerun and Johnny Boulger was protesting to the meeting steward (referee). I also said that Garry should be excluded for causing the crash but he said that he had been knocked off by the rider behind him, i.e. me, and that I should be excluded from the rerun, so that is gratitude for you. I tried to reason with the steward, but was told to "Shut up or go home." The steward also called Boulger "A trouble maker" so there was much heated argument during which 'A' grade rider, Phil Sedgeman, was all set to thump the steward. I asked Garry to own up that all of this was his fault. He had fallen off first and caused the mayhem, but insisted that he had been knocked off by the rider behind him and refused to leave the track. Eventually, with tempers running so high, the officials decided to abandon the race completely and would not let us restart. Perhaps that was a wise decision.

John Boulger, Garry Middleton and I had one more race left on the programme, a six rider, six lap scratch race. My Eso was too badly damaged from the previous crash so I borrowed my old Jap from Tony Melrose and it really flew, but every time I tried to overtake Cas, he rode me out to the fence and that gave Johnny Boulger a chance to hit the front. Unfortunately, JB dropped it right in front of me and again I had to execute a very rapid 'lay-down' to avoid him. With the red lights on and John and I trying to untangle the mass of bikes and bodies, 'Cas' proceeded to do not one lap of honour, but three, waving to the crowd and claiming victory. What a guy. He certainly knew how to get the crowd going, but was not quite so popular with his fellow riders.

I was always treated very well when I rode in Mildura. The first time I rode there, a lady presented me with a large carton of freshly picked grapes. They were huge and juicy and unlike anything I could get back home in Glasgow. The Sunraysia region was definitely 'the fruit basket of Australia'.

The Mildura clubroom was open until 3am for the after-meeting barbeque and get-together. Then we headed back to the motel where we hopped into the open air pool to cool off until 4.30am by which time the manager kindly asked us to leave as we were keeping the other guests awake. Such were the joys of Australian speedway.

9. A title to my name

My debut season in Australia was proving to be a wise decision on how to spend the British speedway close season. It was an ambition of mine to do so and something I would recommend to any young up-and-coming British rider. I learnt to live away from home in a different country and environment, with Christmas Day falling in the middle of summer and instead of Santa Claus arriving on his sledge pulled by reindeer, he can usually be seen water skiing behind a speedboat with his sack of toys slung over his shoulder.

I learnt to look after my bikes – and myself – and rode on tracks which are quite different from anywhere I had raced in Britain and in different weather conditions. On top of that, there is the laid-back sunshine-way-of-life of Australia. I returned to Europe fitter and faster and ready to take on the world.

Despite not being part of the British touring team, I got plenty of Interstate bookings at other tracks along with my Saturday nights racing in Melbourne and by February, the main event of the season was due to be raced for at Melbourne's Brooklyn Raceway: The Victorian State Championship.

This State Championship dates back to the early dirt track years in Australia when the meeting was held at the Geelong Velodrome in the 1926–27 season. The first winner was an Australian, Billy Pilgrim. After the war, World Champion Lionel Van Praag won the title in the 1946–47 season and thereafter, the Victorian Championship was only won by a non-Australian rider on six occasions. Sweden's Ulf Eriksson, England's Gerry Hussey, Scotland's Ken McKinlay, England's Roy Trigg and multi World Champion Ivan Mauger of New Zealand have all achieved this feat.

That summer in Australia proved to be one of the hottest and driest on record. On the day of the 1968 Victorian Championship, I had been waiting for parts for my Eso. After rebuilding most of it on the Friday evening, I got up at 6.30am to finish the job. As I worked on the bike, the temperature climbed up to 102°, pretty hot for me and, when I eventually finished in the early afternoon, I collapsed into bed to recover some strength. After three showers to cool down and waken up, I was ready to head for the track where, by evening, the temperature had cooled down to 83°.

The Championship was run on the lines of the Grand Prix, with the top four riders going into a Grand Final. I was top scorer going into the final, having dropped my only point to Garry Middleton. He also qualified for the Final along with John Boulger and Johnny Dewhurst. As I expected, Cas was up to his old tricks, trying to unsettle his opponents. He held the race up as he fiddled around with his bike – there was no two minute warning – then when he eventually came up to the start, he broke the tapes. No tape exclusions either.

After repairs to the starting gate and more time wasting from Mr Middleton, the final had now been held up for around 10 minutes, which could not happen in the GPs these days where BSI run a very tight ship for the television cameras and the fans. As luck would have it, as we rolled round to the tapes for yet another rerun, the fingers of my left hand clamped tightly shut with cramp and I could not operate the clutch lever. This time I held up events while an ambulance man massaged my wrist and fingers until I was ready to go.

Bert's first meeting at Brooklyn Speedway, Melbourne, 11 November 1967.

Bert leading Johhny Dewhurst in heat three of the Victorian Solo Championship,
17 February 1968.

Left: Winner of the Victorian Solo Championship, February 1968.
Right: Melbourne speedway badge.
Bottom: Riding against Colin Pratt (left) and Nigel Boocock (right) in Melbourne, January 1968.

59

I think the cramp was caused by the heat, the vibration of the handlebars and holding the clutch too long. I had been advised to take salt tablets to help counteract the salt lost from the body when sweating inside my one piece speedway leathers, but had not done so.

After some further delays, the Grand Final got underway. I got into the lead by the second lap and then my fingers cramped again. Luckily they were clamped around the handlebar and the track was big and fast so I didn't need to use them until after I passed the chequered flag. I just had to stall the bike as I could not pull in the clutch. Second place went to John Boulger with Garry Middleton third. Johnny Dewhurst was second when he seized the engine on his Eso.

After the presentations, I had to take the cylinder head off of my bike for scrutineering so that my engine could be measured as 'someone' had protested that it was oversize. It took the officials threequarters of an hour of measurements and calculations before they gave me the all-clear. Nowadays, Jim McMillan and his FIM Grand Prix machine examining team could have done the job in quarter of that time. The Australian machine examiner had originally said that my motor was oversize, much to the delight of Mr Middleton, but eventually it was proven to be under 500cc so the celebrations could begin.

There were many Scots in the crowd at Melbourne that night and they got almost as big a kick from my win as I did. They celebrated by singing *I belong to Glasgow* at the top of their voices. It was an emotional evening for a young Scot so far from home.

So that is how a one-handed Scotsman added his name to the list of Victorian State Champions. The meeting had been sponsored by Craven Filter Cigarettes with a nice silver trophy and fortunately, no cigarettes as I didn't smoke. The last car race finished at 1.30am and the meeting ended with another giant barbeque at the track. At the time, this was illegal as the whole state of Victoria was dry as a bone with bush fires starting everywhere, so there was a ban on all open air fires. However, we were in a safe area surrounded by fire extinguishers. The following day, my fellow Scotsman, Jim Clark won the Tasman Cup car race so it was a good weekend for Scotland. He, Graham Hill and Jack Brabham were due to race in the Australian Grand Prix the following weekend.

I still had a few more meetings to race in Australia before heading back home, including another South Australia versus Victoria test match in Adelaide. Our Victorian team including Johnny Dewhurst, Garry Middleton, Peter Bradshaw and me, plus individual events in Sydney and Melbourne.

Meanwhile, back in Edinburgh, despite a huge petition from Monarchs' fans, demolition had started on the Old Meadowbank stadium and promoter Ian Hoskins had been searching for a new home for the Monarchs within Edinburgh without any success. So despite petitions from many thousands of Monarchs' fans, speedway was lost to Scotland's capital city.

I received an airmail letter from Ian telling me that he had found a track at the Albion Rovers Football Club in Coatbridge, some 10 miles east of Glasgow and that the team would be transferred there and known as the Coatbridge Monarchs. My first reaction was "Where the heck is Coatbridge?" Although it was much nearer to my Eastwood home, I had no idea where it was. I soon discovered that Coatbridge was once the heart of the coal, steel and iron industry in Scotland and it was destined to become a very important heart of Scottish speedway. The Monarchs made their home at Cliftonhill for two years until closing and

60

transferring most of the team to Wembley. But in 1973, after leaving Glasgow's famous Hampden Park stadium, the Glasgow Tigers moved in to Coatbridge to maintain the speedway connection with the town.

I had been offered the chance to stay in Australia and race up in Queensland during the Australian winter, but I still had ambitions in British and world speedway. After hearing from Ian Hoskins that the Monarchs would still be in the league, I headed back to the UK accompanied by my nemesis, the guy who tried to get me excluded from so many races – Garry Middleton.

Garry was just as madcap off a bike as he was on it. On the way back to the UK we had a rickshaw race in Hong Kong and he tried to pay his driver to run my rickshaw off the road.

That evening when I returned to the run down Hong Kong hotel where we were sharing a room, I opened the door and saw Garry, standing in front of a mirror holding a book and repeating, "You WILL be World Champion, You WILL be World Champion". I looked at the book he was holding and I saw the title *Teach yourself self-hypnosis*. Cas had heard me coming up the stairs and started his chanting as I opened the door, more mind games from Cas the Gas. Travelling with Garry really was an eye opener. We came back via Germany and popped over the border to the Jawa factory in communist Czechoslovakia.

At the factory, we met the bosses of Motokov and Garry tried to talk his way into becoming a Jawa works rider by telling them that he was the next world speedway champion, but all to no avail. We did, however, manage to purchase a new Jawa engine each at a discount which, when we brought them back home with us, caused a few problems with the sole UK importer, Barry Briggs. Briggo got word of our 'smuggling' game and sent me a very stern letter stating that I had avoided paying tax, and import duty and that he would have to report me to Customs & Excise for evasion of taxes. That letter had me shaking in my speedway boots, but we talked it over, cleared the air and have remained friends to this day.

When I became the sole UK importer for Scott USA Goggles in the 1980s, I understood Barry's position better because it wasn't fair that the importer did all the hard work, advertising and sponsorship then someone else would bring in the same product through the 'back door' without incurring the same expenses. It happened to me with Scott so perhaps that was my comeuppance for doing the same to Briggo all those years ago.

My 'trails of the unexpected" travelling with Garry was not yet over as I was soon to discover. Landing at Heathrow Airport, my return to Britain was not marked by cheering crowds waving flags and photographers from the speedway magazines, but instead by a couple of stern-faced Customs officials.

Before I had left Australia, my friends in Melbourne had given me a farewell party and presented me with the gift of a large toy Koala bear complete with tartan scarf. This Koala was quite heavy because it had a musical box inside. When I wound the key, it would play *Waltzing Matilda* much to everyone's amusement. When we landed in Heathrow, Customs officials took Garry away for questioning about some new duty free transistor radios which he, as an Australian, was bringing into the UK. Garry, as usual, managed to talk his way out of a possible fine by insisting that as he was a famous international speedway rider, he needed the radios to check on the weather forecasts in the different countries he was riding in. I am not sure what the Customs officials said, but I saw them look at each other and shake their heads in disbelief and wave him on.

Meanwhile as I had been hanging around waiting for Cas the Gas, the Customs officials must have thought that I looked suspicious – I always had a guilty look when confronted by policemen or Customs officers – and as I had just arrived from Hong Kong, they thought that I may be smuggling something into the country. They called me over for a thorough search. They emptied my bags, including the one with my leathers, boots and trophies and even went to the lengths of checking inside the shoulder and elbow pads of my speedway leathers. Frustrated at finding nothing illegal or incriminating, the customs officers started to check my Koala bear and finding that it felt very heavy for a toy, they must have thought that I was smuggling something inside it. They unpicked the stitching, pulled out all the internal cotton wool stuffing only to find the bear's music box inside and no illegal radios or watches. By the time they had finished, the Koala looked very bare indeed and I thought about calling him, 'Fred' ('Fred Bare'). I think that they were quite disappointed so they just pushed the bear back to me. I had to refill the stuffing and try to put the bear together again, but at least they did not impound my Koala for smuggling or quarantine.

I had left Australia at the end of their summer season with the Arnold Schwarzenegger message "I'll be back" and true to my word that is what happened.

Earl Vienet sent me an offer by airmail letter to ride in Melbourne the following season and this time I would have my fare paid and a weekly guarantee to ride at Brooklyn Raceway, so my perseverance had paid off.

Bert showing his Koala bear to his Coatbridge team-mates.

10. Back to reality

My first ever close season trip to Australia had been a great learning curve in my speedway apprenticeship. However, leaving the blue skies, warmth and sunshine of Australia and arriving back in Glasgow on a drizzling, grey, cold March morning with the rain glistening off the cobblestones and tramcars trundling along in the cloudy gloom was a bit of a shock to the system. After the dazzling blue sky brightness of Australia, Dear Old Glasgow Toon looked very grey and dull. Yes, it was back to reality, but it was home.

My new track at Coatbridge was to prove a good one for me. The experience I had gained from my winter racing in Australia was invaluable, and at last I was beginning to show some on-track improvement. I was chock-full of enthusiasm for the new season and new challenge. The Monarchs soon got to grips with the spectacular new track at Coatbridge. It was 380 yards long with steep banking on the corners. It provided some memorable racing and unusual incidents, but more of that later. The new Monarchs built up a good following from locals who had never seen speedway before, plus the 'die hard' loyal fans who had followed their team west from Edinburgh to Coatbridge. The close proximity to Glasgow made Coatbridge an ideal 'away' track for Glasgow Tigers fans to visit, so Scottish speedway was alive and well and living in Coatbridge. Every week, a large contingent of Glaswegians in their red and white scarfs filled the second bend terracing and cheered like mad for whoever the Monarchs were racing against that night.

Many a visiting English rider wondered why he got so much support at Coatbridge and now you know. The presence of the Tigers fans created a lot of friendly rivalry between the two sets of Scottish supporters. It gave Coatbridge a unique atmosphere and meant that the teams from south of the border had some extra vocal support.

On the Monarchs team front, Bill Landels had stayed in Australia, but we had a pretty good squad, spearheaded by the Scandinavian duo of Bernie Persson and Reidar Eide with home grown Scots, George Hunter, team captain Doug Templeton, Alex Hughson, Brian Collins and myself with Brian Black, Lex Milloy and Jimmy Tannock also getting the occasional call-up to ride in the Monarchs' colours. When Reidar first joined us, he didn't know any of our names, so because I always wore glasses, I was referred to as "Him with bike on face". That name stuck for a while.

Fresh from a winter's racing, my debut at the new track did not go as well as expected because I was dogged by mechanical trouble. Before I left Australia, I had blown up my best motor in Melbourne and decided to send it down to Adelaide for one of the top tuners to give it his magic touch, ready for the new British season. This was the first time I could afford to have someone prepare an engine for me. Previously I had carried out all the mechanical work myself, partly because I knew a little bit about mechanics, but more because I could not afford to employ an engine tuner.

The engine was ready just prior to my departure from Melbourne so when I flew home, I carefully carried it my hand luggage, something which is impossible to do in these days of weight restrictions, health & safety and security. I also used to carry a sharp tyre-cutting knife in my hand luggage, so you can imagine what would happen if I tried that in today's air travel climate. There was one flight I boarded where the hostess said "Let me put that bag in the overhead locker for you". She bent down to pick up my bag holding the Jawa engine and her knees just buckled. "OK", she said with a painful look on her face, "you can just put the bag on the floor between your feet."

My 'magic motor' from Australia was fitted for my first meeting at Coatbridge. It was the Champagne Derby against Glasgow Tigers, but that saw me in all sorts of mechanical trouble. In my first race, the bike packed up when the ignition timing slipped. I missed my next ride while retiming the magneto and was sitting behind George Hunter for a 5–1 in my third race when the engine seized. So much for my ace Australian Jawa tuner. I finished the meeting riding Alex Hughson's Jap. Fortunately, the rest of the Monarchs were on form and we ran out winners on aggregate 99–93, a wee bit too close for comfort.

Over at Glasgow White City, Jim McMillan had quickly taken over the number one spot which had been vacated when their Australian star, Charlie Monk, had his transfer request granted. Jimmy had only started riding a couple of seasons earlier at Cowdenbeath. He and Brian Collins were two of the best riders to emerge from that open licence track. Jimmy Mac had the added advantage of guidance from Doug and Willie Templeton, and he did so many laps practicing on their bikes in his early days that he just about ran both bikes into the ground. The only downside was that Jimmy had to wash the bikes and work on them.

The season progressed well for Coatbridge at home, but our away form let us down at times. Highlights were usually the local derbies against the Glasgow Tigers, which brought out the best, and the worst, in both teams. The farmer brothers Templeton were always tough riders. Dougie was captain of the Monarchs while his brother Willie was a heat leader for Glasgow Tigers. On one occasion, there had been a bit a shoulder charging during the race and as the race finished, everyone was surprised to see Doug and Willie swinging punches at one another as they rode down the straight on the 'cool-down' lap.

The crowd loved it and, as they returned to the pits, the 'discussion' continued with arms flying and bikes being knocked over like skittles. It all looked very serious, but it was 'heat-of-the-moment' stuff and in the bar at the end of the meeting, they were laughing and joking and sharing a drink, so there were no hard feelings. It wasn't just the Templetons who got caught up in the electric atmosphere on the Scottish Cup. I fell foul of Reidar Eide, our flame-haired Norwegian with a temper to match.

We had a 'coming-together' on the track and when we got back to the pits, Reidar pulled down his facemask and snarled at me through gritted teeth, "Harkins, I will keel you" and that was from my own team mate. I was a bit wary in my next outing with Reidar, but all went smoothly with no more tantrums. I later discovered that Halifax's Eric Boocock had also had the same warning, and Booey also lived to tell the tale. Although 'Reidar the Slider' had a short fuse, thankfully he did not carry out his murderous threats.

From my own point of view, the close season in Australia had helped a lot and I began to move up to third heat leader and, much to everyone's surprise, I also had a good run in the World Championship qualifying rounds. I scored 13 points at Newcastle to take third place behind World Champion Kiwis, Ivan Mauger and Barry Briggs; 14 points at Glasgow White City to finish second behind Swindon's Bob Kilby with my friendly rival, Jim McMillan only one point behind on 13. After third and 13 points in my first round, second with 14 points in my second round, by the law of averages, I should have scored 15 points for first place in my home round at Coatbridge the following evening. Speedway doesn't work that way. Swindon's Martin Ashby won the Coatbridge World Championship Round with a 15 point maximum. I finished a bit lower with 10 points, but still enough to qualify for the next round.

Unfortunately, that run of form did not continue and I was knocked out of the World Championship at the British semi-final at Sheffield, so it was back to square one and the bread and butter of league racing again.

Ian Hoskins, forever on the lookout for new horizons, arranged to take a Scottish Select over to Ireland for an open meeting in an attempt to re-establish the sport which had flourished at Shelbourne Park in Dublin in the 1950s with Ronnie Moore and his Wimbledon teammates. In those days, the riders were flown over from England, but we travelled the slower and cheaper way, by boat. We were met by old time Irish rider, 'Spud' Murphy who drove us out to the stadium in his 'radio car' which was fitted with loudspeakers on the roof. All the way through the busy city of Belfast 'Spud' kept up his 'Come to the speedway' commentary giving the pedestrians an earful about the thrills and spills of speedway racing in Ireland. Inside the car, we were being deafened with the sheer volume of the PA system. When Spud ended one of his adverts, Jimmy Tannock, in his strong Glaswegian accent told him what to do with his microphone. A stream of bad language erupted in both Irish and Glaswegian accents, but unfortunately the mic was still switched on and, as we were stuck in a traffic jam, the gathering crowd heard every word loud and clear.

The meeting itself turned out to be a rather casual affair in front of a sparse crowd, so the verbal fisticuffs on the mic had not persuaded many people to come to see if this argument would continue on the track. The organisation was a bit slap-happy too and Ian Hoskins had to assist the announcer and the referee who were not too sure about the jobs they had to do. FIM Speedway Grand Prix this was not. The first race after the interval was sent underway by the start marshal before the referee had returned from his tea-break, but it was Doug Templeton who suffered most from their 'Irish speedway rules'. Doug was all ready to go out for his race when a local photographer asked him to pose for some shots for the local paper. Obliging as always, Big Dougie sat on his machine and smiled for the camera. It was only when this budding Mike Patrick kept asking for shots from different angles that he realized that the other riders had gone up to the starting gate, but when he tried to get onto the track, his way was barred by a rather large pits marshal. While Doug had been posing for photos, the track officials had replaced him with the local reserve and when Mr T protested that he should have been in that race, the pits marshal told him "Don't worry, Jock, you can go in the next one." Somehow I cannot see that happening in British speedway.

We never worked out who won the event, but at the reception afterwards, we were sitting around talking to some of the locals when the sound of raised angry voices came from outside. Suddenly, the door burst open and two locals tumbled in, wrestling and punching each other as they fought around the room. The Irish riders calmly lifted their drinks out of the way and continued talking as the two fighters made their way around the room and back out of the door. It transpired that this was a local rider having a dispute with the promoter over his points money. Later on they were the best of friends, laughing and joking together, something else not seen in British speedway – promoter versus rider fisticuffs, I mean.

65

Leading Ronnie Moore at Coatbridge.

Trying out new goggles.

With Wayne Briggs at Coatbridge.

Loading up the bike after a rained-off meeting.

The Monarchs' stay at Coatbridge only lasted two seasons, but thanks to our go-ahead promoter, Ian Hoskins, there was always plenty going on to keep the fans, and even the riders, entertained. Everything from cycle speedway races to pie eating contests, a visit to the speedway was always full of surprises.

We had international meetings in 1968 and 1969: Scotland 62 England 46, Scotland 47 Australia 61 where I collected an 18 point maximum, and Scotland 62 Norway 46 at Glasgow and the following evening at Coatbridge, Scotland 56 Norway 52. It was at this last match that an incident occurred which has gone into Scottish speedway folk lore.

Scotland could field plenty of home-grown riders including Jim McMillan, George Hunter, Ken McKinlay, Doug and Willie Templeton, Bobby Beaton, Brian Collins, Alistair Brady and me and 'Honorary Scot' Charlie Monk. We could put up a good show against most nations. Norway were pretty strong too, with Reidar Eide, Oyvind Berg, Ulf Lovaas, Edgar Stangeland, Einer Egedius and Jon Odegaard, so the teams were quite evenly matched.

Reidar Eide and I were rival captains in the Scotland versus Norway international and Ian Hoskins had organised the meeting with his normal flair and razzmatazz. As usual at meetings involving Scotland, 'Hossy' always booked a pipe band to pipe the teams onto the track for the Grand Parade. The rousing bagpipe tune *The Black Bear* became the marching-on tune for the Scots. During the interval, the crowd were entertained by the Pipe Band marching around the track playing *Scotland the Brave* and other stirring tunes to fire up the Scots.

Reidar and I were out in the first heat after the interval and we lined up at the tapes, with engines revving and, as the green light came on, I noticed some flashes of colour on the first bend. Suddenly the tapes flew up, we charged towards that first bend and I quickly realised what those 'flashes of colour' were. It was the Clan McGregor Pipe Band still marching around the track. The referee had failed to notice them on the track and started the race. He also started a panic in the hearts of the bandsmen because someone had closed the gate from the track to the car park. The pipers quickly realised that they had four fire-breathing, methanol-drinking, unsilenced Jawas with no brakes bearing down on them and there were drums and bagpipes being thrown over the fence followed by a mad scramble of 'kilties' trying to get over the wooden safety fence. The poor laddie who was playing the big drum tried to throw it over the fence, but it hit the top and rolled back down the banking. The Coatbridge crowd certainly got their money's worth and found out the secret of what a Scotsman wears under his kilt.

Such a shame that all this happened in our pre-televised speedway days, otherwise I am sure that a film clip of the action would have won an award as 'best wildlife film' or perhaps even a BAFTA award. The riders and the pipe band survived the incident, but the referee was given an appointment with the local optician and a free guide dog.

At that time, when every Scottish rider apart from Ken McKinlay still lived in Scotland, the team spirit and camaraderie was first class. We frequently travelled together or met up with other riders en route for our raids across the border. I was still living in Glasgow, so Newcastle, a mere 150 miles away, was the nearest English track and the only one I did not need to leave home at 8am to arrive in time for the meeting.

I lived in the quiet Glasgow suburb of Eastwood and my lockup/garage was a couple of miles from my house. The lockup had no water supply so I used to wash my bike in the street in Fyvie Avenue. I used to get busy with a water bucket, washing powder and scrubbing brush, so I soon had my bike sparkling clean again. The same could not be said for the gutters in the street. No power washers in those days. Had I been racing at Newcastle or White City, the gutters would be grey, after Halifax, coal mine black and Sheffield, a nice warm red. If any of my neighbours been connoisseurs of speedway they could have guessed where I had been riding the previous evening by just glancing at the colour of the street.

Once the bike, leathers and boots were clean, it was down to the lockup for the rest of the usual maintenance with tyres, clutches, carburettors and chains to be attended to, plus tins of black boot polish used on the leathers and boots long before my days of coloured leathers and white boots. I then loaded the bike onto my car ready for an early start the next morning. The routine bike maintenance didn't always go as planned and I am sure that the following escapade must have happened to other riders too. The method of lubricating the chains during maintenance was to clean them off and then boil them up in a tin of black grease called 'Lynklife' and then hang the chains up for the excess lubricant to drip back into the tin so the same tin could be used time and time again.

The grease was usually melted by lighting a small tin of methanol under it until the chain sank into the liquid grease. This method worked well but when methanol is on fire, it is invisible and one cold evening, while working inside the small lockup, one of my 'friends' knocked over the tin of Lynklife and also the tin of methanol which caught alight. I tried to kick the burning tin out of the door, but only succeeded in setting my shoes and socks on fire. As we burst out of the door, I kicked off my burning shoe and it hit one of my friends on the backside, setting his trousers alight with an invisible flame. Fortunately, we managed to extinguish the fire with sand and loose dirt and saved the lockup and my bike from a fiery end. We vowed to be much more careful next time.

Amid all this 'organised chaos' I still found time to negotiate another trip to Australia, but Earle Vienet had sent me an airmail letter saying that the track had been hit by a small cyclone which blew down the referee's box and some of the track lighting pylons. The roof of the referee's box was found in the next field, so they were struggling a bit financially. Earle also mentioned that I must have been talking about Melbourne too much when I got back to Britain because during my season there, I had sent an airmail article to *Speedway Star* editor, Paul Parish, describing the way of life and the benefits of riding in Australia during the European winter. Paul must have liked what I had written and he asked me to send regular *The Speedway World of Bert Harkins* stories to the magazine. That is where my amateur journalist writing began, something which carries on to this day. Earle Vienet was now getting letters forwarded on from the *Speedway Star* from 'World Champion' riders in Britain wanting to spend their winter season at Brooklyn Raceway. He had not heard of some of the applicants, so he passed the letters onto other Australian promoters who may have been short on international talent. One rider whom Mr Vienet did know, was Ivan Mauger. I had passed details onto Ivan and he had contacted Earle with a proposal for spending the season at Brooklyn Speedway, but Mr Vienet turned him down. Ivan wanted a bike supplied plus a large (undisclosed) sum of money, but the promoter said that as speedway in the State of Victoria had lapsed for some years, Ivan would only be known to a few keen followers of the sport like himself and they (the promotion) would not get value for their money unless he could draw in extra crowds to Brooklyn Speedway.

Earle Vienet sent me an airmail letter about my contract – and here come the blushes – he told Ivan that (quoting from Earle Vienet's letter to me) "It would not be a proposition because as far as I was concerned, Bert Harkins would be a far bigger draw card in Victoria than himself because everybody who now follows the sport here have seen Bert on the circuit, on television or read about him in the papers." Earle Vienet also went on to joke "If Ivan went on to win another World title then he might end up as famous as you."

Ha! This letter, and others, just came to light when I was researching i.e. rummaging through old boxes of photographs, letters and cuttings which had been stored in my garage over the years. I had forgotten about this airmail letter. I wish that I had found it earlier because I could have teased Ivan about this whenever we met.

Despite the financial difficulties caused by the cyclone, I was contracted by Mr Vienet to ride again in Melbourne at the end of the British season with my fare paid and a $40 guarantee per meeting. Londoner Roy Trigg, who had been a valuable member of the British Lions test team the previous year, fancied a trip to Melbourne with me. So once again, it was a case of "Have bike, will travel" and off we went for another magical mystery tour, 'Down Under' at the end of the 1968 British season.

11. Australia revisited

This time, the outward journey to Australia was a bit more luxurious than the ill-fated *Fairsea* which eventually broke down and drifted in mid-ocean for some time. We were booked onto the P&O liner *Oriana*, a sleek ship with all mod cons including stabilizers to stop the ship from rolling too much – a much appreciated accessory after some days of turning green on the previous voyage. The *Oriana* was due to sail from Southampton in November, so that meant that I could fit in a full British season before leaving. The ship left Southampton six hours late, owing to a dock strike which meant that no baggage was loaded between 5pm and 9pm, so the grand liner did not pull away from the docks until almost midnight. The strike caused quite a few problems on board and it meant that many passengers, myself included, did not get their luggage delivered to their cabins until the following day. The cabins had been allocated in Southampton and when I eventually headed off to my cabin, I found a family in there, husband, wife and two kids. The purser allocated me another cabin down on 'G' Deck. This was well down below the water line in the bowels of the ship which I did not like. I told the purser that this cabin was also occupied, a little white lie, but he was too busy dealing with a queue of people that he did not check if that was true. Fortunately, he upgraded me to a 4-Berth cabin on 'C' Deck, Cabin C249. This was a more expensive cabin that the one I had originally paid for and my cabin partners were two middle-aged gentlemen.

At that time, there was a popular television show called *Double your Money*, hosted by Hughie Green. If you had relatives in Australia, the first prize was a free trip 'Down Under' to visit them. Contestants had to answer three questions on Great Britain and then Hughie Green flew out to Australia – nice work – to ask the relatives three questions on Australia. It turned out that one of my cabin mates was the winner of that competition. He was on his way, all expenses paid, to visit his brother who had emigrated many years earlier. That promised to be an emotional reunion and all thanks to a television show.

My Glasgow cycle speedway and school friend, Johnny Speirs, was travelling with me to Australia to visit his brother, George, and he was allocated a 2-berth cabin to share with Garry Middleton. After a night and day of Garry's endless chat and wild ideas, John moved into the spare bunk in my 4 berth cabin. The trip promised to be an interesting one because, apart from 'Cas the Gas' and my English mate, 'Triggie', Roy Trigg, and me, the passenger list included Kings Lynn's Howard Cole. He was the youngster I had seen on a mini speedway bike in the *Picture Post* magazine all those years ago. Howard was heading for Auckland in New Zealand for a season at Palmerston North track. Also on board was Halifax's Australian Duke, Bob Jamieson. It certainly was going to be an interesting voyage. After being delayed by that dock strike in Southampton, the *Oriana* had set sail on fireworks night, 5 November, a very appropriate day considering that they had allowed a group of speedway riders to be among the 'normal' passengers. Soon we left the cold and wet of Britain far behind us.

The voyage was much faster on this bigger ship, only about three and a half weeks, so there was no chance of getting bored, not that there was ever any chance of being bored in that company. We went through the usual scrapes that befall travelling speedway riders such as losing almost all of what little money we had on the ship's 'Las Vegas Night' – I only had

£1 to lose – and upsetting first class passengers in their tuxedos and dinner suits when we entered the ship's cinema during a film. How were we to know that the 'balcony' was reserved for first class and that we should not have wandered in wearing shorts and T-shirts? Fortunately the captain didn't cast us adrift on a lifeboat as punishment. We were well fed on the *Oriana,* but afternoon tea often created some problems. We sat at our allocated table and there was a stand with small cut sandwiches and cakes on it, just enough for everyone to have one each. Garry would always grab the best cake as soon as he sat down, leaving the rest of us with the sandwiches and the other not-so-nice cakes. When approached about being greedy, he just explained that "In Australia, we always have the cake before the sandwiches" so that also caused some friction at afternoon tea.

We also got into a spot of bother when the ship docked at Durban and we went off on a safari tour in the local game reserve. As luck would have it, our old tour bus broke down in the middle of the lion park. We were about to get out and push when we were surrounded by a group of hungry-looking lions, so rather than giving the kings of the jungle food poisoning, we sat in a bus and let the driver take care of things, although we did ask Garry to get out and have a look under the bonnet.

Despite our various mishaps, we all reached Australia safe and sound, well fed and rested after a pleasant trip. Our first port of call was Fremantle in Perth. During the stop-over, I disembarked to visit some relatives who lived nearby. In typical Harkins fashion, I mistimed my return to the ship, having spent hours catching up on family gossip. As I ran back to the quay, all the gangplanks had been pulled up except one which was just in the process of being moved. I yelled for the captain to 'Stop the bus', or something equally stupid and the passengers lining the deck rails gave me a huge cheer as I scrambled up the gangplank and collapsed on the deck. The *Oriana* set sail for Melbourne and I almost 'missed the bus'.

When we reached Melbourne, Roy Trigg, Johnnie Speirs and I disembarked. We said farewell to Bob Jamieson and Garry Middleton who were heading for Sydney and Howard Cole who was bound for New Zealand. They stayed on for the rest of the 'cruise'.

Settling down in my winter base with Tony and Louisa Melrose near the beach in Seaford, it didn't take long to renew my acquaintance with the Melbourne track. In fact it was only in my second meeting there that I did another 'Flying Scotsman' act in a dreaded handicap event and finished up with all sorts of bumps and bruises. I began considering asking for danger money to ride in the handicap races as they were very 'hairy' to say the least.

Triggie and I had our hands full beating all the locals because, in addition to the established stars such as Johnny Dewhurst and 'Trapper' Peter Moore, Dave O'Conner, Peter Bradshaw and Mal Carmichael were all riding very well. The 'new' Australians were showing a lot of skill and speed and it was only natural that their eyes were set on a trip to the Britain in the near future. All three eventually made the trip, but Dave O'Conner returned to Melbourne after finding the going very tough. Poor Mal and Peter lost their lives in the tragic road accident in Lokeren in Belgium on 14 July 1970 when returning overnight from racing in Holland. The minibus carrying the West Ham party was in collision with a heavy lorry and Martin Piddock, Gary Everett. Phil Bishop and Dutch driver Henrikus Rommanoes also lost their lives. Colin Pratt, Garry Hay, Stan Stevens and mechanic Roy Sullivan all sustained serious injuries that night, making it the worst ever speedway disaster.

In Australia, Roy Trigg and I had been getting plenty of Interstate bookings and one which we looked forward to was New South Wales versus Victoria at the new Liverpool Raceway in Sydney. As flying from Melbourne to Sydney would be very expensive, we decided to save on our travel expenses and take the Scotsman's way out. We drove there in Tony Melrose's trusty Volkswagen.

It was only a short drive from our base in Melbourne; around 13 hours and we were in Sydney with a very overloaded VW and trailer. Arriving at Liverpool Raceway, I met up with my old Edinburgh team-mate and *Fairsea* buddy, Bill Landels who had enjoyed a couple of very successful seasons at Sydney Showground and was riding for the NSW team.

It was my first race on the big, fast D-shaped track and I was ahead of NSW's Garry Middleton and Victoria's Johnny Dewhurst and chasing Big Bill. Going into the third bend, Bill left a gap on the inside which was large enough to drive a bus through and naturally, I dived for that gap. It was then that I wished that I had been driving a bus. Bill came diving down from the banking heading for the white line and crunch. His rear wheel and my front one met and I went bowling head-over-heels down the track.

It reminded me of the 'Reserve trophy finals' at Edinburgh's Old Meadowbank. We landed in a tangled heap of bikes and bodies. Fortunately the ambulance and the medics at the track were quick on the scene. I woke up with an oxygen mask on my face and another pair of damaged spectacles. That was my first ever race at Liverpool, a track where I later spent another two winter seasons, and by some unfortunate coincidence, in my last ever race there before the track was tarmaced in 1974, I was involved in another nasty crash on the same pit bend with Bill Landels once again. We had come 10,479 miles from Edinburgh in Scotland to Sydney in Australia just to continue crashing into each other.

Readers' note: By the time you have finished reading this book, you, dear reader, will be feeling as many bumps and bruises as a speedway rider so I am considering supplying a tube of muscle-easing cream with every copy.

The remainder of that winter season went well and everything was building up to the climax of the Melbourne fixture list, the Victorian Championship. I was determined to hold onto my title, but it looked like being a tough assignment because, in addition to Triggie and the local flyers, Peter Moore, Peter Vandenberg, Johnny Dewhurst and others, we also had Gordon Guasco, Greg Kentwell and Garry Middleton from Sydney and Ove Fundin, five times World Champion, from Sweden. As would be expected with such a field, the track record took a pounding during the meeting and according to the timekeeper, it was equalled or broken five times.

By the end of the qualifying heats, the finalists were: Ove Fundin on 10 points, Roy Trigg on 9, Peter Moore with 8 and I was unbeaten with 12 points. In the Grand Final, I gated first but Roy squeezed past on the first turn and try as I might, I could not pass the flying Londoner. Triggie took the win and the title, I was second ahead of Ove and Peter Moore. Roy was the new Victorian Champion and to say I was disappointed would be an understatement. Even counting the points from the final, I still came out on top with 14 points against 12 for Roy, 11 for Ove and 8 for Peter, but that is the same way that it goes in today's Grand Prix series, the winner has to ride their very best race in the Grand Final.

In full flight at Melbourne in January 1969

To make matters worse, when he had mechanical trouble in an earlier heat, I had lent my bike to Roy which helped him to qualify for the final. Oh well, we were good friends and I guess I could not have lost my title to a nicer person, but it still hurt.

During the event, my three lap track record of 52.5 was equalled once and shattered four times. I equalled it in my first race, then broke it next time out. In my last heat race I broke the record again and set it at 52.2, the fifth time that the record was toppled on that night.

A few weeks later, Roy and I were on our way back to Britain along with Australian riders, Geoff Curtis, Peter Bradshaw, Paul Sly and Bob Tabet on a ship and jet trip. The idea was to sail from Australia on the Greek Chandris Line ship, RHMS *Patris,* to Djibouti in the Horn of Africa – 12 days at sea from Freemantle – and then fly, via Athens to London. A very relaxing trip we thought, until we found out that there was civil unrest in Djibouti. We saw army tanks lining the runway as we waited to taxi out of Djibouti Airport, but fortunately we got clear before any trouble began.

12. Back in Scotland

We arrived in London the day before Coatbridge Monarchs' first meeting at Coventry on 26 March 1969 and dashed down to Southampton to collect our new Jawas from Barry Briggs. It was then that I had my first surprise. In my absence on my Australian trip, it seems that Rider Control had allocated me to Newcastle but as usual, everyone knew about it except the rider concerned, in this case me.

Newcastle was one of my favourite tracks – grippy and bumpy with tight corners – and I always enjoyed racing there with their friendly Geordie fans. However, I had no wish to leave Coatbridge and I appealed against the transfer. As time was running out, I was given special dispensation to ride for Coatbridge at Coventry while the whole matter was ironed out. It seems that before my name came out of the hat, first Olle Nygren and then Charlie Monk had been allocated to the Diamonds, but both had turned down the move to Brough Park.

Five days later, Newcastle were due to ride at Newport and they were still hunting for a rider to replace me. I then received a booking to ride for the Diamonds at Newport as a guest in place of their missing heat leader – Bert Harkins. I was very pleased to be guesting for the Harkins chappie because it saved the fans from having to make any programme alterations, but I wonder if any other rider has ever guested in place of himself? The smile was soon wiped off of my face. The Newport track was fairly narrow around the football pitch with 'square' corners. At the end of the straight, there was a banner advertising beer and it read: 'Take Courage'. The riders certainly needed plenty of that around the place.

Coming down the home straight, my machine got hooked up with the footrest on Norman Strachan's bike. Wee Norm wisely abandoned ship, but I was caught between the bikes until we were stopped abruptly by the safety fence and that was the end of my riding for the night. Following X-Rays at the local hospital, the doctor seemed a bit annoyed by having his time wasted by a self-inflicted speedway casualty and declared that nothing was broken and I was free to go. A touch of déjà-vu.

Driving a car and changing gear with only one arm is not too easy, but I couldn't lift my left arm. Despite lowering my handlebars as much as possible, I could not complete my races at Oxford or Wolverhampton. On returning to Glasgow, a letter arrived about a week later. It was from the hospital in Newport and, from memory, said something like "Dear Mr Harkins, on further examination of your X-ray plates, we have discovered that you have broken your shoulder blade.

Please do not do anything strenuous and take this letter to your local hospital as soon as possible". So, I was out of action even before my red Australian suntan had worn off.

After such a bad start to the season, things could only get better, and they did. My scores improved, although Glasgow's Jim McMillan out-scored me in the World Championship Round at Coatbridge. I failed to progress past the British semi-final, but had the consolation of scoring an 18 point maximum for Scotland against Australia just three days later. Unfortunately, the Charlie Monk-led Australians beat us 61–47, but the score line belied the fighting spirit of the Scotland squad.

My own long apprenticeship was paying off as I began knocking up a few maximums. The one against Australia proved that although I may have larked about off the track, when the helmet was pulled on and the goggles were down, life was taken very seriously.

Having said that, there have been a few occasions when I was less-than-serious on the track, but not, obviously while I was racing. Take the occasion when the Monarchs came down to Wimbledon for a league match. It wasn't the kind of night to go racing because the rain was teeming down. Wimbledon team manager, Cyril Maidment got the sawdust down in the puddles and when it mixed with the shale, the surface was raceable and was the best way to get a meeting on when the weather was wet.

During my second race the top to bottom zip on the front of my leathers came apart spitting out all of its teeth as it gashed wide open letting in the wet shale and cold air. This was in the days before dirt deflectors diverted the shale so my broken leathers soon filled up with soggy red shale.

As Angus Kix (alias editor, Eric Linden) reported in *Speedway Star:* "I swear to you that I heard Bert yell 'Oooosh' in a Scottish accent then wobble and shudder and fall back to stone last. Right out in the cold, so to speak, was Harkins the Haggis Eater." Thus he described my discomfort.

Unable to fix the zip, and only having the one set of leathers, I donned a pair of swimming trunks I had with me and wore them over my leathers, thus helping to ease the 'The Wind Around The Trossachs' and carried on with my other races.

Angus Kix went on to write: "Nothing daunts this young Scot though. Protected against the weather, he proceeded to tackle his next race with such gusto that he became Coatbridge's only other race winner apart from Reidar Eide and finished the night as their joint second highest scorer."

He continued "I forecast that it will not be the last time this young man finishes that high up on the Monarchs score chart. I predict that he will go one higher on occasions and that the occasions will get more plentiful as the matches roll along." He finished up the article by writing: "I also predict one other thing. Monarch Harkins will have a new zip by now. Either that or he will really have found out why they call Scotland, The Frozen North." Ah yes, praise indeed from the hallowed pages of *Speedway Star*.

Our speedway had plenty of fighting spirit north of the border, especially in the Scottish Cup matches which were always sure to stir the blood. Glasgow Tigers had been moved from their White City stadium. It had first opened in 1928, but was due to be demolished to make way for the M8 motorway.

The Tigers found a new home at the famous Hampden Park Stadium in the Mount Florida area of Glasgow, home of the Queens Park Football Club and venue for many Scotland versus England football internationals. The stadium was vast with a capacity of over 100,000; although they did squeeze in 150,000 in 1937 in the days before Health & Safety concerns reduced the capacity. The size tended to take away some of the atmosphere, although the sound of four unsilenced speedway bikes racing and echoing around the grandstands gave the place a unique special effect.

Apart from Wembley, Hampden Park was the most prestigious stadium in the UK and the riders had luxurious conditions in the spacious football dressing rooms. There were proper wardrobes, under-floor heating and always hot showers. How the other half live. It was a far cry from many of the draughty speedway dressing rooms with their lukewarm or cold showers and a nail hammered into the wall to hang your clothes on.

The speedway track was built around the outside of the football pitch. The floodlights were trained on the football pitch and left a dark shadow as we raced into the third turn, but that didn't slow down home stars Charlie Monk and Jim McMillan. The opening night meeting against the Kings Lynn Stars on 11 April 1969 brought in a crowd of almost 11,000 so speedway in Glasgow was back with a bang.

In the home and away Scottish Cup matches at the end of August, the Tigers had beaten the Monarchs by 11 points in the first leg at Hampden so the following evening at Coatbridge was the big decider urged on by a huge crowd from both clubs.

In the second leg, racing was, as usual, fast and furious. Doug and Willie Templeton, again riding for opposite teams, were indulging in a bit of handlebar and elbow bashing in yet another show of 'brotherly love'. Tensions were running high when, a few heats later, Edinburgh's Reidar Eide gave Tigers' captain, Jim McMillan, a tough four laps with frequent inspections of the wooden Coatbridge safety fence. As they returned to the pits, Jim's elder brother, Bill who was riding for the Tigers, took exception to our Reidar's tactics and grabbed the Norwegian's handlebars. The Coatbridge pits were long and narrow with little room to manoeuvre and a 'Handbags at dawn' scuffle broke out. Oyvind Berg, Glasgow's third heat leader, and Reidar's fellow countryman, had to push his way through the melee to retrieve his front wheel which he had loaned to Jimmy Mac because he (Oyvind) was out in the next heat. Doug and Willie Templeton saw Bergie joining the fray and mistakenly thought that Bill, their nephew, was about to be outnumbered. They forgot their own differences and rushed to the other end of the pits like a Tsunami tidal wave, pushing bikes and bodies out of the way. Poor Oyvind did not know what was happening as the two burly farmers bore down on him, but in his best broken English he yelled "I haf only come for mine wheel".

Dougie and Willie, gentlemen as ever, apologised profusely. They began changing wheels, topped up the fuel and oil for Oyvind and got him out onto the track before the two minutes time allowance had ended. Such was the camaraderie and rivalry between the two teams.

The Monarchs managed to pull the first leg deficit back to a nail-biting last heat decider. I beat Charlie Monk for a 4–2 to make the final score Glasgow Tigers 77 Coatbridge Monarchs 78. We had scraped home by one point to win the Scottish Cup. The fans had witnessed two great meetings and the riders were friends again, but Glasgow promoter, Les Whalley, was less than enthusiastic about the 'boots and elbows' racing and reckoned that the Monarchs' riders were ducking under the tapes. Mr Whalley then took the centre green microphone to announce to the fans that his team would never again race the Coatbridge Monarchs in anything other than official league fixtures. It had been a controversial meeting, but the fans had witnessed racing that would keep them talking for a long time to come.

Personally, I believed that Les Whalley had made a big mistake. The fans were yelling for more and Messrs Whaley and Hoskins should have got together and booked their rivals in on the first available open date. The paying public would have flocked in to see an action replay. They would have been certain to get their money's worth instead of having to watch a team from south of the border, tired from the long drive up to Scotland and trying to cope with the bumps and banking of Coatbridge or the vastness of Hampden Park. Sadly, the Glasgow promoter stuck to his word and the Scottish Cup was dead.

Les Whalley may have put paid to the Scottish Cup contests, but it was still a good year for Scottish speedway, despite our skipper, Doug Templeton, and George Hunter suffering injuries. Wayne Briggs found life difficult following his return to Scotland from Exeter. Wayne had been truly brilliant in his early days with the Monarchs and looked all set to emulate his elder brother, Barry, but a number of serious injuries took the shine off the young Kiwi. Reidar Eide had a great season which culminated in him winning the Scottish Open Championship after a run-off with Newcastle's Ole Olsen. I scored 12 points to finish fourth.

At the other end of the team, Brian Collins and Alex Hughson were making good progress. Over at Hampden Park, Blantyre's Bobby Beaton was starring with Jim McMillan and being hailed as the best thing since another Blantyre born Glasgow Tiger– Ken McKinlay.

As the season drew to a close and the weather got cooler, I began to get itchy feet for another trip to Australia. However, we had had a lot of laughs during our travels around the speedway tracks of Britain. I recall incidents such as when we were heading south to ride at Hackney and, to cut expenses, seven riders plus team manager, Tommy Hughson and mechanic, Arty Fisher, travelled in two cars with the bikes piled onto the trailers.

I was travelling with Alex Hughson and George Hunter in George's Ford Cortina and trailer when, as we were bowling down the A1 at a high rate of knots, there was a loud scraping noise and we were overtaken by a wheel. It turned out to be a trailer wheel, our trailer wheel. You may think that controlling a one-wheeled trailer down the busy A1 at 70mph (slightly over the speed limit for towing a trailer) is difficult. Well, it is, but not if your name is George Hunter. Behind us, Tommy Hughson saw what had happened and carefully eased his Jaguar and trailer into the middle of the road, 'team-riding' to prevent anyone overtaking our five-wheeled chariot. Once again 'The Hunter luck' shone down on us, because just when the wheel had overtaken us, George spotted a layby ahead and calmly steered the car and trailer to safety in a shower of sparks and clouds of dust. Saved again. We searched the bushes and undergrowth and found the offending wheel which George quickly repaired. Then it was back on the road for our 'Make it a date, Friday at Eight' meeting at Hackney.

With our vehicles covering many thousands of miles from Scotland during a busy speedway season, and cars not being a reliable as they are today, mechanical problems often occurred. Once, George Hunter and I were motoring down to Poole and luckily we had left a day ahead of schedule. We were making good time until George's usually trusty Cortina began to splutter. It then sent up a heavy smoke-screen from the exhaust. We had blown a hole in a piston. George nursed the stricken Ford off the main road and we limped down to Eric Boocock's house in Wakefield where we quickly pulled the engine out of the car. Eric drove us into Wakefield to buy some pistons. We rebuilt the engine and were back on the road that same afternoon, having completed a super-quick pit stop that would have made the Formula 1 teams proud. It just shows that in speedway, we may be rivals on the track, but we really are just one big speedway family when anyone is in trouble.

And so the end of the season approached once again and I prepared to 'follow the sun'. When I left Coatbridge at the end of the 1969 season, I did not know it at the time, but it was to be the end of me racing for the Monarchs in Scotland for almost a decade.

The 1969 Coatbridge Monarchs: Brian Collins, George Hunter, Alex Hughson, Tommy Hughson (team manager), Reidar Eide, Wayne Briggs and Bert Harkins with captain Doug Templeton on the bike.

Enjoying a pie with Doug Templeton in 1969.
The pies were for a pie-eating contest for the supporters.

The speedway seasons in Britain and Australia were beginning to overlap, so the slow ship travel on The *Fairsea* was ruled out in favour of joining the jet-set and getting there quickly to avoid missing any meetings. This time my contract for the Australian season was with Frank Oliveri at Liverpool Raceway near Sydney, after two seasons at Melbourne. I had enjoyed my time there, but it was right to head for Sydney and even stronger opposition.

A chance conversation with Australian journalist and former speedway sidecar passenger, Peter White, who was in London working for Dave Lanning, led me to modify my winter plans. Dave was general manager at First Division West Ham and Second Division Eastbourne. He was also team manager for both teams. Dave was also working full-time for the *TV Times* weekly magazine and wrote a weekly column for *Speedway Star.* In return for his board and lodgings at the Lanning household, Peter White was given the job of being team manager for both sides on most of their away trips. So he made his 'working holiday' pay and visited all the tracks in Britain that year. He was also team manager for Australia for their test matches in both divisions, so he had an exciting summer in British speedway.

At the end of the season, Peter, like me, was preparing to leave England to fly to Sydney. The information he gave me made me change my flight plans and had a major effect on my speedway future. Thank you Peter White. He told me that there were a couple of speedway meetings in California the following week in which I may be able to ride on my way to Australia. I jumped at the chance and Peter gave me the telephone number of Costa Mesa promoter, Harry Oxley. I was so keen that I did not even think of reversing the charges to the USA when I phoned. Harry sounded very keen for me to come and offered to organise a bike for me to ride. He invited me to stay at the Oxley family home in the wonderfully-named, Sierra Madre in Southern California.

American speedway was an unknown quantity for me. I had only seen photos of their 'Class C' and flat track racing which didn't look too much like speedway to me. However, I was very keen to find out so I rushed around to arrange an American visa, change my flight and I took off into the sunset, heading for Los Angeles, City of Angels. It was another world adventure and if the speedway didn't work, perhaps I would become a cowboy after all.

13. Speedway, American style

I arrived in Los Angeles on the evening of Thursday 16 October 1969, all alone except for my leathers, favourite handlebars and ever-present tartan helmet. Waiting at the airport was DeWayne Keeter, the American who raced for Leicester that year and Costa Mesa promoter Harry Oxley, along with a few suntanned Californian riders who had come along to see what this new 'foreign' rider looked like. I think they got a shock when they saw this pale, skinny bespectacled character with ginger hair, not what they imagined an international speedway rider would look like.

Peter White arrived on a different flight and somehow we managed to meet up in the busy LAX international airport. Next morning, Harry took us over to the Orange County Fairgrounds to have a look at the track which is now known world-wide, the one and only Costa Mesa. At first I thought that we had arrived at a cycle speedway track, but Mr Oxley assured me that this compact little stadium with the 180 yard track was indeed used by 500cc speedway machines. Someone brought along a Jap for me to ride. It had a Huck Fynn frame and 22 inch rear wheel. It looked strange because it had no fuel tank, the fuel was carried under the seat. I blasted around for a few laps without any mishaps. Harry was pleased and so was I, except that I was wondering how four bikes could compete when it felt that when my front wheel was on the inside line, my rear wheel was brushing the fence. Harry just laughed and said "Oh, there's room for four alright". What he did not tell me that they also ran handicap racing with six riders in each race.

'Happy Harry' had kindly offered Peter White and me a bed in the busy Oxley family home in Sierra Madre which we gratefully accepted. What we did not realise at the time was that it was just the one bed for the two of us. This was long before it was classed as acceptable for two men to share the same bed and we didn't know one another too well either.

The Oxley household was hectic and noisy with Harry and his wife Marylyn, son Brad, and daughters, Susan, Robyn and Lori all yelling at each other at the top of their voices. I thought that I had landed in the middle of a family feud, but found out that was their normal volume for speech. I soon got used to it.

In the evening, Peter and I settled down to our new surroundings in Brad's room. Early in the morning, I heard a bang like gunfire, jumped upright in bed and hit my head on the shelf above holding all Brad's schoolboy motocross trophies. I brought the shelf and all the trophies down on Peter's head; that was the last – and only – time we shared a bed.

For once, my timing of events was spot on. Ivan Mauger and Barry Briggs had visited the States the previous year and ridden at the Whiteman Stadium, but that had closed down. Costa Mesa was the new venue run by 1937 World Champion Jack Milne, and Harry Oxley, who at the time was manager of Jack and Cordy Milne Brothers motorcycle shop. Ivan and Barry were still in England, preparing for the British League Riders Final at Belle Vue, so I was about to become the first European rider to race at Costa Mesa, quite an honour indeed.

The travel brochures spin the magic tales that the USA will take your breath away and leave an indelible impression on your memory. Those glossy brochures certainly told the truth, but the impressions that California left on me were not just on my memory. After my first night at Costa Mesa, I had cuts and bruises and the biggest 'impression' was the tyre marks which ran up my back. I could not sit down for a week.

On the Friday evening, it certainly was a memorable debut for me, the first British rider to race at the Orange County Showgrounds track. The grandstand 'bleechers' were packed full and the floodlights and noise of the crowd yelling for their favourite rider, all egged on by their flamboyant announcer, Larry Huffman gave the whole place a fantastic atmosphere. It was almost like entering the Roman Coliseum with a grudge match between the Christians and the lions, but I was determined not to be eaten by these Californian lions.

I had been lent a Jap machine by a local sponsor, but my first race already saw me in trouble. I made a good gate on this borrowed machine, but veteran flat track racer and former American tourist to Britain, Don Hawley, was pushing hard on the inside. I tried to lean on him coming out of the second turn, but his right thigh caught my handlebars and lifted my front wheel off the track. I was thrown off in front of Don's machine. As I was bouncing along underneath his bike, I had a close-up view of the engine crankcases, then the track, then the engine and so it went on. The fence at the other end of the straight halted my bouncing progress. Fortunately, on such a small track we were not going too fast, so I was able to hobble back to the pits to inspect the damage to man and machine.

The borrowed Jap looked rather the worse for wear and I felt rather second hand too. The ever-helpful Americans helped to dust me down and brought another bike for me to ride. After a 10 minute delay while everyone helped me to get my breath back and replace the lens in my famous specs, I went out and won the rerun. So Scottish honour was restored. This was to be the pattern for my exciting first evening at Costa Mesa, race, crash, win, race, crash, win. All-in-all, I had eight races and managed to demolish six borrowed bikes. One crash occurred when the left handlebar rubber, something we did not use on our bikes at the time, came off in the middle of the corner. In Britain we didn't use handlebar grips, just rolls of Elastoplast wound around the 'bars, usually with a length of a spoke or even a pencil underneath, just to give that extra grip for the fingers. The idea of using Elastoplast was to give the rider a better 'feel' of the throttle and handlebars. However, the resulting vibration gave many riders the 'speedway rider's condition' of 'white finger' when circulation to the fingertips seized up.

Later, when motocross handlebar rubbers had improved, riders began fitting grips such as the Scott Hurricane grip. They were fitted with grip glue or even hair spray to stop them sliding off the way that happened to me on that borrowed bike in Costa Mesa. I am sure that when riders began using proper grips, sales of Elastoplast must have tumbled because for many years, almost every rider taped his handlebars that way.

I thought the Americans were friendly people. They kept lending me their bikes and I soon discovered why the local riders wore knee and shin guards. Speedway at Costa Mesa was a contact sport and the riders needed plenty of protection. That is why I soon renamed it 'Shinbone Alley'.

My encore, or 'Grande Finale' came in the six rider handicap final. I battled through from my back mark of 50 yards. On the bigger tracks in Australia, 50 yards would be almost scratch. As I tried to go around the outside of one rider, he swerved to the right and I ran over his wheels. I was launched into the air once again and landed in a heap at the fence.

Legend has it that some of the Hollywood stars occasionally came along to Costa Mesa on a Friday night to watch the action. There were big stars such as Steve McQueen, who was later taught to ride a speedway bike by Barry Briggs, and Robert Redford. On this particular October evening, I was told that as I flew over the handlebars I landed beside the fence at the feet of film star Ann Margaret, one-time girlfriend of Elvis Presley. It shows how dazed I was when I say that she could have performed a strip tease and given me the 'Kiss of Life' and I probably would not have noticed.

Unfortunately, when I recovered I did not see Ann Margaret to have a chance of having my photograph taken with her, just to make Elvis jealous, so I don't know if Harry Oxley had been telling me the truth. He did say that Ann Margaret had leaned over the fence and asked me how I was, but knowing Harry, that could have been a bit of 'promoter's licence'. But I like to believe that it was true.

I had earned my spurs the hard way at Costa Mesa and if I had had a dollar for every bump and bruise I would have been a very rich young Scotsman. The crowd loved it, the promoters, Jack Milne and Harry Oxley, loved it and, despite all my aches and pains and the infamous jet-lag, I kind of enjoyed it too!

I even gained a new nickname that night after bouncing down the back straight underneath Don Hawley's bike. Harry and presenter Larry Huffman named me 'Bouncing Bert Harkins' and that name stuck every time I returned to race at Costa Mesa.

My first impressions of Californian speedway certainly made a lasting impression on me, in my head, in my heart and with the tyre marks on my body. Costa Mesa was like nowhere else with its wild and wonderfully enthusiastic fans where, if someone sat high in the grandstand, they certainly could get 'high' on the smoke drifting along in the warm night air.

The announcer-presenter-showman, Larry Huffman, was like no speedway presenter I had seen in Europe or Australia. He wasn't hidden away in the referee's box like he would be in Britain, but stood beside a table at the starting gate in full view of the fans. Larry wore a tuxedo and bow tie and looked like a Hollywood movie star introducing the Oscar Awards. He began the meeting gently with rider introductions, but as the races went on, and the racing became fast and furious, Larry racked up the enthusiasm. He took off his bow tie and leapt onto the table, ripped off his jacket and waved it wildly above his head. He turned up the volume and got the fans up to fever pitch. He made our announcers at home seem like funeral undertakers. Larry's enthusiasm was infectious as he stoked up the crowd to yell louder and louder for their favourite rider. This was speedway, American style.

Even the riders and the organisation were different. Mechanics and anyone else going into the pits had to wear 'whites'; that is white shirt and white trousers. This was fiercely enforced by Londoner Freda Wenn and her husband, George. No 'whites', no pit entry. Everyone respected that rule so there wasn't a mishmash of colours in the pits or in the centre. It was not a centre green because there was no grass.

It may sound strange now, but riders were different too. At the time when all riders in British speedway had black leathers, they all had fancy coloured made-to-measure leathers festooned with sponsors' names and professionally painted helmet designs, so the fans could easily recognise their favourite rider. Mechanics were different too, with their 'whites' and wheeling in two or more bikes plus a large wheeled tool chest, spare wheels and multiple sprockets. This is quite normal in today's speedway. However, in 1969 in Britain, everyone had black leathers and used plain open face helmets with helmet covers. Riders had small tool boxes with just the correct number of spanners required and perhaps only one or two rear sprockets suitable for that track.

Bikes were also different. Some riders still using low flat track-style handlebars and 22 inch rear wheels. Ivan Mauger and Barry Briggs had run training schools at Whiteman Stadium the previous year, so some riders were already riding more 'European style'. At home we rode Japs and Jawas with high handlebars – normally the left handlebar higher than the right – and low seats, all the better to wrestle the bikes around the corners. Nowadays, with the lower centre of gravity laydown engines and leading link forks, the modern bikes are very different to ride. Riders have reverted to having low motocross handlebars and high saddles. They also bring huge tool chests on wheels into the pits. Speedway British style is now speedway, American style!

The Californian riders all had large vans, kitted out inside like luxury apartments with carpets all around the floor, the walls and even the roof and an onboard fridge, power steering, cruise control and air conditioning. The latter was essential for those long hot road trips in America. Murals on these vans were anything from an action shot of a speedway rider in full flow to a beautiful and colourful ocean sunset. On the side of former flat track racer Steve Fortune's van, the legend 'Wheels of Fortune' was painted, very appropriate.

Bikes were carried in a section in the back of the van so it was a home-from-home for the riders. At that time, the only riders using vans in Britain were second strings or reserves. They were small vans such as the Morris Minor 1000 which took a bike minus the front wheel inside. The stars and heat leaders had cars with trailers or bike racks on the back or Citroen Estates with two bikes inside. The British vans were not too comfortable to drive and not very fast either, but now it has all changed. Almost all riders in Britain from GP riders to juniors now have vans kitted out like the Americans of the early Costa Mesa days. We have come the full circle.

One item we did not have in British speedway and was a pleasant surprise to me was 'overage'. If the crowd was over a certain figure, the riders got a bonus paid to them the following week. It was almost like double points money and encouraged the riders to put on a show for the crowd.

One thing I did learn in America was about helmets. I was using a lightweight open face Italian helmet, painted tartan of course, with a chin-cup fastening. During my encounters with the Costa Mesa dirt, I had damaged the helmet and given myself an aching jaw because of the chin cup which pulled my jaw to one side. Fortunately, a couple of guys from Bell Helmets were at the speedway that night. They took a look at my damaged helmet and invited me to come down to their office at Long Beach. The next day, I drove to the Long Beach headquarters of Bell Helmets and met Race Department manager, Don l' Heaureux and rider rep 'JJ', Jim Johnstone who gave me a tour of the factory and showed me how the fibreglass Bell helmets were built. This tour taught me the error of my ways as far as head safety was concerned. Even although my own helmet was ACU approved, it was not up to the high Snell Foundation standard of Bell as JJ proved to me in various tests both on my own helmet and with Bell's. They then measured my head – no, it wasn't big – and supplied me with a couple of perfectly-fitted helmets, a Magnum open face and a Moto Star full face, plus gear bags, jackets, T-shirts and tear-offs. It was my first major sponsorship and I used their helmets for the rest of my career.

At home Bell helmets were very expensive compared to other makes on the market. But their advertising slogan summed it all up for me: 'If you have a ten dollar head, buy a ten dollar helmet. If not, buy a Bell.' They certainly saved me many a time.

I also learned that in Californian speedway, red does not necessary mean 'Stop', it just meant 'Danger'. I found this out the hard way when the red flags came out during one of my races at Costa Mesa. I was in the lead and put my hand up to show the other riders I was slowing down, as we did in British speedway. 'Wild Bill' Cody came charging past, hooked my left handlebar and sent me flying off the back of my bike. Bill later apologised. I realised that the red flag only signified that there had been a crash and the track ahead was probably blocked with riders and bikes. Just keep going and try to avoid the carnage as best you can.

Two days after my introduction to 'Speedway, American style', I was due to leave on the next part of my tour and fly to Australia. Harry Oxley asked me to stay on for another couple of meetings which were being held the following weekend. I was able to change my air ticket and postpone my departure for one more week to fit in two more meetings in California.

After my debut as the lone foreigner at Costa Mesa, Barry Briggs, Ivan Mauger and Jim Airey all flew into Los Angeles International Airport, having finished in that order in the British Riders' Championship at Belle Vue a few days earlier. The Californian speedway scene was hotting up with all these 'foreigners' arriving. My experience of riding the tiny Costa Mesa track, eight races in all, stood me in good stead for the following week's battles. Even so, I was still 'in the wars'. On the Friday night, the racing was fast and furious as usual and even world class riders like Ivan, Barry and Jim had their problems on that 180 yard circuit. After coming straight from Belle Vue's big Hyde Road track, Briggo reckoned that he got so dizzy at Costa Mesa that after the race, he had to ride four laps in the opposite direction in the pits to unwind himself. It says a lot for the spectacle of racing at Costa Mesa that all the riders, including us 'foreigners' watched every race just to see what would happen next.

Rick Woods, who later rode for Newport, was the big star at the time and the way the lanky Californian threw his Jawa around the little track had to be seen to be believed. Steve Bast was every bit as good, but much neater and smoother than the spectacular Woods. Rick just didn't realise that sometimes you could ride faster by using a little less throttle. Many a time he battled though from the back in a handicap race, built up a good lead and then careered into the crashwall – safety fence to us – while still on the back wheel. He was terrific to watch. Sonny Nutter, Mike Bast and 'Wild Bill' Cody all rode extremely well, but Rick was the most spectacular of all.

On Friday 2 November two Kiwis, one Australian and one Scot lined up against the local 'hot shoes' and what a night it turned out to be. Jim Airey, more accustomed to the wide open spaces of the Australian circuits, settled down to the 180 yard Costa Mesa very well. However, riding against the super-keen Americans, who were determined to beat the visiting international stars, was like a mixture of stock car racing and roller derby on bikes. We all got knocked around a lot that night and I lost count of how often Briggo picked me up, dusted me down, cleaned my glasses and sat me back on the bike for the next rerun.

Ivan collected a hard knock in his handicap race when he locked up in the middle of the corner. One of the Americans T-boned his bike and sent him high-siding off of the wrong side of his machine. Ivan was dazed and had slight concussion, but recovered enough to gain his revenge in the rerun. Threading his way through from the back mark position in the handicap race, he drew alongside his rival, slowed gently, lifted his right leg and expertly guided his footrest into the American's front wheel. He paused just long enough to ensure that the wheel would collapse due to the loss of spokes, then went on to win the race. That's 'a cool Kiwi'. Costa Mesa, with its packed grandstands and tiny track floodlit under a starry sky was a blaze of colour and excitement which someone once described as like 'Watching a race in your own living room'.

To me, it was more like the Coliseum in Rome where Christians were thrown to the lions and, after that bruising meeting, I think that the score was Christians 1, The Lions 10.

On the Sunday, we were all due to race in Santa Barbara, some 100 miles north of Los Angeles up Highway 101. Harry Oxley had arranged for us to ride in a charity meeting there to raise funds for the local San Marcos High School. We would be racing on their narrow running track. We all travelled to Santa Barbara separately, arriving at the pre- booked motel during the night. Next morning, we met the American riders for breakfast and it must have looked as though the foreign visitors were here for an 'old crocks race'.

I could hardly walk, as my bruises and muscles had seized up and had to be helped to the breakfast table. I soon stopped feeling sorry for myself when I saw the other boys. Jim Airey had his hand bandaged because he had caught his fingers in someone's wheel at Costa Mesa. Barry Briggs then hobbled in painfully. He had broken a toe during our 'friendly' race meeting at the Orange County track and to beat us all, Ivan arrived driving a new pair of crutches. He had torn some ligaments while demolishing someone's front wheel. We were a sorry looking bunch.

Despite the various injuries, the Santa Barbara meeting went very well and we raised some money for the local school. The track was around the playing field, about 440 yards and, because it was their running track, there was no safety fence, just a deep ditch on the outside. I had handling problems with a special framed borrowed Jap I was riding. On the straights, the bike only wanted to go one way and that was straight up, saving wear on the front tyre. At the end of the straight it did not want to turn into the corner, so I think the frame must have been designed for a drag racing bike which is only ridden in straight lines.

DeWayne Keeter, who was riding a similar machine to mine which had been perfect for him on the small Costa Mesa track, also had his work cut out to get the beast to turn at the end of the long straight. About three times DeWayne lost the battle with his bucking bronco machine and disappeared over the edge into the ditch. He should have got extra prize money for entertaining the crowd. Evel Knievel could not have made a more spectacular leap.

And so my time in America was drawing to a close and, although there were two more meetings the following week and I was tempted to stay, I had promised Australian promoter Frank Oliveri that I would be at his Liverpool Raceway Speedway for my first meeting on Friday 31 October. So, like the John Denver song said "My bags are packed, I'm ready to go" and I was soon "Leaving on a Jet Plane," but unlike the lyrics of the song, I knew that I would be back – in California – again.

14. Down Under again

Yes, my bags had been packed and I did go, but when I landed at Sydney Airport, my bags were nowhere to be seen they had gone 'walk-about' as the Aborigines would say. Eventually, they traced my luggage and found it in Tokyo. So I had to leave the airport in just the clothes I was wearing and wait for my luggage to catch up with me.

Liverpool Raceway in the 1970s was a hotbed of solo, sidecar and car racing. All the top solo riders would appear there, everyone from Barry Briggs and Ivan Mauger to Ole Olsen and Jim Airey, John Langfield and the British Lions touring team. No wonder the Green Valley circuit was called 'The Place of Pace'.

In addition to the solo scratch races, the programme also featured the spectacular six-rider handicap races with less experienced riders starting at the gate and the top faster racers starting 120 to 130 yards behind. By the last lap things would get very hot and hectic as the riders all bunched up racing towards the chequered flag.

Prize money was good and in the handicap races, there was a season-long point score award which was heavily sponsored. Each week, points earned in the handicap races would count towards the overall championship, like the modern Grand Prix system. The winner at the end of the season, would take home a brand new 250cc Suzuki Hustler motorcycle plus a large cash prize from a local soft drinks company. To earn the big points, riders still had to qualify through the handicap heats to the handicap final so it was a pretty tough job.

That Liverpool Raceway Handicap Championship had already started when I arrived in Australia, so I had given the other riders a couple of weeks start. However, each week throughout that season I kept qualifying through the heats and into the final and sometimes winning it too. So I gradually pulled the points back and in the last meeting of the season I eventually gained enough points to win that Championship. I became the proud owner of a brand new Suzuki motorcycle and some much needed cash.

I could not ship the Suzuki home, so I sold it before I left Australia and, with that and the cash prize from the soft drinks company, I put a deposit on a block of land in Engadine in South Sydney. I was becoming an Australian land owner!

The trophy presentation was a bit of a washout as at the end of the meeting. The heavens opened and everyone had to run for cover. I did, however, manage to ride a couple of laps of honour on the Suzuki in the pouring rain, waving to the fans who had braved the downpour to cheer me on. It wasn't too difficult because the Australian rain was much warmer than Scottish rain and almost like having a warm shower while riding a motorcycle.

That winter season at Liverpool Raceway was a good one with great racing in all the classes, cars, solos and sidecars, so the fans flocked to the Green Valley circuit in their thousands every week. Frank Oliveri even brought Japanese rider, Junichio 'Jimmy' Ogisu over from Tokyo to add to the international flavour of the Australian season. Jimmy was Japanese champion on dirt tracks, but eventually all the tracks were tarmaced over and the style of racing changed.

Speedway was big business in Japan. Betting was allowed and vast sums of money changed hands each night. With so much money involved, riders were kept well away from the crowd so that there could be no contact between them and the betting public. The chances of a fan getting a pre-meeting autograph were zero. The previous year, Perth promoter Aub Lawson had visited Japan and witnessed speedway in the Far East. He had invited Jimmy to come to Claremont Speedway in Perth and so began the first of Jimmy Ogisu's many visits to Australia.

We raced at Liverpool Raceway every Friday night throughout the Australian season and sometimes had extra meetings Interstate as well. It was at one such meeting that a young lad came up to me in the pits, pointed at Jimmy and said "Are you his interpreter?" When I replied "No, Junichio is my interpreter" he looked at me blankly because he had not understood my reply in my Scottish accent. I think that he probably understood Jimmy more than he did me.

Between meetings, Frank Oliveri employed Jimmy to do odd jobs around the stadium repairing the fence, painting and doing some general maintenance. One very hot day, Jimmy was up a ladder painting the outside of the referee's box when a big Australian Holden saloon car charged into the stadium, slid to a stop under the referee's box in a cloud of dust and out jumped Barry Briggs.

Jimmy had previously met Barry in Tokyo when the Kiwi stopped off in the Land of The Rising Sun to check out Japanese Speedway. Barry even donned all the armour and competed in a few races in Tokyo. Jimmy got a real surprise to see Barry again so in the true Japanese custom of politeness, he turned around, bowed and said 'Hello Mr Bliggs', then promptly fell off of the ladder with paint and brushes going everywhere.

Although outclassed in this kind of speedway in Australia, Jimmy was a popular addition to any race programme and was welcomed by the local fans and riders. He also became the first – and only – Japanese rider to race in Britain when he competed in the prestigious Internationale meeting at Wimbledon. Racing on the small Wimbledon track against some of the best riders in the world was very difficult for Jimmy, but he was a welcome and colourful addition to the line-up.

Jimmy returned to Japan to coach the young Japanese riders, but we kept in touch over the years with the occasional letter and Christmas card. Jimmy's English was not too good and my Japanese was non-existent, so nothing much was heard much was heard until the winter of 2011 when an email message popped up on my computer screen. It read: (sic) "Tokyo-London. It arrive Heathrow 06.30 hours. Go for lunch of Knowledge WSRA. Would you tell me how it goes?"

The 'WSRA' referred to was The World Speedway Riders' Association, a social organisation for former speedway riders of which Junichio was a member, but what was "lunch of Knowledge WSRA"? And then the penny dropped – or perhaps the Yen. Jimmy had come over to Britain to attend the WSRA Norwich Lunch, a popular annual event put on by Pam Hedge, wife of Wimbledon and England star, Trevor. Jimmy had just attended the Australian Veteran Riders Association Dinner in Sydney and now he was flying in unannounced to attend the Norwich lunch. Fortunately, Pam Hedge was able to fit us in on the day as this event is always a sell-out. There was a huge queue of former riders waiting to shake Jimmy's hand, welcome him and have their photographs taken with him.

Run off with Jim Airey for the 1969 New South Wales Championship.

Runner-up in the 1969 New South Wales Championship. Howard Cole (right) was third.

Runner-up in the 1969 Jack Adams Trophy. Garry Middleton was the winner, Bill Landels was third.

During his short stay in Britain, Jimmy managed to visit the Rushbrook family in deepest Essex where he had stayed when he had raced in the Internationale at Wimbledon some 41 years earlier. We arrived at the house and Jimmy, in true Japanese style, got out of the car and started taking photographs of the front of the house. Suddenly the front door opened and an irate lady came out and angrily asked what we were doing. The Rushbrook family had moved; we had come to the wrong house.

Fortunately, we found the correct house and Jimmy was welcomed back like a member of the family. All those years ago, when Stephen Rushbrook was a young lad, Jimmy had given him the open face helmet and goggles he wore in the Internationale as a souvenir before he went back to Japan. Stephen had kept them safe for all that time.

By modern standards, the open face fibreglass helmet was quite heavy, but the goggles were very unusual. Instead of the normal clear Lexan lens in the goggle frame, these goggles had a fine wire mesh lens held into place with Elastoplast. "Could not see in wet shale with normal goggles", explained Jimmy, "but these much better when it is raining." I had never tried wire mesh lenses, so took Jimmy's word for it. These goggles and the Japanese helmet are now on loan from Steve Rushbrook to the Speedway Museum.

As I mentioned, Jimmy had attended the annual Australian VSRA Dinner in Sydney where Ove Fundin was guest of honour. The great Swede gave Jimmy a set of his old yellow leathers to give to the Speedway Museum. They are on display with Ove's fellow Swede Bengt Jansson's leathers and their autographed Swedish body colours. After the Australian dinner, Jimmy flew to Tokyo, stayed there for seven days, then back onto a plane for London where I met him as outlined above. Jimmy was the first – and only – Japanese rider to race in England and first to attend the 'Knowledge' Lunch.

Rain seemed to follow speedway around quite a lot, especially in Scotland although it was possible to race on a wet track once the sawdust was put down, so we did not have so many rained off meetings. At one sawdust-soaked meeting at Edinburgh I decided I did not want my freshly polished black leathers to suffer from flying wet shale so took out my favourite striped pyjamas, the ones with the wee teddy bear embroidered on them, and wore them over my leathers. I thought "Well, if Peter Craven can wear his pyjama trousers under his leathers, then surely I can wear my pyjama jacket and trousers on top of my leathers?" This was in the days before Yorkshire's 'Flash' Roberts began making waterproof over-suits for speedway. My pyjama outfit seemed to go down well with the fans even if the referee had his doubts about the legality of such clothing. I guess my pyjamas were not 'ACU approved'.

Being Scottish I was always proud of my heritage and tried to 'Fly the flag' for Caledonia as often as possible, hence the tartan helmet and later on the tartan-striped TT Leathers. I had also been known to wear the kilt over the top of my leathers from time-to-time, not when racing obviously, but for the pre-match parades. I even had a full Scottish team, 'The Bert Harkins Haggis Bashers' dressed in kilts at Wimbledon, but more of that later. I usually wore the kilt over my leathers for the pre-match parades in Australia and that always went down well with the fans. The only problem was that it was great when I was winning races, but a bit embarrassing if I had a poor meeting.

One hot summer's evening at Liverpool Raceway, I donned my kilt for the introductions as usual and also my tartan 'See you Jimmy' hat. I think that I was the original model for this tartan hat with the ginger wig. At that time, I wore a tartan 'Tammie' and my hair was long, red and curly. I think that I should have got commission on the sales. Nowadays, with much less hair on my head, I can don one of the 'See you Jimmy' tartan hats with wig and it just looks like many of my old speedway photographs.

On the evening in question, after presenter Steve Raymond had made the rider introductions, we all did a lap of honour around the big Liverpool track. I stopped on the back straight to make a practice start, revved the Jawa motor, dropped the clutch and with the track being very grippy, the front wheel flew high in the night sky and my kilt went flying over my eyes and head. I crashed straight into the hard wooden "safety" fence. Fortunately, the only thing I hurt was my pride. I stood up, bowed to the crowd, as Jimmy Ogisu had taught me, and hurriedly picked the bike up. I bump-started it and rode back to the pits with a red face and steamed up glasses.

At the end of the Australian season and packing up to go home, my luggage was overweight so I had to leave my kilt with Australian speedway sidecar ace Bob Levy in Sydney. Many years later, former Yarmouth rider Jim Courtney, secretary of the Australian Veteran Speedway Riders' Association travelled from Sydney to the UK and presented me with a heavy parcel. It was my original kilt, moth-eaten and with some Liverpool shale stained into it, but still in good enough condition to be used around the tracks again.

Apart from it being the beginning of me wearing the kilt at race meetings, Australia was also where my famous white boots were born. I had been told about a company in Sydney who built made-to-measure boots for horse riding and other activities so I thought I would see if they could make me some speedway boots. "No worries, mate", the owner said, "just tell me what you want and we can make it for you." I then designed the boots with a large heel on the right boot, a smooth sole on the left boot and hidden full length zips. I then decided that I would add a bit of colour so I ordered them in white leather. White was not the ideal colour for speedway boots with all that wet shale flying around, but in my schooldays I had seen photos of Exeter's Goog Hoskin and the Falcons' team all kitted out in white boots and thought that they looked good. Prior to that, there had been photos of 'The White Ghost', Ken LeBreton wearing white boots and leathers. Swedish star Olle Nygren also had them. My theory was that my opponents could see my left leg easier and would not run over it in the corners. That idea was good in theory, but it didn't work out that way in the years to come. These made-to-measure boots cost the princely sum of $20. These days it would probably cost that for a tin of boot polish! The white boots became a bit of a trade mark for me, but were difficult to keep clean. After scrubbing them with soapy water, I used Kiwi White, which was meant for trainers, and they came up as good as new. I used so many tubes of Kiwi White over the years that I should have been sponsored by them. When I finally retired from speedway and did not need it any more, their sales must have slumped.

By the end of the 1969–70 Australian season, I was getting ready to head back to Scotland to ride for the Monarchs again when I received a short, but urgent, telegram sent to me c/o Peter White in Sydney. It was from Ian Hoskins: "Monarchs transferred to Wembley, will you ride there? Urgent! Signed Hoskins." I thought for a nanosecond and replied: "Yes please!"

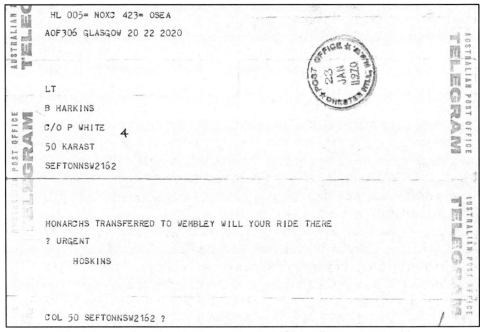

The telegram from Ian Hoskins asking Bert if he will move to Wembley.

15. On the way to Wembley

During my winter in Australia, I had no idea that the Monarchs were about to lose their home track, so I was quite unprepared for the changes that were about to come into my speedway and personal life.

Frank Oliveri gained many new friends with his New Year's Eve "Seeing out the old speed year" meeting on 31 December. After an action-packed race meeting there was a monster midnight firework display followed by free beer on the infield. That certainly appealed to the Australian fans.

The Liverpool meetings were always hotly contested with riders such as Jim Airey, John Langfield, Howard Cole, Roy Trigg, Greg Kentwell, Bill Landels all battling against the local hot shots Gary Hay, Bob Young, Barry Van Praag Ted Lindskog, Bob Humphries and others. In that end-of-the-year meeting, John Langfield won the International Stars Scratch Race from me, Jim Airey and Howard Cole. Airey got his revenge by winning the AC McGrath Scratch race. Jim and I were also scheduled to compete against each other for the International two-lap match race championship. The Australian won the first race after I had reared at the gate – no excuse – in 35.6 seconds, breaking Bill Landels's two lap track record. I won the second race and broke Jim's track record by lowering it to 35.1 seconds, so the scene was set for a great third heat decider. I trapped in the run-off and led the two lap race until the final bend when 'Alf', as Jim Airey was known, pipped me on the run to the chequered flag.

Later I evened up the score by winning the Shelley's Suzuki Handicap Grand Final from the 130 yard back-mark, ahead of Greg Kentwell (120 yards), Barry Van Praag (60 yards), John Langfield (110) with Ted Lindskog falling and both Jim Airey (130) and Howard Cole (120) retiring with bike problems. All-in-all, a nice way to end the Auld Year and see in the New, especially as a Scotsman can get very emotional being so far from home on Hogmanay.

My last meeting in Australia was on Friday 13 March, unlucky for some, but lucky for me because I finished off the season in style with the following results:
Stars Scratch Race final first;
AC McGrath Scratch Race heat first;
Handicap heat first;
Handicap final third;
AC McGrath final second.

Not a bad way to end my winter season at Liverpool. Two days later, I returned my sponsored Holden Ute (pick-up truck) to AC McGrath Holden before heading for Sydney Airport. I was sad to leave Australia, but was looking forward to riding for Wembley. This time, my travelling companion would be my 'friend' who pipped me for my second Victorian Championship, Roy Trigg. We had quite an itinerary booked to fly to London with Qantas Airways. I wanted to fly via California to visit friends and pop into Bell Helmets at Long Beach to collect my new helmets for the new season. We flew from Sydney to Auckland in New Zealand, then onto Tahiti where we got off the plane while it refuelled – small fuel tanks in those days – and strolled around the airline terminal grounds in the warm sunshine.

McGrath Monarchs in Liverpool: Bill Landels (Scotland), Howard Cole (England), John Langfield (Australia), Greg Kentwell (Australia), Jim Airey (Australia) and Bert Harkins (Scotland – on bike)

Leading Bobby Campbell at Liverpool Speedway November 1969.

I was asked by a nice American family with two children if I could take their photograph with the Qantas aircraft in the background. This was before the days of 'selfies'.

We landed at Los Angeles International Airport around 5pm local time and eventually managed to get through the long queues at passport control and then customs. I guess they wondered why someone would be coming through the airport carrying a crash helmet, did this guy not trust the pilot? At least I wasn't carrying a musical Koala bear this time.

On clearing customs, I was surprised to hear some bagpipe music drifting through the closed doors of the arrivals hall. 'That's a coincidence', I thought, 'An American radio station is playing Scottish music.'

The doors then opened and as I stepped out, I saw a full pipe band with kilts swinging marching down the aisle towards me blowing full blast on their bagpipes. I politely stepped aside to let them pass, but the six foot tall drum major leading the band stopped beside me, marking time to the music and throwing his mace in the air and said out of the corner of his mouth: "Keep walking, Bert, we've come to pick you up." Poor Roy Trigg was left to carry my bags as I was whisked away at the front of this pipe band.

Sure enough, this was my surprise welcoming committee and they marched me all through the International Airport along the corridors and even down the escalator before going out to the car park where they stood in a circle blasting out those Highland airs.

As we were marching through the airport, huge crowds, including passengers from our flight from Sydney, formed on either side of the aisles, clapping as we went by. I recognised the family I had taken the photo of in Tahiti, so I gave them an embarrassed wave. When the playing stopped and the pipers were having a wee dram to refresh themselves, that same American family came up to me and the father shook my hand and said "Oh, Mr, Stewart, we didn't know it was you otherwise we would have taken your photograph in Tahiti." I am not sure if they thought that I was racing driver, Jackie Stewart, singer, Rod Stewart or the kilted Scottish entertainer, Andy Stewart. I guess I will never know the answer.

I was really surprised at this welcome as the Californian speedway season was still about four weeks away and I had only told a couple of people that I was flying home via LA, but as I looked around, I saw familiar faces from the Californian speedway scene. I realised that they had put on this great reception as a big surprise, and it certainly was. Cheryl Funk, who had started the American branch of The Bert Harkins Fan Club when I first rode at Costa Mesa, had helped organise this Highland extravaganza. The Californians really know how to put on a show, but with all the security and health & safety issues these days, such an event would never be allowed to happen at an international airport.

In the autumn, Peter Oakes had reported in the *Speedway Star* on the impact I had made on my first American trip. He said that despite the appearance of Ivan Mauger and Barry Briggs, the "number one hit in the American season [was] Bert Harkins. He reported Cheryl Funk saying: "It is obvious why he [Bert] is one of the leading motorcycle racers in Scotland. If you get a chance to talk to him in the pits after the race you know that he is as entertaining off the track as he is on. He has a beautiful personality and a never-ending sense of humour. For instance, he said that anyone who would like to join his fan club can do so by writing their name and address on the back of any old $100,000 bill and sending it to him. In return, you will get a free lifetime membership card."

Peter's article also reported how Steve Bast had given me the first trophy he had ever won. In exchange, I gave Steve the Scottish plaid scarf I had been wearing since I started racing. This was the background to my amazing welcome.

I also saw Roy standing in the crowd holding my luggage and his jaw was still open in amazement. I guess that no-one in speedway has ever had a welcome like that. Photos even appeared on the front page of the American motorcycle racing magazine, *Cycle News,* but unfortunately my copy was lost somewhere on my travels. I should have bought all of the copies at the time.

From the airport, we were whisked off to a 'Welcome back Scotty' party before heading back to Harry Oxley's house for the night. I was lent a car by one of my Californian friends, and although I had stayed at Harry's place the year before, in those pre-satnav days, I got a bit lost trying to find my way in the dark.

I spotted a telephone box so pulled up alongside it to phone Harry for directions and that was a mistake. I was talking to Harry on the telephone when a police car came round the corner and stopped right in front of my car while another police car came from the other direction with blue lights flashing and blocked me in. Then I realised the problem. I had parked with two wheels up on the kerb as we sometimes do at home, but these were wide Californian streets and people did not park on the 'sidewalk'. One policeman approached Roy in the car while the other questioned me. I was still on the phone to Harry Oxley so I made my apologies to him: "Sorry Harry, there is a big policeman with a gun who wants to talk to me" and I put the phone down. That was another mistake because Harry could have talked to them in their own language – American English – not Scottish English.

"OK, Buddy," the patrolman drawled, "what are you doing and why have you parked on the sidewalk?" Well, when I get nervous I am liable to start speaking very quickly and my Glasgow accent comes to the fore. Besides I was not too comfortable with this cop with his gun which did not help and I jabbered away "Och, ah've just arrived in yer wonderful country and ah'm lost an' trying to get directions", I babbled in my nervous Glaswegian tongue. The policeman was not tuned into my Scottish accent and did not understand me. So, with his hand on his gun, the cop said "Have you been drinking, buddy?" to which I quickly replied without thinking, "Och no, ah always talk like this". He must have thought that I was trying to take the mickey and was shaking his head in disbelief as he wrote out the parking ticket.

16. Life with the Lions

Wembley had always been a magical name, no matter what sport was taking place between the famous Twin Towers and to have league speedway returning there after a gap of 14 years was an exciting prospect.

I remembered my early visits to Wembley when my friends and I used to come down to London on the overnight bus from Glasgow, a long and tiring trip to watch the World Final. Now I had a chance to join this famous team and race regularly at this cathedral of speedway. The things that impressed me most about those early World Finals, apart from the racing, was that when the race started, the grandstands and centre green were all in darkness and only the thin ribbon of track was floodlit. Sixteen riders in polished black leathers with chrome plated Jap speedway bikes whose chrome plated handlebars, wheels and rear mudguards sparkled under the lights gave the packed stadium a unique atmosphere.

New Zealander Trevor Redmond, a former Wembley rider, promoter at various tracks including Glasgow and Kiwi team manager, along with local Wembley businessman Bernard Cottrell, had purchased the Coatbridge licence. They were preparing to resurrect the famous Wembley Lions. Despite protests from the disappointed Scottish fans, the Coatbridge Monarchs were no more and the riders were moved to other tracks. However, the resurrection of Wembley was good news for speedway in general.

Ove Fundin would be coming from Sweden to captain the Lions. So after all those years ago, when he had come over to speak to me after I had travelled down from Scotland for a second half junior race at Wimbledon, we were going to be team mates. Small world, eh?

Reidar Eide, Brian Collins, Wayne Briggs and I were transferred to Wembley for the 1970 season. The second string and reserve places took some time to settle, and included Brian Leonard, Tim Bungay, Stan Stevens, Des Lukehurst and a youthful Dave Jessup who was signed from Second Division Eastbourne. George Hunter was signed by Newcastle and Monarchs skipper Doug Templeton moved west to the other end of the M8 motorway to ride for Glasgow Tigers.

The difference between Coatbridge and Wembley could not have been more pronounced. From draughty dressing rooms with lukewarm showers at Cliftonhill to the spacious football dressing rooms at Wembley complete with hot showers, several deep baths and a huge communal 'swimming pool' bath. This was luxury indeed.

Our team manager was former Wembley legend and double World Champion, Freddie Williams. He proved to be an excellent manager because he understood the riders' temperaments and the Wembley track. He was a valuable addition to the team. I became good friends with Freddie and his wife Pat and family. They were to be instrumental in changing my on-track and off-track life forever.

Another former Wembley Lion involved was former team captain Bill Kitchen, who was national official machine examiner and track inspector, so with Freddie, Bill and Trevor Redmond, half of the old Wembley Lions team were on hand to help out us 'new boys'.

But all was not sunshine and light. Owing to the extended football season, the Wembley speedway track could not be laid in time for the start of the British League season, so our 'press and practice' day consisted of all the team members wearing the new Wembley Lions body colours to pose for photographs around the track. We could not ride the bikes on the track so the photographers made do with shots of us sitting on the famous Wembley tractor or digging holes to help get the track ready.

We still got a lot of publicity for speedway because just the name 'Wembley' was enough for newspaper sports editors to send photographers, reporters and even feature writers along to the Empire Stadium.

The problem with the late opening was that by this time all of our opponents had been racing for about eight weeks and would be completely 'race fit'. The new Lions had a series of 11 away matches before our debut at Wembley. I had also ridden as a guest for Glasgow Tigers at Hampden Park the evening before our opening meeting at Wembley, so it was the usual rush to clean and prepare the bike and head back down the M74, M6 and M1 to The Smoke in time to face Len Silver's Hackney Hawks at the Empire Stadium.

Prior to our first home meeting Bernard Cottrell had organised a welcome party and press conference for us in his office in Cottrell House opposite the stadium. This gave us an opportunity to meet our new team mates and share a glass of champagne together – pity I didn't drink. Mr Cottrell and TR had also arranged a sponsorship deal with a local restaurant in Wembley High Street, called, appropriately enough, *The Captain's Table* where we could all eat free of charge after each home meeting. The advert in the Wembley programme read "Eat where the Lions eat – The Captain's Table". Many supporters came along, so the sponsorship helped both the restaurant and the Wembley team.

The Wembley name was invaluable in terms of sponsorship because many companies wanted to be associated with it, no matter what sporting team carried the famous name. Swiss watch company *Jaeger-LeCoultre* sponsored me with one of their latest watches which had an alarm clock built into it. This was invaluable for my overseas trips and early rises.

Second half races were also heavily sponsored, and at the time of the Skol Six Day cycle race in the nearby Wembley Arena, the lager company also sponsored the Trophy Final at the speedway on the Saturday evening. I won a crate of Skol lager but, as I didn't drink, the rest of the team had a nice party in the dressing rooms after the meeting.

I also won a very expensive Breitling gold watch at Wembley but unfortunately, that was stolen in a break-in at our house some years ago when we were away. Also stolen in that burglary was the gold watch which was presented to my dad when he retired from the Glasgow Fire Brigade after 25 years' service, which was a great sentimental loss. The thieves even took my XR350 Honda motorcycle plus other items and to add insult to injury, they loaded everything into my Mercedes van and stole that too.

Our first ever home meeting at the Empire Stadium, Wembley versus Hackney, was a great success with over 20,000 present. That included a few hundred who had travelled down from Scotland to support their former Monarchs in their new home.

Initially, the BBC's Bob Danvers-Walker was the track announcer, but soon BBC Radio 1 DJs Ed Stewart and David Hamilton became part of the Wembley presentation team and did a very good job. The benefit of having such household names on board was that we often got 'plugs' on their BBC radio shows. Ed 'Stewpot' was hosting the ever-popular *Junior Choice* programme on Radio One and he got the message over to the younger generation.

I remember 'Diddy Dave' once announcing on his Saturday morning show that "Bert Harkins will be somewhere on the M6 or M1 driving down from Scotland for tonight's speedway at Wembley, so if you see him on the road, toot your horn." Quite a few cars blew their horns on that trip south, but I think that was more to do with my bad driving rather than that they had recognised me.

Also with their show business connections, they were able to persuade pop singers Leapy Lee of *Little Arrows* fame and Troy Dante to come along to Wembley and have a match race on speedway bikes, along with Dave and Ed. Now I am not sure whose idea this was, but I can see the thoughts of TR the showman behind it all. Get some pop stars along and the young fans will love it. Trevor always said that 'Everyone is special' so he always had some publicity stunts in mind.

The main problem with this great idea was that neither David nor Ed had ever ridden a motorcycle and we were going to let them loose on 500cc fire-breathing, methanol-drinking speedway bikes.

Ed had to wear my leathers, boots and tartan helmet while Troy Dante, who was supposed to have ridden a bike before, borrowed my Jawa. Ed was about six feet tall, so he had great difficulty in getting into my leathers. He could not do up the zip properly – shades of my burst open zip at Wimbledon a year or so earlier – this time I did not have a pair of swimming trunks to hold the zip together so Ed had to rely on the body colour to keep out the wind and hide his modesty.

The four man 'race' was probably the slowest ever recorded at Wembley. I think the timekeeper used a calendar instead of a stop watch but, all credit to them, at least they had the courage to try to ride a speedway bike. They circulated the Wembley track at just above walking pace until Troy Dante tried to go faster than the others and crashed my bike, bending the front forks. The things we do for speedway. Sadly, Ed passed away in 2016, but 'Diddy David' is still touring with his *David Hamilton's Rock & Roll Years* stage show and still gives speedway a 'plug' whenever he can.

We met up at one of his shows last year. He brought his scrapbook which contained a lot of show business and speedway cuttings including a picture of him checking what was worn under my kilt.

When I signed for Wembley, I was still living in Glasgow and wearing a groove in the motorway driving up and down each week. The offer to sign for Wembley had come so late and so quickly that I did not have time to organise accommodation nearer London, nor did I even ask Wembley to provide something for me. I just was not a hard-nosed businessman when it came to negotiating contracts, I just wanted to ride speedway and was grateful for the opportunity to do so.

I sometimes stayed with my long-suffering cousin in Hayes in Middlesex where I had been on my ill-fated World Cycle Speedway Final trip to London and also occasionally with friends in Watford. By mid-season, Freddie Williams offered me a room in *Delgarth*, the Williams family home in Harpenden, Hertfordshire. This really helped to cut down my travelling time.

Riding at Wembley was a great experience, we may not have had the huge crowds that attended the World Finals or those of the old Wembley Lions of the 1940s and early 1950s, but the club was still very well supported.

The 1970 Wembley Lions: Dave Jessup, Bert, Tim Bungay, Freddie Williams (team manager), Ove Fundin (capt – on bike), Wayne Briggs, Reidar Eide, Brian Collins. (JSC)

In the pits at Wembley.

Bert leading Brian Collins and John Boulger at Wembley. (JSC – Mike Patrick)

Left: Bert's former Coatbridge team-mates Reidar Eide and Wayne Briggs who moved with him to Wembley. Right: Ove Fundin in Wembley colours. (Both photos JSC)

Walking up the tunnel from the dressing rooms and onto the track and seeing that crowd and hearing the noise was an awesome experience. For the riders in the 90,000 World Final crowds, it must have made the hair on the back of their necks stand up.

After each meeting, riders from both teams would head to The Long Bar in the grandstand to meet the fans before heading to *The Captain's Table* for a late dinner. Like many riders, when racing, I never ate before the meeting so by the time it ended, I was getting rather 'peckish'. It was quite a sight to open the doors of The Long Bar and be engulfed in a wave of kids running towards us, autograph books in hand. Wembley had a very loyal following of young fans and Saturday night at Wembley was their big night of the week. With no school the next day they could really enjoy themselves. Occasionally, I still meet a few of these kids who are now fully grown adults. They remember their days as Junior Lion Cubs with pride.

Not everyone was quite so happy about the return of Wembley to Saturday night speedway. King's Lynn promoters, Maurice Littlechild and Cyril Crane thought that their Saturday night crowd was down as so many fans from the Norwich area had gone to Wembley to see their hero, Ove Fundin riding for the Lions. Ove was a God in that part of the country and later received the Freedom of the City from Norwich Council, an ancient honour which allows you to drive your flock of sheep through the city. I don't know if Ove has ever taken up that offer.

When Wembley were due to race at Kings Lynn, there was great anticipation that Ove was coming 'home' and there was a huge turnout at the Norfolk track to see the return of their multi World Champion. Unfortunately, Ove's flight to the UK was fog-bound in Copenhagen and he didn't turn up, so there were many disgruntled fans that evening. Poor Trevor Redmond was the one who had to break this unpalatable news to the fans over the centre green mic. The Stars fans were not too impressed, but even that master showman, TR could not do anything about the weather.

Despite that disappointment all those years ago, Ove is still held in high esteem with the Norwich and Kings Lynn fans and many others throughout the speedway world. He is a regular visitor to the annual Norwich Lunch along with his wife Joanna. He is still riding his BMW motorcycle at an age when others look for a comfortable armchair, pipe and slippers.

In 1970, Ove was living in Sweden where he had a thriving transport business and flew over to Britain for the Lions matches. I was made captain for the matches where he was missing. Eventually Ove left Wembley for good at the end of July and I continued as captain until Wembley closed at the end of the 1971 season. Many riders did not like going out in heat one, preferring to watch and see what the track was like before taking their first ride, but I always enjoyed that first heat. Normally the track was well-prepared and grippy and that gave me a chance to make a flying start against the opponents' number one and give some feedback on track conditions to my team mates.

After Ove left, Trevor Redmond brought in a young Californian, Steve Bast, to ride for the Lions. Steve was American champion and one of the very best riders at Costa Mesa. I had raced against him many times in America and seen how talented he was on a motorcycle.

Unfortunately, by the time Steve came over, on 13 August, the season was well underway and he found the change of tracks, food, weather and lifestyle just too much to handle. He became very homesick for the Californian sunshine and beaches so on 25 August, flew home after only a few race meetings. Had he arrived at the beginning of the season, persevered and got over his homesickness, I think that he would have been just as good as Bruce Penhall, Scott Autrey and other American stars who came along later. I always thought that it must have been very difficult for young riders from California, Australia or New Zealand to give up the sunshine, food and comfortable lifestyle in their home countries and travel the world to race in Britain. Everything was different to home. The food, weather, speedway tracks, houses, traffic – the list goes on. So hats off to all those riders from across the world and Europe who came here and learned their speedway trade in this country.

A new rider signed by Wembley at the start of the 1971 season was a young unknown 19-year-old Swede, Tommy Jansson. Tommy only rode three meetings for the Lions before he was released, but his smooth style and obvious potential shone through. I was very surprised and unhappy that he was dropped. It was a very hasty decision because Tommy could have been a great asset to the Wembley Lions. Tommy later returned to be a star at Wimbledon. We raced together both at Wimbledon and in Australia. He had the potential to be World Champion. Sadly, Tommy lost his life in a track crash in the Swedish Final at the tender age of 23. Wimbledon, and speedway overall, were never the same again.

Personally, I loved riding at the Empire Stadium. It was a technical track, but one that gave the rider tremendous satisfaction if he rode it well. My own form was going well and I was enjoying my new home between the Twin Towers, so it was with great pride that I heard that Glasgow's Jim McMillan and I had been selected to represent Scotland in the World Best Pairs Semi Final at Belle Vue. Nothing excites a Scotsman more than being selected to ride for his country.

Not that it was going to be easy against the might of England, Australia, New Zealand, Australia, Denmark, Norway and West Germany. Critics reckoned that we may have been able to beat the Germans and stay away from the bottom of the table, but Jimmy and I surprised them all. We scored 13 points each to finish second, only one point behind the New Zealand pairing of Ivan Mauger and Barry Briggs but, more importantly, three points ahead of the England duo of Nigel and Eric Boocock. Australia, with Jim Airey and Charlie Monk were in fourth place, while Ole Olsen scored all but one of Denmark's 13 points. Norway, with Reidar Eide and Oyvind Berg also had 13 and the West Germans finished in last place with seven points to their name.

The Scotland versus England tables were turned in the World Best Pairs Final in Malmo, Sweden on 2 June when Ivan and Ronnie Moore won the title for New Zealand ahead of Sweden. Third place went to England with Eric and Nigel just one point ahead of Scotland. Jimmy and I were not too far away from being World Champions.

Back at Wembley and the Lions were roaring again. In 1971, Norway's Sverre Harrfeldt joined the team. He had previously been at West Ham and had suffered very serious injuries in the 1968 European Final in Poland. Sverre was an all-action rider. He was idolised by the Wembley fans and when he scored his first maximum for the Lions, it almost lifted the roof off of the grand old Empire Stadium.

The Scandinavian influence continued at Wembley when Trevor Redmond brought in Sweden's Gote Nordin in mid-season and the stylish Swede was another fans' favourite in his short spell with the Lions. Gote was a neat rider with a very upright style on the bike.

1971 Wembley team: Dave Jessup, Tony Clarke, Brian Leonard, Bert (capt- on bike), Gote Nordin, Freddie Williams (on bike), Sverre Harrfeldt, Brian Collins, Peter Prinsloo.

He was just as much of a gentleman off the track as he was on it. Reidar Eide had moved on at the end of the 1970 season, so Sverre and Gote became our Scandinavian riders,

Our 'home grown' riders such as my fellow Scot, Brian Collins, Brian Leonard, Tony Clarke – another 1971 recruit from West Ham – and the young Dave Jessup, all improved when riding for Wembley. Trevor Redmond added to the international flavour of the team. He brought in a Rhodesian, Peter Prinsloo, who he had seen racing in Rhodesia (now Zimbabwe). It was a tough task for Peter to be thrown in at the deep end with Wembley.

Trevor Redmond even 'poached' Kings Lynn's announcer/presenter Martin Rogers from the Norfolk track to take up residence in the Wembley announcer's box. TR was doing everything to portray Wembley as a glamour club.

My own season at Wembley was going very well and I was enjoying my 'Life with the Lions' and still knocking up the miles both here and on the Continent where I was getting regular meetings in Germany, Austria and Italy. There were no Swedish, Polish or Danish leagues for us to ride in, so those countries were the ones to go to for Sunday racing.

17. A broken leg, Sir? Coming up!

The 1970 British season was over. I finished with a league match at West Ham on the Tuesday then flew out to California. I hit a slight spot of bother at the Los Angeles International Airport customs when they discovered a 'bomb' in my hand luggage with wires protruding out of the zip. The bomb was a spare magneto I was taking out with me, but I must admit that it did look rather suspicious. Fortunately, the customs officer was also a keen motorcyclist; he believed me and let me through with my precious cargo. The next day, Thursday, I was already putting in some practice laps on borrowed bikes at Costa Mesa in preparation for my return to 'Shinbone alley' the following evening. I was due to race in a couple of their end-of-season meetings on my way to spending the rest of the British winter racing in Australia.

Friday night at the Orange County Fairgrounds on a balmy October evening and it was balmy in more ways than one. I was back to the hazy, crazy world of Californian Speedway. Promoter Harry Oxley was yelling at the top of his voice. At the pit gate, Freda Wenn was yelling at the mechanics who were not wearing 'whites'. Announcer/presenter Larry Huffman was doing his famous 'Huffman Hop', leaping up and down on his table at the starting gate and whipping the crowd into a frenzy of excitement. The fans were warmed up and eager for action and they always got their money's worth at Costa Mesa.

I lived up to my 'Bouncing Bert' nickname. I had eight races in which I used six bikes and had two wins, three engine failures and three falls, pretty much a typical night's racing at Costa Mesa.

The following weekend I was booked to ride at Costa Mesa on the Friday evening and on the Saturday at Indio in the Colorado Desert region, not far from Palm Springs. In the warm evening air at Indio, all was going well until Rick Woods speared me in the middle of the corner and broke my left leg. That was the end of my American season, only two weeks after my final British meeting in October. I was quickly whisked off to Indio Hospital where I was seen by Doctor Koenig. He was a sort of American Carlo Biagi (a British doctor who regularly treated speedway riders) and one of the top orthopaedic surgeons in Palm Springs, the famous desert hideaway for film stars and Barry Briggs. Doctor Koenig decided that the best and quickest method of repairing my injuries was to insert a steel pin in my leg and a screw (metric, I think) in my broken ankle. This proved to be quite correct.

I was laid up in that hospital for a week, but despite the anguish of getting injured so far from home, there were lighter moments to brighten my day. Many of the riders came past the next day to see how I was, but I felt a bit too groggy to appreciate that. Harry Oxley and the American fans were very good to me, paid my hospital bills and even had a collection for me. I was also entertained by a local Mexican motorcyclist by the ominous name of 'Jose the Madman'. He was a regular visitor who came past each day. When I say 'came past', he usually came past my window on one wheel while waving at me. That certainly kept me entertained. Oh boy, was Jose an entertainer. He used to have quite an audience of nurses, patients and orderlies watching his one man stunt show until the local highway patrol officer came along to take him away.

Indio is some 120 miles from Los Angeles and had a fair percentage of Mexican residents. In hospital, one of my nurses was an elderly Mexican lady who had difficulty understanding my Scottish accent. I was in a private room at the hospital and each day, she came in to check that I was still there and had not escaped during the night. I always chatted with her, although I don't think that she understood me. One day she could take no more, gave me a puzzled look and said "Where are you from, boy?" and I replied in my best Loch Lomond accent, "Oh, I am from Scotland". "Scaatland?" she said in amazement. "How long have you been in the United States?"

"Oh, about two weeks" I said, to which she looked really surprised and said in all seriousness "Wow! How did you learn to speak English so quickly?" I tried not to laugh because it would hurt my leg, but little things like that helped brighten my day.

I began to wonder if I had some unusual symptoms or injuries as I seemed to have an endless stream of nurses and orderlies visiting my room. Each would ask a couple of unimportant questions and then back out of the door laughing. This went on for some time until I asked a passing doctor what was wrong. "Oh, don't worry", he reassured me, "It's just that they haven't heard an accent like yours before and they like to hear you talking."

During that stay in Indio my hair got rather long and curly. One morning I was asleep with my back to the room door when a new nurse wakened me with "Good morning, Mrs Harkins, time to take your pills". Boy, did she get a shock when I turned around – a topless haggis. Needless to say, I had a haircut the next day.

My leg healed fairly quickly and I was eventually released from the hospital on crutches and told that the cast had to stay on for at least four weeks. That was quite heart-breaking because I had a contract to race at Liverpool Raceway the week after my accident. I then had to make a big decision. Did I return home to convalesce before the British season or continue on to Australia on crutches with my leg in plaster, in the hope that I may still be able to race there before their season ends?

It was still only early November, so I thought that if I headed home, I would have the full British winter to go through. However, if I went to Australia, it was their summer and the sunshine may help my healing process, so the decision proved to be quite straightforward. Australia here I come, again. I phoned Liverpool manager Mike Raymond and explained that I had been 'delayed' on my way to Australia and may be a little late in arriving. After my November appointment at Indio Hospital and armed with copies of my X-ray photos, I hopped – literally – onto a Qantas aeroplane and headed for Australia, crutches and all.

I arrived in Sydney in mid-November and spent a few weeks hobbling around Liverpool Speedway acting as team manager for the 'Fred Williams Marines' and generally getting in the way. This was not our Welsh double world speedway champion, Fred Williams. This Fred Williams was one of the largest water ski and speedboat companies in Australia who sponsored me in my racing campaigns down under.

Eventually, by mid-December, the cast came off and I had a few practice laps at Liverpool on a hot afternoon. That was brought to a halt by some thunderstorms and the practice session was rained off. Next evening, I made my comeback at Liverpool with a modest three points from four rides. It was not my best performance, but my leg felt OK and the following week I scored 10 points to finish fourth in the New South Wales Championship.

Above: Racing against Peter Moore (left)
in the Victorian Championship in 1970.

Right: Bert being interviewed by Ken McPhail
in Australia in November 1970.

Below: Howard Cole, Jim Ryman and Bert in action at
Liverpool Speedway in Australia in February 1971.

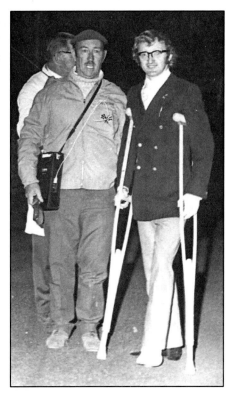

That Australian summer season consisted of sunshine speedway all around Australia, barbeques and water skiing. The latter activity was a little tricky because I couldn't swim, but then my fun came down with a bump, again. My Australian friend, Ray Schriever, lent me his Honda 450cc road motorcycle to get around. One wet February evening while riding home in the pouring rain, I hit a puddle. This was no ordinary puddle; it was an Australian puddle. It concealed a pothole six feet deep and as the Honda's front wheel disappeared into the hole, I became the first Scotsman in space as I 'disappeared' over the handlebars. I broke the scaphoid on my left wrist and collected a few other cuts and bruises. Another hospital visit; this time the plaster was moved from my leg to my arm. The doctor said that I could be out of action for three months.

The damage was not too bad, apart from Ray's motorcycle, and after three weeks on the sidelines watching the other boys collect the prize money I 'modified' my leathers and cut some of the plaster away to enable me to use my fingers on the clutch. I made my second comeback of the winter season and was back racing again. It is amazing what can happen when an Australian dollar bill is waved in front of a Scotsman.

On the big Australian tracks it was not too difficult to ride with this injury and my comeback meeting at Liverpool saw me rattle up 10 points from five races. By the beginning of March the hospital cut the rest of the plaster cast from my arm and wrist, but were puzzled as to why I could move my fingers so well. "Oh, the plaster must have just broken off" I told the nurse as she replaced the plaster with an elastic bandage. I think that the Castrol 'R' stains and tyre marks on the plaster must have given her the idea that the arm had not been in a sling all the time.

Above: Wedding day: Barry and June Briggs, Bert and Edith, Raye and Ivan Mauger.

A less formal wedding photo!

Left: Bert and Edith at the WSRA Dinner Dance in 2008. (JSC - John Chaplin)

Above: Bert and Norman Christie.

Below: Bert (riding) and George Huner (passenger) show their skills at Cycle Speedway at Coventry in May 1973.

Left: Scott Autrey, Bert and Edward Jancraz riding for the Rest of the World in Australia.

Bottom left: Flying the flag. (JSC – Mike Patrick)

Bottom right: With Briggo at the 1985 Golden Greats meeting at Edinburgh. (JSC – Mike Patrick)

Right: The 1978 Edinburgh Monarchs: Dave Trownson, Alan Morrison, Alan Bridgett, Bert (Capt – on bike), Brian Collins, Rob Hollingworth, Steve McDermott, Neil MacFarlane (team manager).

Left: Bert's leathers, helmet and four valve Jawa on display at the National Speedway Museum.
Right: Bert and former Edinburgh legend Jimmy Tannock.
Below: Bert with an overenthusiastic Scottish fan (JSC – Mike Patrick)

18. World Championship dreams

With Wembley having a late start to the 1971 season, I was able to keep racing in Australia until the end of March, fit in a stopover in California before arriving back in UK on 4 April. I was fit and ready-to-go apart from a strapped up left wrist.

The Lions' first meeting was at Wolverhampton on Good Friday where I collected nine points, but my Wembley and Scotland teammate, Brian Collins, broke his collarbone. By a strange coincidence, our fellow Scot Jim McMillan also broke his collarbone at Hampden Park the same evening. Not a very promising start to a new season.

I raced regularly in Germany on my free Sundays and, at the beginning of the 1971 season, Freddie Williams said to me "You have got to come over to our house and meet our new au pair, Edith, she is from Germany." Well, Freddie always gave the riders good advice on the track, so I did what he suggested and eventually, some three years later, that au pair, Frauline Edith Kemnitz, became Mrs Edith Harkins, so Freddie and the Williams family have a lot to answer for.

The Williams family are a unique sporting family. Freddie was twice World Speedway champion and the only Welshman to win that title. His brothers Eric and Ian also had very successful speedway careers. Freddie's wife Pat was an Olympic ice skater, son David became a professional golfer and daughters, Jayne and Sarah were expert horse riders. Today, Jayne is still competing and winning in many of the big events in the horse world such as the Windsor Horse Show where she is often introduced to the Queen after beating the Queen's horse, a rather awkward situation indeed. Now there is a third generation of champions with Freddie and Pat's granddaughter, Joanna, winning the same ice skating championship that her grandmother had won in the 1950s. A very talented family indeed.

On the World Speedway Championship trail, the Wembley riders were always at a slight disadvantage, because, owing to the late start of the season at the Empire Stadium, we did not have a 'home' round at Wembley in the three-round World Championship qualifying stages to boost our chances. However, if a rider wants to qualify for the World Final, he should be able to ride any track in any conditions, so we could not complain.

My own World Championship rounds consisted of the usual mixture of rushing around the country and living out of a suitcase. My troubles began when my car seized up in Glasgow and with no time to carry out repairs, I had to hire a van to take my two bikes around, load it with everything but the kitchen sink and head south. This was not like a modern van, it was an 'economy' model. I had to pad the rattling doors with sponge rubber and stuff rags into the holes in the floor and then I could settle down and 'enjoy' my drive down to London. Despite magneto trouble, I collected nine points at West Ham and then spent the next day working on my bikes at Roy Trigg's place in Streatham, or, as I thought it was pronounced, 'Street-Ham'. Luckily for me, Roy's crate of spares had just arrived back from Australia so I was able to borrow the necessary bits and pieces I required. Next round was north to Sheffield where I collected a further 10 points. My third and last round was due at Kings Lynn, but two days of heavy rain put paid to that. I met a very tired Willie Templeton there. Willie had left his farm in Fife early on the Thursday morning, driven down to Wimbledon for his World Championship round on Thursday evening, back up to Glasgow on Friday for a league match with the Tigers, then back to Kings Lynn to find that the meeting was rained off. Quite often the Scottish based riders put in a seven or eight hour day just to get to a track and then had to race. The joys of being a long distance speedway rider.

By the time I got home to Glasgow after the rain-off at Saddlebow Road, I got a phone call from Trevor Redmond to tell me that for my World Championship round I had been reallocated to Cradley Heath. At Cradley I had won my first race and was cleaning my famous spectacles when the frame on the glasses broke in two. As I wasn't carrying a spare pair at the time, I repaired the broken glasses with duct tape and a strip of Elastoplast from my forehead to my nose held the things in place. At the time, I was given a lot of help from Pete Jarman. 'Old Speedy' volunteered to lead me out onto the track, sit me on my bike and point me in the right direction saying "Just keep turning left, Haggis and you will be OK". Fortunately, things were not too bad and my only real trouble was focussing on the tapes as, with the vibration through the handlebars, I was seeing six tapes instead of three.

My marathon rent-a-wreck tour ended on the A74 in Scotland at 4am on a cold, wet morning when the headlights began to dim and the engine died. With some fiddling around under the bonnet with torches and spanners and the help of a friendly truck driver, I got the van running again, but with no heater and no lights. I had to wrap a travel rug around me and wear my crash helmet and goggles for the rest of the journey. Ah yes, the joys of being a speedway rider in the swinging 1970s.

Anyway, with my three 'away' rounds I had scored enough points to reach the semi-finals, scored nine points at Sheffield to finish sixth and therefore managed to qualify for the 1971 British Final at Coventry. These were the days when the British Final was contested by top Commonwealth riders such as Ivan Mauger, Barry Briggs, Ronnie Moore, John Boulger, Jim Airey and Geoff Curtis as well as top home riders, Nigel Boocock, Eric Boocock, Ray Wilson, Howard Cole, Tony Lomas, Martin Ashby, Bob Kilby, Dave Younghusband and Arnold Haley. It was almost like a mini World Final.

Several hundred Wembley fans had made the trip up the M1 motorway to cheer me on and there were plenty of red and white scarves in the crowd that night. I scored nine points in my first four rides and had a good chance of being on the podium, but in my last race I was up against the three Kiwi World Champions and finished behind all of them, but my nine points were still enough to finish fourth and get me to the next round, the Nordic/British Final at Hampden Park in Glasgow.

I had previously qualified for a World Best Pairs Final in Sweden along with fellow Scot, Jimmy McMillan and that first individual World Final place was edging closer. From the Nordic/British Final in Glasgow, eight riders would qualify for the next stage, the European Final at Wembley and from there, the top eight plus one reserve would go directly to the World Final in Sweden. My chances of reaching that World Final were beginning to look good. I had been riding well and if I could get through the Nordic/British final then I had a home meeting at Wembley.

Not too many riders were beating me around Wembley, but meanwhile, there were still league matches to race for Wembley and a Scotland versus England international at Glasgow.

For the record, the Nigel Boocock-led England beat us Scots 60–48 and I notched up 11 points from my six rides.

My high scoring continued until Wolverhampton came to town on 24 July, just six days before the Nordic/British Final at Hampden Park. We beat the Wolves 48–30, but Ole Olsen was flying and I just could not match him. The only point I dropped to an opponent that night was to Ole. I tried to figure out just what he was doing to beat me so easily at Wembley. We met again in the second half trophy final and Ole out-gated me again. I sat almost on his back wheel to see where he was getting the grip when I hit a rut on the second bend and with lightning speed, the bike stood up on its back wheel and ran straight into the safety fence. I don't remember too much about it, but this was before the engine cut-out cord was compulsory and the bike was stuck on the wire fence above me with the engine revving hard until Ole came round again and pulled off the spark plug lead. Thanks Ole, because that saved me from having a haircut with my spinning rear wheel.

That was the end of my night's racing. I was whisked off to Wembley Hospital and it looked like the end of my World Championship dreams. I had broken my collarbone and the Nordic/British Final in Glasgow was only six days away. An impossible dream.

With my left arm in a sling and without the aid of a team of Grand Prix mechanics, I tried to get my bike ready for Hampden Park, still in the vain hope that I may be able to take my place there. I had never broken a collarbone before and obviously it hurt, but I did not know if I would do more damage if I tried to race. I phoned Barry Briggs to ask his advice, because Barry had often defied the odds to ride through injury. I also rang speedway's top surgeon, Doctor Carlo Biagi at Peel Hospital in Galashiels in the Scottish Borders. Carlo had patched up so many speedway riders and rugby players that he was the person everyone went to when they were injured. He treated everyone from world champions to reserves equally. He helped so many riders to keep on track when other doctors said it was impossible.

With a broken arm or leg, a 'normal' doctor would slap you in plaster and tell you to come back in six weeks, but Carlo understood the speedway riders' mentality and if it was possible, he would patch you up to let you race. If he said 'No', then the rider knew that he had to listen to the medical advice.

Everyone had a 'Carlo story' to tell from going back to the days when he was the track doctor at Southampton speedway and he saved Belle Vue's Bob Duckworth from having his foot amputated. He returned to his beloved Scotland and in his later days at Edinburgh's Powderhall Stadium, he was always 'The speedway riders' friend'.

Stories such as when Bengt Jansson was unofficially in a ward in Peel Hospital in Scotland with a broken ankle and a senior doctor was due to visit and make his rounds of the wards. 'Benga' was hurriedly helped out of bed and hidden in a cupboard until the inspection was over. Then when the 'inspection' had passed, he was reinstated back into bed and hospital life went back to normal, or as normal as it could be with Carlo in charge.

It wasn't just broken bones that Carlo would help with as Jim McMillan, George Hunter and I found out one evening at the end of the season. The three of us were due to fly to Australia to ride for the British Lions and had to have various injections for smallpox and malaria before we left. With all our racing commitments, we ran out of time to have our final injection, so we rang Carlo to see if he could help. "Och", he said, "you should have had that last injection a week ago, but meet me in the pub at Clovenfords – Carlo's local – and I will see what I can do."

We drove to the Borders and met Carlo who was holding court with some friends at the bar in the pub. He was carrying a bag and said, "OK, lads, follow me into the toilet". We wondered what was going on and didn't want to be seen all rushing to the Gents together, but did as Carlo requested. We went into the toilet one at a time at short intervals. Inside, Carlo had put his bag on top of the washbasin, opened it and pulled out the biggest needle we had ever seen. "OK lads, roll up your sleeves".

He then proceeded to give the three of us injections. We worried that if anyone came through the toilet door from the pub they would think that they had walked into a Scottish drugs den and telephone the vice squad. On the drive home that night, we could not move our left arms, so I steered the car with my right hand while Jimmy Mac changed gear with his right hand.

But back to the Nordic/British Final. Both Briggo and Carlo gave me advice. Carlo said that he would check me out before the meeting and strap me up tightly so that my shoulder would not move and cause more damage. I was determined to ride so I also lowered my handlebars so that I did not have to stretch so much to reach them. I altered my clutch lever and even my seat. In the 1970s, everyone had their own style of handlebars and they were usually set quite high to help wrestle the bike around the corners. Normally, the left bar was slightly higher to enable the rider to 'pull down' on the corners while the right bar was lower so that the wrist and throttle would be almost in a straight line to help with throttle control. Just look at photos of Ivan Mauger's right hand and arm and you will get the idea.

At the track, Carlo strapped me up like a chicken, gave me some painkilling injections which were more painful than the injury itself and I was ready to go. I was the lone Scot left in the World Championship that year with Jim McMillan and George Hunter having missed out through injury. There was a lot support and expectations from the 10,000 strong crowd, most of whom were Scots at Scotland's biggest ever speedway meeting.

With the top eight riders qualifying for Wembley, I had a glimmer of hope that I could hang on and make the cut, but I was too tentative and not comfortable on the bike. A last place plus three thirds in my first four races did not bode well. In my last race, heat 19, I made the gate against Ray Wilson, Nigel Boocock and Denmark's Kurt Bogh, but my success was short lived. 'World Cup Willie' dived underneath me going into the pits corner, ran over my left leg and brought me tumbling onto the Hampden Park shale. The partisan Scottish crowd erupted with indignation and anger and poor Willie was booed the whole way around that vast Hampden Park track. Even during the presentations at the end of the meeting, the jeers continued and it is said that Ray had to have a police escort out of the stadium.

Obviously I was bitterly disappointed that all my efforts had come to nothing, but in analysing my own performance later, I realised that I probably could have ridden harder, faster and much less defensively. At least I had tried and given it my best effort on the night. My crash with Ray was probably caused by me going into the corners much slower than I would have had I been fully fit; but hindsight is a wonderful thing, so Ray, the crash was not entirely your fault.

The Lions celebrating another home win in 1971.

Just ahead in the Internationale at Wimbledon, May 1971.

If riding six days after breaking a collarbone sounds dramatic, then all that pales into insignificance when compared to Jason Doyle winning the 2017 World Championship while carrying a multitude of serious injuries. They certainly breed them tough Down Under.

And so my World Championship dreams were over for another year and I was out of action for another three weeks as my injuries healed. By a twist of fate, my comeback meeting was a British League match riding for Wembley at Leicester who were led by their captain Ray Wilson.

Fortunately there was no repeat of our 'coming together' and we raced to a 39–39 draw. Somehow, crazy situations seemed to happen to me when Leicester riders were involved. In one race at Leicester's Blackbird Road Stadium, the tapes were broken. I was certain that it was either Ray Wilson or John Boulger who was the culprit, but the referee excluded me for the offence. I protested, but the ref would not listen to me and put the phone down. It takes a lot to wind up this Scotsman, but when something does, watch out. I was incensed at the injustice of it all and that the referee would not listen to me so I refused to leave the track. Eventually a policeman came up to the starting gate and escorted me back to the pits with my arms flying in the air like a windmill. My then girlfriend, Edith, thought that this was hilarious and that is when she realised that it does not pay to come between a Scotsman and his points money.

I was always a good gater and on occasions I had the feeling the referees were trying to catch me out. This was confirmed years later when I was invited to a Referees Association Dinner and one referee actually admitted that much to me. Ivan Mauger, among other information in his 'Little black book', kept notes on the various referees and how they handled the starts, a very handy piece of knowledge as a rider does not want to be competing with the referee as well as the other three riders in a race.

Despite failing to qualify for the World Final, it had been a successful season and, in October I packed my bags and prepared for another 'Have bike will travel' winter season in Australia. I reflected that Wembley had been successful at raising the profile of speedway and that we would be back there bigger and better in 1972. How wrong could I be?

19. Australia with the British Lions

My form with Wembley and in Australia had at last been recognised by 'the powers that be' and I was selected for the British Lions in their tour of Australia during the British winter. No booking my own flights and contracts, no hassle of arranging my crate of equipment and bike to go to Australia – with help from Dick Barrie and Meadows Airfreight – and no hassle of arranging my own transport for the various meetings in Australia. It was now a team effort and Lions skipper Nigel Boocock was the ace organiser to get us from A to B and beyond.

The Lions team consisted of four Englishmen: Malcolm Simmons, Tony Lomas, Chris Pusey and Nigel Boocock, and three Scots: George Hunter, Jimmy McMillan and me. However, to the Scots' dismay, we were often referred to by the Australians as England instead of Great Britain, but we didn't let that upset us too much.

The Australians always loved nothing better than to beat England, so the seven round series of test matches were always high adrenaline affairs. There was controversy about the Australians using the banned Nitro fuel additive which was always a bone of contention when we rode against them.

Australian tracks were usually big and fast. Each track had their own riders who performed like world champions on their home circuit, so throughout the series the Australians brought in a home expert or two. Throughout the series, Australia used 22 riders and we used the same 'magnificent seven' wherever we rode.

The Sweden team was also in Australia at the same time and after our match in Sydney, we went our separate ways. The Swedes headed north to Queensland while we headed south to Adelaide and Melbourne. Our schedule was pretty tight at times with us riding in the fourth test against Australia on the Friday and the fifth test in Melbourne the next night. It was a 600 miles journey. Many times we only had one meeting per week and the rest of the time was taken up with machine preparation and numerous press, radio and television interviews. Promoting the test series was part-and-parcel of our job in Australia and we enjoyed it.

Jimmy Mac was once interviewed by a keen young radio reporter who asked him "Tell me, Jim, what do you like about Australia?" Before Jim could reply, the budding reporter said: "Is it the sunshine, the surf, the beaches, the suntanned girls, the barbeques and the Aussie milkshakes?" by which time Jimmy had nothing else to add other than saying "Yes".

Even skipper Nigel Boocock, who was always one for giving good press and public interviews, slipped up. The North Queensland Racing Drivers Club invited the team to their annual cabaret dinner. When Nigel gave his after-dinner speech on behalf of the British Lions team, he thanked the club for "their hospitality here in Rockhampton". Oops, we happened to be in Townsville at the time.

It wasn't surprising that Nigel made that mistake because our Queensland tour took us north from Sydney to Brisbane, north again to Rockhampton then back to Brisbane to catch a flight further north to Townsville before returning to Rockhampton and Brisbane. Confusing, eh?

It was during this hectic tour that a radio reporter asked me "Where do the Lions go from here, Bert?" to which I replied "From here we travel to Townsville, Rockhampton and

Brisbane" which was a good answer except that we were in Townsville at the time and the programme was going out live. We were always asked strange question by reporters such as "Why don't speedway bikes have any brakes?" and the classic question asked by a reporter to George Hunter: "Tell me, George, how do you find Australia?" "Och", said George, "Ye just sail down to the bottom of South Africa and turn left." Exit one confused reporter.

Townsville is a lovely town in tropical North Queensland and a week after we left, it was hit by a cyclone. We had raced at Savanna speedway, which was similar to Glasgow White City with long straights and tight corners – but with sunshine. The track was heavily watered when we went there and the wet sandy surface covered our goggles like the Lone Ranger's mask without the eyeholes.

An interesting point about Savanna was that there was a drag racing strip alongside the speedway track. When the 'drags' were running, the track staff lift the tubular grandstand by crane and turn it around to face the drag strip. The drag cars and bikes were very popular and two former Glasgow Tigers riders, 'Cowboy' Bob Sharpe and Brisbane-based Kiwi, Peter Dykes, were regular competitors. That season, Bob Sharpe held the Australian motorcycle record and Peter Dykes was one of the fastest men on the 'rail cars'.

Peter had the unpleasant experience of arriving at the end of the quarter-mile travelling at around 200mph and finding that his parachute, which helps slow the car, failed to operate. The car disappeared off the end of the drag strip, somersaulted over a 10 foot high wire and landed upside down in a muddy swamp in the woods. Rescuers had difficulty in finding Peter because it was a night meeting. After a frantic search they found Dyksie half-drowned in a swamp and pulled him out to safety. Peter was wet and knocked around, but otherwise unhurt. It made me think that I would stick to speedway, it was much safer and there was no risk of getting drowned when you raced.

At the tropical Townsville Speedway, the only things missing were dressing rooms and showers, and they were very important in the heat. We did, however, overcome this by standing under the water-truck for a shower, much to the amusement of the local fans. Fortunately, the motel where we were staying was air conditioned and had its own swimming pool where we spent most of our spare time. Malcolm Simmons and I were non-swimmers so Simmo bought an underwater facemask for his efforts to learn to swim. We practiced hard and eventually progressed to the deep end, but the sight of both of us trying to swim towards one another with Simmo wearing his frogman's mask caused us to double-up with laughter and sink in a stream of air bubbles. We were not ready for a cross Channel swim.

Poor Jim McMillan was banned from the pool because he had contracted some kind of dreadful 'lurgy' called 'Tropical Ear Disease' which meant that he had to stay away from water. It did not affect his racing, but did affect his washing habits.

Other memories of that trip include the promoter Noel Ross taking the team out in his speedboat to Magnetic Island. It was a lovely tropical island off the coast of Queensland. We hired a mini-moke beach buggy to drive around the island. We were bouncing along a dusty road, seven of us in a four seater. I was leaning out of the open side with my cine camera and Jimmy McMillan was hanging out of the other side with his 'Box Brownie' camera when suddenly a car appeared. It seemed that there was only one policeman on this island and yes, you've guessed it, we had found him. He stopped our jeep, counted heads and said:

116

"Right, you three get out and walk". So Jimmy, George Hunter and I had to get out. The 'friendly' island policeman sent our car on its way and stayed around to make sure that we walked. You can imagine three pale-skinned Scots trudging along in the 100° heat. We felt, and probably looked like, deserters from the French Foreign Legion.

We survived that ordeal only to find out that our flight to Rockhampton was leaving at 4.30am the following morning. I think that the airport authorities wanted us there early so that we could help load the milk, newspapers and mail onto our plane.

Rockhampton was hot and sticky and after racing that evening we spent an uncomfortable night under mosquito nets in a very humid motel with no air conditioning. The things we had to do to represent our country abroad.

Back in the less humid, but still hot climate of Sydney, my former Edinburgh team mate, Bill Landels and his wife Liz put on a barbeque party at their new Sydney home. They invited the visiting Swedish and British teams and the Australian riders. All nationalities were having a great time and then the party really livened up when Bill's Scottish brother-in-law, Ian made his entrance playing the bagpipes. The Scots in the group immediately went into a furious Highland Eightsome Reel and were soon joined by their Australian, Swedish and German friends. Bernie Persson, who was nicknamed Mick Jagger on the tour owing to his long hair, and 'Benga', Bengt Jansson were both very good at the reels. They had both raced for Scottish teams and learned Scottish country dancing the hard way at the Edinburgh Monarchs' Supporters Club dances.

On the track, I hadn't been exactly setting the house on fire for the Lions, and had not scored very well in The Governor's Cup individual event on the big Claremont circuit the week before the final test. I was dropped to reserve for the big decider. Australia had won the early tests in Sydney, Brisbane and Adelaide, but we fought back to win the second Brisbane test and also in Melbourne and Perth so the British Lions went into the final decider at Claremont Speedway in Perth, Western Australia, tying with Australia on three wins apiece.

In the days prior to the deciding meeting when we were getting our bikes ready, it was discovered that my bike had lost a lot of compression in the engine. Some skilful mechanical work by my fellow Scots, Jimmy and George, breathed new life into the motor. It proved to be a master stroke because I romped to a 17 point haul in that final test and equalled Anders Michanek's track record around the 641 yard (586m) Claremont track.

Great Britain won the match 77–31 in front of a 20,000 crowd and the Ashes 4–3, so all-in-all, a very successful test series for the Lions.

Perth was a lovely city with very friendly people, so friendly in fact that the local motorcycle shop lent Malcolm Simmons and I a couple of Yamaha motorcycles to do some sightseeing. On our free Sunday we were asked to be guests at Collie Speedway, some 130 miles away in a charity meeting for the family of Des Noble who had been fatally injured at Claremont Speedway at Christmas.

We rode on our Yamaha motorcycles from Perth in the heat of a lovely sunny 90° afternoon. We had a pleasant ride north in the lovely Australian bush and saw an evening of good racing with bikes and cars combined in the programme. By the time the meeting finished, around 11pm, the sun was long gone and the evening was decidedly cooler, how much cooler we were about to find out when we set off on our ride back to Perth.

We had dressed for the daytime heat with jeans, thin windcheater jackets, open face helmets and thin speedway gloves which were fine for the riding in the midday heat, but were quite inadequate when faced with a long cold ride home. We suffered quite a lot on that ride and even stopped a few times to put our gloves on the hot engine to warm them up, then run up-and-down to warm ourselves up. We eventually made it back to Perth, shivering with the cold and thought 'That is a lesson learnt, Australia can be so hot during the day then so cold at night'. A 260 mile round trip by motorcycle was fun while it lasted during the day, but not such good fun in the cool and even cold of a West Australian evening.

Before we had left Britain on this tour, I knew that Malcolm was a really good all-round motorcyclist and an excellent trials rider which takes a lot of throttle control. This tour proved to me just how good he was. We had lots of fun on these borrowed motorcycles and Simmo could ride for ages on the rear wheel, changing gear as he went along, something I never quite mastered. My wheelies were OK, but Malc was the master of one wheel riding. We used to have contests to see who could ride the furthest on the back wheel and Simmo always won, skilfully changing gear with one wheel in the air. Eventually, our stay in Perth was over and it was time to hand the motorcycles back to the friendly dealer.

We had a bit of time to spare before catching our flight so I said "Let's just have another little ride before we go back to the motorcycle shop." Big mistake. We were larking around pulling wheelies again when I overdid it, looped the bike and came off the back. I then watched it sliding down the road in a shower of sparks and broken headlights. Oops. We rode back to the shop all set to offer my apologies for bending their motorcycle but when we arrived, the shop was closed so I just had time to leave a "Sorry IOU" note and hightail it to the airport.

Somehow, I managed to miss the flight from Perth in Western Australia back to Melbourne on the opposite side of Australia. I telephoned Edith, who was still back in Melbourne to tell her what had happened and she said "Can't you catch the bus or take a train?" Edith did not realise the vast distances in this southern continent as even a train journey between these two great cities would take over two days. It was not like catching the train from Glasgow down to London.

Away from the test matches against Australia, we also had a lot of Interstate meetings all around Australia from Perth to Queensland, including a three-way International between Australia, Sweden and Great Britain in Sydney. In between racing, there were the usual barbeques, water skiing and beach parties. It was at one of these Sunday BBQs by the river when we spotted a large speed boat cruising down the river towards us. Sitting on the bow, was a suntanned blonde lady with long flowing blonde hair and her light cotton dress blowing in the warm breeze. We all wandered down to the water's edge to see this lovely apparition sail by. As the boat got closer, we suddenly realized that the 'blonde' we were all admiring was actually a 'blond'.

It was our Swedish friend, Olle Nygren, his hair covered by a long bleached blonde wig, wearing a flowing dress and sitting on the front of the boat like a figurehead. The rest of the Swedish team were in the boat. They had been water skiing, but we never found out where Olle got the dress from or if it was part of his normal Swedish wardrobe.

118

The 1971–72 British Lions on parade before a meeting.

The 1971–72 British Lions. Bert, Jim McMillian, George Hunter, Malcolm Simmons, Nigel Boocock (capt – on bike), Chris Pusey, Tony Lomas.

Ready for action with the Lions in Australia.

A relaxing moment with Nigel Boocock, Jim McMillian and Chris Pusey.

Although the Swedes were racing in Australia, our paths seldom crossed. When they were racing in Perth, for example, our British Lions would be racing in Brisbane, or vice versa. In the three-pronged test match at Sydney Showground, it was Great Britain 41, Australia 40 and Sweden 26. Simmo got a 15 point maximum for the Lions while the Swedes didn't seem too happy with the huge Showground track with the concrete wall 'safety' fence. No air fences in those days and there were a number of fatalities and serious injuries to car drivers and solo riders at that track over the years.

On our trip to Queensland, where the British Lions were due to race a couple of meetings at the Ekka Showground in Brisbane, Malcolm Simmons, Tony Lomas, Edith and I headed for Surfers Paradise to spend a few days between races. On the journey there in our hire car with Simmo driving, fast as usual, was overtaken by an unmarked police car. The driver drew alongside and held up a sign saying, 'Police. Stop!' We thought it was a joke and laughed as we wondered why they could not afford sirens or blue lights in Queensland. Malcolm just pulled over to find out what the problem was. It seemed that we were speeding and as the undercover cop was not a speedway fan he wrote us out a ticket on the spot. $30 later, we were on our way again.

Tony Lomas said "OK, Malcolm, you were driving too fast so I will take over and drive the rest of the way." With our new co-pilot in the driving seat, we set off again only to be overtaken again some 20 minutes later by another car with the driver holding a sign out of the window which said 'Police. Stop!' I felt like holding a sign of our own out of the window saying "No thanks", but the long arm of the law had caught us again and we collected another speeding ticket. Two in one day, that must have been a record. This time the fine was only $15, so it looked like the Gold Coast police were giving us a quantity discount.

The Ekka track was big and almost a circle. It was difficult to know what part of the lap I was on. I found that when I crossed the line at the end of the race, I did not know where the pits were until they opened the pit gate.

The starts in Australia were always controversial for us. The Australians usually had a flying start, so it was a case of 'if you can't beat them, join them'. We then began to make good starts as well. The orange-leathered John Langfield was always a controversial character. He almost brought the house down when he disagreed with a decision. He rode round to the starting gate, pulled off his helmet, climbed over the fence and up the tower to the referee's box. He just wanted to make sure that the official understood that he was not too happy with him. The crowd went wild in their support for their home hero, but later John and the referee had a beer together at the after-meeting barbeque. So there were no hard feelings once they had had a few 'tinnies'.

We were kept pretty busy during the tour with race meetings all over this vast Australian continent. In January, for example, in one week we flew from Sydney to Melbourne, then Melbourne to Adelaide on the Thursday, raced the fourth Australia versus Great Britain test on the Friday, where we lost narrowly by 57–51. Then we flew back to Melbourne for the British Lions versus Victoria Challenge at Brooklyn on the Saturday, which we won 64–44. After the meeting, we left to drive to Warnabool. We eventually arrived at the Motel at 4.30am on the Sunday morning. It was always better to drive in the cool of the evening because the cars we were using did not have air conditioning.

121

At the end of the Australian season, it was time to head back to Britain, leaving the British Lions and hopefully re-joining the Wembley Lions although I had not heard from Trevor Redmond during the British off season. One evening, a few days before I was due to fly out of Sydney, I got a long distance phone call from the UK. It was Sheffield promoter, Frank Varey, and I wondered why he was calling me?

"Ah, ye booger", came the Yorkshire voice down the phone line. "Ah've bin tryin' to reach ye in America, in New Zealand and all around Australia and now I have caught up with ye at long last in Sydney". I was still puzzled why Frank was spending so much time and effort and running up hefty telephone bills in trying to track me down because I had only seen him to say 'Hello' to when I rode at Sheffield for Edinburgh or Wembley. "OK, lad, Wembley has closed down and ye are allocated to Sheffield in the new season." To say that I was surprised was an understatement because I had not expected Wembley to close, especially as we were getting good crowds for our league matches. I was quite shocked and also disappointed.

Later, I thought that the British promoters should have done much more to keep the track alive. The Wembley name was iconic and known worldwide and helped the reputation of speedway, so it was a great loss to our sport when it closed.

This was becoming a habit for me. I had left Edinburgh's Old Meadowbank to race in Australia and when I came back to Scotland, it had closed. I left Coatbridge for the winter and when I came back it had closed and I was transferred to Wembley. I came back this time, Wembley had closed and I had been transferred to Sheffield. What next, I asked myself. No wonder I never had a testimonial later in my almost 20 season career as I was being moved to a different club almost every year.

Once again, football fixtures had affected speedway at the Empire Stadium and there was no way that the Lions could run a full season. So despite Trevor Redmond's valiant efforts to find another track for his team, TR had to give up.

With Wembley closing its doors, I would have preferred to have stayed with a London club and been transferred to Wimbledon, but it was too late in the day to ask for a change. For some reason, the Wembley riders were allocated far and wide and not to any London clubs which is a pity as I am sure that the Lions' fans would have followed them had they still been riding in 'The Smoke'. My team was split up with Brian Collins heading for Poole, Dave Jessup to Leicester, Tony Clarke to Newport, Peter Prinsloo went back to Zimbabwe before returning to ride for Exeter, Brian Leonard went to Swindon; and 1970 Lion Reidar Eide joined me at Sheffield. Sverre Harrfeldt and Gote Nordin retired from British speedway, a sad end to a promising team. West Ham had also closed so London and the wider world of speedway had lost two great names.

And so the 'Wandering Haggis' was on his travels again, another track, another team and another challenge, swopping the Scottish haggis for some Yorkshire pudding. I left Australia, disappointed that Wembley had closed but looking forward to a new horizon in Sheffield. There were no direct non-stop flights from Australia to the UK, so how is this for a route home from Australia: Melbourne-Perth-Singapore-Bombay-Beirut-Athens-London-Glasgow, changing flights or crew at every stopover. I left Melbourne on the Sunday evening after a farewell (again!) barbeque and got back home to Glasgow on the Wednesday evening. It was a marathon trip.

20. My part in Briggo's downfall

Sheffield was another home track to learn. It was big, fast and very well prepared thanks to Frank Varey's hard work on the tractor. After every meeting Frank could be seen grading the track and getting it in tiptop shape for the next meeting. Sheffield was almost a 'home' track for me, being only four hours drive from Glasgow. The Glasgow Tigers Hampden Park stadium was only about 10 minutes away, but I had signed for the other Tigers in the Steel City of Sheffield.

The Sheffield track was big and a 'D' shape. There really was only one straight, the 'home straight' and the other side of the track curved into one long corner so the bike was turning all the time. Despite my successes on the big wide and fast Australian tracks, I always liked small tracks with tight corners where the riders had to work a bit harder and use more throttle control. However, I never had any hang-ups about track size or shape and just took every one as it came along.

Frank Varey and team manager Terry Thornhill took a great interest in their riders and ran a happy team. The Tigers had lost their star man from the previous season, Australian champion, Jim Airey and Sweden's Bengt Larsson. Frank and Terry put together a pretty good team. Bob Paulson was appointed skipper. The 'terrible two' local lads, Doug Wyer and Reg Wilson, could put the wind up most riders when they were on the track. They came up from the Second Division. I thought of them as 'Butch Cassidy and The Sundance Kid' but didn't know which was which. Australian Bob 'Bluey' Valentine was fresh from racing in Australia and Rhodesia, along with Arnold Haley, whose party piece was to walk along on his hands, plus my former Edinburgh and Wembley team mate, Reidar Eide and me, so we were quite a solid team.

The Sheffield track required a fast engine and good tyres which may sound very obvious, but on some tracks that was not always an advantage. At Wimbledon for example, a used rear tyre was much better than a brand new tyre, possibly because the stock cars polished the track surface and a used tyre would give better grip. Also, on some smaller tracks, riders could get away with a little less engine power, but at Sheffield the rider needed as much power as he could obtain and also a new rear tyre every meeting. To help keep the home team's bikes up to scratch, Frank Varey allocated spares such as pistons, valves and other engine parts free of charge to his team riders. There was no excuse for the Tigers riders to be short of power.

Owlerton Stadium is one of the best in the country with a glass fronted restaurant and bar. The team for that 1972 season looked capable of hitting the heights. We had a no-nonsense promoter in Frank Varey as Reidar Eide was to later find out. Reidar had a reputation of being a hard negotiator when it came to points money and travelling expenses. Many a time Ian Hoskins had to dig deep into his pockets to persuade Reidar to return to Scotland after going home to race in Norway. It is rumoured that the flame-haired Norwegian often invoiced Ian Hoskins for ferry crossings which didn't exist, but Ian always paid up and Reidar repaid him with 100 percent effort on the track. By contrast, Frank Varey was a tough

Yorkshireman who took no prisoners, so when Reidar started to do his 'Oliver Twist' act and ask for more, Frank soon put him in his place, physically.

As a pre-war dirt track star, Frank has been there, done that and got several T shirts. His tales of his adventures in those early swash-buckling days could have filled a book and there was a book written in 1937 about him by Victor Peters called *Frank Varey The Red Devil of the Speedway*, Frank's nickname before Mike Broadbank came along. He was given the Red Devil name or rather *El Diablo Rojo* when racing in Argentina on his red painted Scott dirt track machine and wearing a red jersey over his leathers. Frank told me how he travelled down to Argentina by Zeppelin airship, in the height of luxury in the late 1920s. It was quicker than going by ocean liner. Comfortable cabins, plush restaurant, a piano in the lounge, there was even a 'smoking room'. The Zeppelin was air travel for the rich and famous, but this mode of transport was finished after the Hindenburg disaster in 1937 when the airship caught fire while docking in New Jersey.

Prize money was very good for those intrepid pioneer dirt trackers. Frank recalled when, as a young lad, he wanted to buy his first house. "You are too young to get a mortgage", the estate agent told him. "Not to worry", said Frank and pulled out a wad of cash to buy the house outright.

My season with my new club, Sheffield, was busy as ever fulfilling all the Tigers' fixtures plus long track meetings in Germany and Scotland (Motherwell), ice speedway at Aviemore in the Scottish Highlands, speedway in Germany and even pony trotting harness racing at the Motherwell long track. On top of this, I even had an entry in the Scottish road racing championships, but my deal to borrow a 250cc Yamaha road race machine fell through. It was probably just as well because I would have had no time to sleep with that schedule.

One of the highlights for me was when Sheffield went down to London to race against the Hackney Hawks early in the season and there were red and white Wembley scarves everywhere on the terracing and in the grandstand. For a moment I thought that I was back at the Empire Stadium. The Wembley fans were cheering on Sheffield, so it gave Uncle Len Silver's Waterden Road stadium a real local derby touch.

My open meetings included heading back to Scotland for the Motherwell long track meeting which was held in pouring rain and cold. The meeting was held around the Motherwell pony trotting track where they staged harness racing. At the interval it was decided to put on a one lap 'match race' between Barry Briggs, Garry Middleton and me just to warm up the soggy spectators. Nothing wrong with that? The catch is that we each had to drive a 'Sulkie', which is the spindly frame on wheels pulled by the trotting pony. It looked easy, but when I was sitting on that frame with my feet almost at shoulder height I suddenly realised that the only thing stopping me from falling backwards were the leather reins, so needless to say, I held them very tightly. It was quite scary, sitting low in this two wheeled racing cart, holding the reins and looking at the horse's backside. I just hoped that it had been to the loo before our race. Briggo, Garry and I took no chances and wore our speedway helmets and gloves. By the time the prancing ponies were lined up at the start, I was wishing that I had declined the offer, but it was too late to back down. Suddenly we were off and charging towards the first turn. I realised that I was in the lead. I remember that after such a flying start, I named my horse, 'Ivan' after the fast-gating Kiwi.

A rare foray into trotting. Motor cycles were easier to control than horses.

It occurred to me as we all rushed towards the corner, that I did not know how to 'turn' the pony on the bend, but fortunately my horse knew more than I did and charged towards the inside rail. I was now beginning to enjoy myself when I heard someone yelling "Oi, Oi, Oi!" It was Briggo. As my four-legged friend had dived for the first turn, poor Barry was getting jammed between my cart and the rail. "Go easy, Haggis." I heard him yell "These things are dangerous." He was right too because, when I looked down, I saw that our wheels were almost touching. The chariot race in that classic movie, *Ben Hur* had nothing on us.

As I tried to pull my pony away from BB, Garry Middleton came thundering around the outside and into the lead. We tucked in behind the Australian, with my horse trying to bite Cass's head off, but it soon gave up. With one-third of the lap to go I realised that the other two had seen harness racing before. Both Barry and Garry had been holding their horses back a little so, as my nag ran out of puff, they staged a great run-in to the chequered flag. One final problem was that no-one had told us how to stop these horses so they just kept trotting around the track until they had had enough. I decided that speedway was safer and I would stick with engine horse power, not the four-legged variety.

Back on the speedway scene, after heading south to Sheffield for our challenge match against Belle Vue, it was back north again and up to the Aviemore ski resort in the Scottish Highlands, 140 miles north of Glasgow, for an indoor ice speedway championship. During the Australian season I had read with interest of the new ice speedway scene being held on indoor ice rinks in Scotland and was keen to try my hand at it. Jim McMillan and George Hunter had competed on the ice when they came back from Australia and I was due to make my debut at Aviemore. After the 90° heat and huge tracks of Australia, it was certainly a change to race on a cool and tiny ice skating rink in Scotland. It was ice speedway, but not as we knew it.

125

Instead of the big ice speedway stadiums and riding 500cc ice racing Jawas with two speed gearboxes and long spikes in the wheels, we were competing on a small ice skating rink using converted Greeves motocross bikes with speedway handlebars and studs, not spikes, in the tyres. It was a fun afternoon and Glasgow's John Wilson and I finished runners-up in the Best Pairs Ice Racing Championship to Alan Forbes and Pete Bremner.

aviemore ice racing

Aviemore Ice Rink Saturday April 8

the aviemore centre 'best pairs' meeting

Meetings were coming thick and fast and on checking my diary for that time I see that I rode at Ipswich on a Tuesday, Sheffield on the Thursday, spent Friday morning getting my bike ready in Sheffield then headed off with Terry Thornhill for a league match at Glasgow that evening. Even back then there were traffic jams on the motorways. We were stuck on the M6 for one and a half hours and then delayed again at Gretna, so had to push on once we had cleared the hold-ups. We went over the border and into Scotland with the usual toot of the horn as we crossed into the land of the Scots. As we reached Lesmahagow, 25 miles south of Glasgow, bang! The piston blew up on my Ford Corsair and we were stuck. I phoned Glasgow speedway to tell them and said that I would hire a car and get there.

With time running out, I hitch-hiked to Hampden Park with some Sheffield supporters who had seen my car stuck with smoke coming out from under the bonnet. By the time I breathlessly reached the pits, heat three, which was to be my first race, was almost underway with Denis Jackson of Berwick taking my place. I was getting ready to race, but the referee disqualified me from the meeting because I had not been there at the start. He said that he had been told that I had returned to Sheffield and would not be riding that night. All that effort in getting to Hampden, preparing the bike and the driving from Sheffield to Glasgow was all for nothing. The Sheffield supporters and team were a rider short and the Scottish fans were deprived of seeing another Scot race at Hampden Park that night, all because of a petty decision by the referee.

Glasgow boss, Neil McFarlane was desperate to get the meeting on before I arrived and as Sheffield eventually lost by four points, I could see why he did not want me to ride at one of my favourite tracks. I guess I could and would have made a difference. C'est la vie.

That year the World Final was due to be held at Wembley. I had failed to qualify, but was looking forward to watching all the action on the Saturday night. Meanwhile, I had some races of my own to contend with. I rode at Sheffield on the Thursday as usual, then back up to Glasgow on the Friday then south to Wembley on the Saturday. I arrived at the Empire Stadium in the early afternoon and parked my car with my Jawa on the back outside the pits while I went round to the Speedway office to collect my pass. I came back some time later to see three burly individuals wrestling my bike off the carrier on the rear of my car. "Hey, what are you doing?" I yelled and then realised that they were some of the Russian contingent here for the World Final.

They didn't speak English – but then again some people say the same about me. Speedway Control Board chief John McNulty then appeared and explained that some of the

Russian bikes had been stolen so could they borrow mine? As my bike was already off the bike rack and getting wheeled towards the pits, I agreed that they could use it. I said that it would have been nice to have been asked first before the 'smash and grab'. It later turned out that one of my former Wembley team mates had been involved in the theft. Not only was he stealing from the Russians, he was stealing from me too because my bike got a hammering at Wembley that night. I guess I could take some comfort in the fact that my bike had made the Wembley World Final even if I hadn't.

This was a very controversial World Final. Barry Briggs was in top form and had beaten fellow World Champion Ivan Mauger in heat two. He looked on form to claim another world title until that fateful heat five.

Briggo made the start and another former team mate of mine from Edinburgh, Bernt Persson, dived under the Kiwi and caught his front wheel. Briggo fell right in front of the two Russians, Grigory Khlinovsky and Valery Gordeev who could not avoid him. The crash launched my lovely Jawa bouncing down the track and over the Wembley safety fence onto the dog track. The loss of my favourite Jawa was huge for me, but nowhere near the loss that Barry suffered when he lost the index finger of his left hand in the crash. A very sad ending for Barry. Most of the 75,000 crowd booed referee Grigory Traunspurger when he failed to exclude Persson for being the cause of the crash. The Swede went on to take second place overall after a run-off with Ivan Mauger while Barry Briggs was rushed to Wembley Hospital. He was transferred to a more specialist hospital where they could deal with Barry's injuries. That accident led Briggo to campaign for better medical facilities for the riders. Speedway could never afford the travelling hospital which follows the moto GP road racers around, but having an expert doctor on hand at every meeting is a big help.

I had to fit a new frame diamond and borrow the front forks from the Sheffield track spare to put my bike together again. Fortunately, the Speedway Control Board later paid for some of the damage. Another rush of meetings was on the cards with meetings at Sheffield on the Thursday where I was pleased to beat Ronnie Moore, then back up to Glasgow for the following evening where Jimmy McMillan beat me 2–1 in the Scottish Match Race Championship. I got my own back by beating Jimmy in the second half, but it was too late then because he was now the Scottish Match Race Champion. Back down to Coventry with Sheffield for the next night where Doug Wyer and I got a 5–1 against Nigel Boocock, an almost impossible task around Coventry. Nice teamwork.

Talking of teamwork, on many weekends I was off to the continent to race in Germany, Austria or even Italy on my free Sundays. One time, when I had a contract to race in Bopfingen in Southern Germany on the Sunday, I also rode at Sheffield on the Thursday and Glasgow on the Friday. I hit mechanical trouble at Glasgow and blew up my engine. Look at this schedule taken from my 1972 diary. 'Thursday: Sheffield. Engine failure when leading. Use Sheffield track spare. After meeting, strip motor in Sheffield workshop, bed 1,30am. Friday: Rise 5am rebuild Jawa. Leave Sheffield 12 noon to drive to Glasgow. Two rides, five paid six then engine blow-up use track spare again. If I did not turn up for my meeting in Bopfingen on the Sunday, my name would be mud with the German promoters, but my Sheffield team mate, Doug Wyer then came to my rescue.

Doug loaned me his Jawa for my trip abroad so after the meeting at Hampden Park, I nipped home to my parent's house in Eastwood, had some of my mum's home cooking and then set off south again to Sheffield at 1am. Saturday was spent on the Sealink ferry from Dover and then driving down through Belgium and Germany. I stopped in Wurzburg for a few hours sleep. I eventually arrived at the Bopfingen track at 10.30am in time for the 11.30am practice. In the meeting, I collected 10 points on Doug's bike to finish behind Australia's Garry Middleton and Norway's Oyvind Berg in the championship. A long, but worthwhile, trip and to get a bed in Bopfingen at last was a welcome bonus.

Next morning I drove to Nuremberg, picked up Edith and headed to Munich to get her visa for the end-of-season trip to California. We got to the American Embassy and it was closed because there was a public holiday in Munich that day. It was then back to Nuremberg, drop Edith off at home and head for the Channel ferry. With fog and other delays, I eventually made it to the ferry port at Ostend around 4am so I settled down to get some sleep in the 'Mercedes Hotel' i.e. my Mercedes 220 diesel car until the 8am ferry. I got back to my digs in Sheffield at Terry Thornhill's house around midnight on the Tuesday. It was a marathon trip, but just one of the joys of being a 'Have bike will travel' speedway rider.

This is nothing compared with the modern Grand Prix riders who could be riding in three or four different leagues plus the GPs and flying to a different country every day. Yes, they have a team of mechanics and helpers to drive the vans and work on their bikes, but it is still a punishing schedule throughout the year.

My own season with the Sheffield Tigers was drawing to a close and it was time to pack my bags and 'Follow the sun' once again.

21. LA and Liverpool

And so it was up, up and away once again in November 1972 back to Australia, from Glasgow to London, onto Los Angeles and then Sydney and this time Edith was coming with me. The stop-over in California took in a couple of race meetings, the chance to meet up with old friends and do some sightseeing before flying on to Australia. This time it was a low key entrance to the Los Angeles International Airport. No Scottish pipe band and no crowds of local riders and fans to welcome me. However, our friends, English ex pats, George and Freda Wenn were there to meet us. We landed at round 11pm on the Thursday evening and I already had a contract to race at Ascot Park the next evening, so there was no time to lose.

Ascot was the famous race circuit in Gardena run by JC Agajanian in South West LA County and was used by cars and bikes. It held the big flat track mile and half mile races where the riders used Triumphs, Harleys, BSA and Norton machines and the show was always very spectacular.

We were going to race on the quarter mile circuit on normal speedway bikes and I would be riding George Wenn's 'Tuned by Wenn' Jap that evening. The track was big, wide and fast, but the clay surface made it very difficult to slide the bike and with a Jap, it was even harder. With our track being inside the normal flat track circuit, the outside 'fence' was just straw bales. With the grippy track, quite a few riders couldn't turn their bikes in the fast corners and disappeared over the outside edge, never to be seen again. During the evening, the clay surface tended to break up under the speedway tyres, sending huge lumps of material flying off of the rear wheels which caused some painful bruises to the following riders. We counteracted that by tearing thick cardboard boxes apart and stuffing strips of cardboard inside the arms and legs of our leathers. I am glad that Kevlar suits were still to be invented, otherwise racing at Ascot would have been even more painful.

I even went as far as shaping a pair of handguards out of cardboard and taping them onto my handlebars with duct tape, the racer's friend. I wasn't gating too well and by the end of the evening, the front of my tartan-painted Bell helmet was full of stone chips, just as if someone had spayed me with a shotgun full of pellets and the black and blue bruises on my legs and arms were turning purple.

I didn't win that night; that honour went to DeWayne Keeter. But I was represented on the podium because Edith was chosen as the Trophy Girl to present the cup to DeWayne. So at least one of us was in the winner's circle. The following week, the meeting at Ascot was rained off. Who says 'It never rains in sunny California'?

It was November. The speedway season at Costa Mesa had already finished and with Ascot rained off, there was no more racing. The rest of the stay in California was taken up with visiting friends and collecting my new helmets from Bell in Long Beach. The long European season was over and it was also time for sightseeing. We did the usual tourist things like Disneyland, Knotts Berry Farm and Universal Studios, plus a motocross event at Carlsbad and road racing at Willow Springs. There was always plenty going on in California.

At dinner one evening with Harry Oxley and his wife Marilyn, Harry once again tried to persuade me to quit British speedway and come back to race in California the following season because I had a good reputation with the Costa Mesa fans. The offer was tempting, with various sponsorships, such as a condominium flat with swimming pool, a sponsored van, good prize money, plenty of race meetings and even better weather than Britain. The financial benefits were much higher than at home. I was certainly tempted, but I still had ambitions on the World Championship scene and I could only do that by riding in Britain, so I said "Thanks, Harry, but no thanks". The bagpipes were calling me home.

Meanwhile some of the top American riders were considering heading over to race in the British League. Mike Bast, younger brother of Steve who rode a few meetings for Wembley, and Scott Autrey were talking about braving the British winter and flying in early to take part in some of the pre-season training schools. Scott, with his long flowing blond hair, had previously impressed onlookers when he had a few practice laps at Wimbledon and later became a major star on the British and European tracks. Another super-keen Californian was Sumner McKnight. He had Scottish ancestry so perhaps we could have used him in our national team. Sumner contemplated making the trans-Atlantic trip in style. He would bring his own mechanic, one-time spanner man for Norwich Stars, George Wenn, while George's wife, Freda, voted the number one cook in the Los Angeles area by the riders would ensure that Sumner never had to eat at a greasy egg and chips transport café. Freda's home-made steak and kidney pie was to die for. That's what I call organisation. He did join Swindon in 1973, but the move didn't work out for him and after a few meetings he returned home.

Three weeks later our California dreaming came to an end and we flew on to Sydney for another season in the sun. We arrived at the LA Airport at 10pm to find hordes of screaming teenagers running towards me yelling and holding placards saying "We love you!" I thought, "Gee, these Yanks give you a big send-off", but the girls ran straight past me and I saw the rest of their hand-painted signs: "We Love You Osmonds!" and "Welcome Home Osmonds". They had come to see their pop heroes returning from a European tour and not to see some Scot getting onto an aeroplane for Australia. Oh well, you can't win them all.

Prior to leaving Britain, I had ordered a new speedway Jawa from Kawasaki sidecar speedway racer and motorcycle dealer, Geoff Grocott in Sydney. The Jawas imported to Australia were different from our European models. They had a chrome rear mudguard and fuel tank while the ones we could buy at home had the blue tank and rear guard. Some early ones which were imported by Fred Jolly in Adelaide still had the separate 'clip-on' handlebars, but later they had the normal Jawa-style speedway 'bars. The first riders I saw with the clip-on 'bars were Long Eaton's Rim Malskatis, Reidar Eide and the Russians when they came to Britain. All this chrome was quite cosmetic, but the biggest advantage with the Australian Jawa is that the rider received a box of spares with valves, valve springs, piston rings and sprockets all included. In Britain these important spares cost extra. Somehow, my new Australian Jawa seemed faster straight out of the box than my bikes at home, but maybe that was due to the clear Australian air.

I used to travel with my own handlebars and saddle when racing abroad so that a new bike just fitted me straight away. Ivan and Barry went one better in California. They had their own bikes there and just rode them whenever the crossed the Pond.

130

My former bed-mate in California, journalist Peter White, was there to meet and greet us. He drove us over to the Sydney Showground and then to Bradwell Park to Ronnie Bayliss's house, the widow of sidecar speedway racer, Bert Bayliss.

My Australian season was filled with racing at the fast and narrow Sydney Showground with the concrete wall and Liverpool Raceway, with occasional forays to interstate tracks in between barbeques, beaches and water skiing. It was a tough life.

One interstate meeting was at the quarter mile 'bush track', Kembla Grange, in Woolongong, some 60 miles south of Sydney, where Jim Airey and Gordon Guasco had originally learned their trade. I was invited to take part in a Sunday open meeting there. I believe it was for charity or raising funds for the club, so I agreed to take part. My fellow Scot, George Hunter, was also invited, but declined because he thought that it was just a bit too dangerous. We would be racing in handicap events against many riders who were a bit wild and not too experienced. I guess that George had a premonition of what would happen on that hot and sunny afternoon.

One rider who was not wild was a young Billy Sanders who was at the beginning of his career. He rode very well with a smooth style, fast and with a lot of throttle control. The track was dry and very slick with small stones, it felt like riding on marbles. It was difficult to find grip, but Billy coped with it very well and beat me 2–0 in our scratch match races. Billy had started his speedway career on a Jap machine which was once ridden in the World Final at Wembley by Aub Lawson, so he had a good pedigree.

Then it was onto the six and eight-rider handicap races. Again, I started on the back mark of almost half a lap with the other local riders starting at different yard markers ahead of me. I had heeded George's warnings about the dangers of trying to pass less experienced riders, so I was very careful and precise in my overtaking moves. By the penultimate lap, I had moved up to third, right behind the leaders, and was working out how to pass them. I was going to dive up the inside, but thought that it was be safer and quicker with a fast blast around the outside. Big mistake. As I almost rounded the two leaders, Chris Quigley hit the leading rider's rear wheel and turned right, straight into my path. He sent me and the bikes crashing into the solid wooden safety fence in a tangle of scrambled machinery.

I was badly knocked around with injuries on my arms, legs, ankles, shoulders and even my fingers. However, at least nothing was broken which is fortunate because I was taken to hospital lying in the back of a pickup truck bouncing along some bumpy roads. At the hospital they told me that nothing was broken and proceeded to strap me up like an Egyptian Mummy. And we thought this was going to be an easy day's racing at Kembla. I guess that George Hunter had been wise not to accept this booking.

I was due to race back at Liverpool Raceway. However, the heat in Sydney was still 90 to 100° which made it very difficult to sleep at night. The thought of donning leathers, gloves, boots and helmet while everyone else was wearing shorts did not appeal to me too much. To make matters worse, even after a few days rest and recuperation I was still swathed in bandages from my crash at Kembla and aching all over. I would have had to pull out of the Liverpool meeting if Bobby Campbell had not straightened out my bike for me because I was in no way fit enough to hobble around with spanners that week.

I was back in action at Liverpool Raceway, looking like Tutenkamun with all those bandages. I was back to winning without crashing so life was good again. I had some good tussles with Ole Olsen, Howard Cole and the other resident flyers at Liverpool. In the Gordon Guasco Memorial meeting, in memory of the talented Australian who had been fatally injured in a track crash at Liverpool in November 1970, I was second to Ole in the scratch race heat, second again to Ole in the final, but managed to beat him in the handicap final, so my Australian season was going well.

Pretty soon it was time to leave the sunshine speedway of Australia and head home to Britain and another change of club. I would be riding for Wimbledon, but there was to be some more action in America before I eventually arrived home.

One race I was persuaded to compete in – without too much difficulty – was the Daytona Series which tried to bring speedway to the East Coast. At that time, there was no real speedway racing as we know it on the East Coast of America, so during the famous Daytona Speed Week, some special meetings were staged.

To run these exhibition meetings, promoter Harry Oxley transported his entire show all the way from California to Florida. Riders, bikes, officials, starting gates and even the announcer, Larry Huffman, were ferried over from the West Coast. The bikes, 24 in all, plus spare wheels, tyres and equipment, travelled by road in a huge truck and trailer accompanied by some of the riders. The other riders took it easy and went by plane.

Ivan Mauger and Barry Briggs flew in from their winter bases in New Zealand and I arrived from Australia via, strangely enough, Atlanta, Georgia. I had turned down a couple of extra meetings in New Zealand because Atlanta was due to stage its first ever pukka speedway meeting so I arranged to race there en route to Daytona. Rain had been falling for two days, but when I arrived on the day of the meeting, the weather was cool, clear and sunny. The track was a long one by American standards – 440 yards – with steeply banked corners, but the rain had affected the surface and the referee called the meeting off. I was really choked because there were no puddles on the track and it was quite raceable. As the Atlanta race was only a one-off speedway event, there was nothing for it, but to head for Daytona.

The Daytona Speed Week brings together motorcycle enthusiasts from all over. They enjoyed a festival of motorcycle racing with motocross, flat track and culminating with the 'Daytona 200' road race. Speedway was something new for the Speed Week and, despite the track, Velusia County Speedway, being 20 miles from Daytona, a large crowd came.

Racing on the East Coast had been limited to 'Class C' style, where the riders rush up to the corners on their Yamahas or Bultacos, slow down, then accelerate hard going out of the turns. So the spectators were not sure what to expect when they saw the spindly looking Jawas being wheeled onto the track. They could not believe that the bikes had 500cc engines. The first race won them over at once. The sight of four speedway bikes power-sliding into the corners locked together had them jumping up and down and cheering themselves hoarse.

The racing was fast and furious and no sooner was one race over, than the next was ready to start. The fans loved it all and as usual, there were a number of spectacular spills. Larry Moon sustained the only real injury. He broke his collarbone in a handicap race crash.

The Velusia track was typically American, 200 yards long with a very slick surface and although it was slightly wider than the Californian circuits, it still looked tiny under the floodlights. Briggo realised just how short the track was when his throttle jammed open and he had to bail out before he hit the fence. He collected a rather colourful bruise in a delicate place and spent the rest of Daytona Week standing up drinking his tea from the mantelpiece.

The introduction of speedway racing to Florida was a great success and left the spectators yelling for more. Unfortunately, the rain clouds had followed me from Atlanta and two extra meetings which were scheduled were washed out.

Financially, the rained-off meetings in Atlanta and Daytona were bad news, but at least I had the compensation of watching the big road race and spending some time on the beach. Daytona Beach was quite a place. As the Americans say "You ain't seen nothing yet". It is the only beach I have been on where cars and motorcycles can drive along the sand. I left Daytona as the only guy with suntanned tyre marks on his chest.

The race meetings were quite successful, but the results seemed to have disappeared into the Daytona Beach sands of time. We also got to see some of the high speed motorcycle racing from the infield near the awesome Daytona banking, very spectacular.

Despite the various big meetings in places like Daytona, Texas and Salt Lake City, the main speedway action still was around the tracks of Southern California. It was at Costa Mesa that photographer Jim Leonard made a sound movie of one of the America versus Rest of The World test matches. The 'World' team on that occasion was Mauger and Briggs (New Zealand), Pusey and Ashby (England), Plech and Jancarz (Poland) and me from Scotland. The USA was represented by Sonny Nutter, the Bast brothers, Scott Autrey, Bill Cody, Danny Becker and Mike Caruso. The film was shown in the car park at Costa Mesa one night after the races and with plenty of action plus a few spills, the racing came over very well. Especially as our World team won the series in the last race.

The outdoor film show over, the crowd drifted away heading for home. There were still a few of us standing around talking when a voice boomed out of the heavens: "Hey, you down there, get into your vehicles and leave the area now." And a shaft of light shone down from the dark sky. I looked up to see this 'Chariot of the Gods'. It was a police helicopter circling overhead with its powerful searchlight illuminating the Costa Mesa car park. I left in a hurry.

Bert in the lead in a tight race at Costa Mesa. Barry Briggs outside Bert,
close to Americans Mike Bast and Larry Shaw.

USA versus Rest of the World at Costa Mesa: Bert leads Rick Woods, Bill Cody and Barry Briggs.

22. Now I am a Don

I was very pleased with my transfer to Wimbledon because, although I had enjoyed Sheffield and they had treated me well, I thought that the move south would benefit my racing career. Many people seemed to think that I was a 'big track' rider, probably because I usually did well on the big tracks in Australia and thought that Wimbledon would not suit me. But tracks did not come any smaller than the 180 yard Costa Mesa circuit where I also did well, so that argument did not hold any water.

I was joining a new-look Wimbledon team in 1973. The Dons' number one and all-time fans' favourite, Ronnie Moore, had decided to stay in New Zealand. 'Slim Jim' Tebby, an ever-dependable second string was going to Newport and Peter Murray to Reading. The replacements were Reg Luckhurst, who was returning to Plough Lane, Tony Clarke –a former team-mate of mine at Wembley – and me. We would join the previous year's Dons: new captain Trevor Hedge, Kiwi Graeme Stapleton, Australian Neil Cameron and the ever-improving. Tommy Jansson from Sweden.

The Plough Lane track could be tricky to ride, so gave us a slight home track advantage. The stadium, which was also used for greyhound and stock car racing – but not at the same time – was very plush and comfortable. It had a glass fronted restaurant on the home straight. Fans could have a three course meal sitting in style watching the racing, but if it all got too exciting, they could finish up with indigestion. The grass centre green was kept clean and tidy with plenty of colourful flowers, and it gave the place a special feel.

From the rider's point of view, the track was always well prepared and the dressing rooms were not too bad, but the pits were something else. Enclosed under the home straight grandstand, they were long and narrow with not much room to move around. Imagine 14 or more 500cc unsilenced speedway machines all in a confined space and all warming up together. The noise was deafening, the exhaust fumes were choking and eye-watering. Usually we warmed the bikes up wearing ear defenders, or even pieces of rag in our ears, and a scarf around our faces. I guess we should have worn our goggles too. No wonder with all that noise that so many former Wimbledon riders are now hard of hearing. Ah yes, the joys of those pre-silencer days.

I had also decided to up sticks from Glasgow and move south, thus cutting down the hours and miles on the road traveling to meetings in England. Thanks to Coventry's Nigel Boocock, who put in a good word for me to rent a house in Rugby for the season while the owners were working abroad. Rugby was the ideal base for a speedway rider, handy for the motorways, making many of the British tracks within two hours' drive of home. It was a far cry from the many hours we Scots spent driving from north of the border. Sometimes I could even get home from a meeting on the same day I had left for that meeting, instead of arriving home in Scotland where the dawn chorus of birds would keep me awake.

My fellow Scot, George Hunter, also moved south and moved in with Edith and me in Rugby. Jimmy Mac came down from Glasgow to stay with Nigel and Cynthia Boocock, so we were quickly turning this part of the Midlands into a mini 'Scotch Corner'.

The Dons started the season well with wins at home against Ipswich, Kings Lynn and Poole and away wins at Reading and Poole, but our run of successes was not to last. London rivals Hackney came to Plough Lane and the Bengt Jansson-led Hawks beat us 42–36 with 'Benga' scoring a 12 point maximum. We were without the injured Trevor Hedge and had to use junior Pete Wigley as a replacement, so the odds were in Hackney's favour.

Unfortunately, in April my father passed away in Glasgow so I missed the meetings at Ipswich and Wolverhampton and the home match against Hackney. The funeral in Glasgow was very moving. As the hearse and the cortege of funeral cars approached the Linn Fire Station on the south side of Glasgow, all the firemen were lined up outside and saluted as the procession drove slowly past. An emotional send-off for a former Glasgow fireman.

Back on the track, the Dons were having a pretty good season until Tommy Jansson was recalled to Sweden for his to do his national service in the Swedish Army.

Good news for Dons fans was that their hero, Ronnie Moore, would be returning to Britain for a short spell to ride for New Zealand in the World League International Tournament. Scotland had been unceremoniously dropped from the World Team Cup and were also not included in the World League. Ronnie needed a few extra races meetings to get back into the swing of British racing again and, as we had an open date in the Wimbledon fixture list, I came up with an idea. I said to team manager, Cyril Maidment: "Why not bring Ronnie back to captain Wimbledon in an open meeting and I will put together a team of Scots?" I said that we could make it interesting for the fans if I got all the Scottish riders to wear kilts over their leathers for the pre match parade. Even better, I could get each Scot to present a haggis to his opposite number in the Wimbledon team. Cyril thought that this could be a good idea, but as I was not allowed to call my team, 'Scotland' by the powers that be, the "Wimbledon versus Bert Harkins Haggis Bashers" meeting was pencilled into the open date. The Haggis Bashers were born.

I then had to chase around friends and family borrowing kilts and visiting the local Scottish butcher to order eight haggisis (or is it 'haggi'?) which included one for team manager Ian Hoskins to present to Cyril Maidment. My Scottish Select team consisted of top Scots Ken McKinlay, Jim McMillan, George Hunter, Bobby Beaton, Brian Collins and me and, as we had run out of true Scots, Wimbledon Australian Rob Jones was drafted in at reserve.

All went well and at the parade, we marched out with each Scot carrying a haggis for the presentation. Imagine my shock when I presented 'Mirac', Ronnie Moore with a haggis and he took one look at it and promptly threw it into the crowd, almost knocking out a spectator at the starting gate. It was sacrilege to treat a haggis this way and I told Ronnie that next time I was in New Zealand, I was going to kick a kiwi. I guess that the spectator could have sued Ronnie for 'Assault with a deadly weapon'.

It was an entertaining meeting and Wimbledon beat us 42–36. I didn't manage to beat Ronnie when we met, but I collected a paid 13 with only Mirac and Tony Clarke beating me from the Dons team. At the interval, Brian 'Pogo' Collins and I tried to perform a Highland Sword Dance in front of the main grandstand and, in the absence of a couple of Claymores, we just used the chequered and yellow flags. Not very elegant, but I think that it raised a smile among the Dons fans. They were shaking their heads and murmuring something about 'Those crazy Scots'.

Wimbledon versus Bert Harkins' Scottish Select in June 1973.
Top left: with Ronnie Moore leading the teams out;
Top right: Doing a Highland Sword dance with Brian Collins;
Bottom: feeding haggis to Brian Collins. (All JSC Mike Patrick)

137

The Bert Harkins Globe Trotters on 6 July 1973. Back: Odd Fossengen (Norway), Graham Stapleton (New Zealand), Bert, Roy Trigg (England) Dick Barrie (team manager); front: Scott Autrey (USA), Etienne Oliver (South Africa), Doug Wyer (England), Chris Quigley (Australia).

The 'Haggis Bashers' was not my only foray into putting a team together. In July, I took a team to Scotland for a challenge match at Coatbridge. This time the team was 'The Bert Harkins Globetrotters' an apt name for a septet of riders I had raced with or against in various speedway countries around the world. It was a tough meeting and a 5–1 in the last heat by Scott Autrey and me gave the Globetrotters a win by one point, 42–41.

The Wimbledon season continued, with weekend trips to race in Germany or Austria fitting in nicely. Normally I would drive across through France and Belgium, but sometimes if I was racing on the Saturday night I would fly and Edith would drive the car and bike over.

A non-league meeting was the Jubilee Charity Show at Canterbury Speedway with Barry Briggs and Dave Jessup. The Men in Black were there giving demonstrations on their vintage dirt track Douglas and Rudge machines. Johnnie Hoskins, who was the Canterbury promoter, asked Barry and I if we would have a match race using the old dirt track Douglas machines. We were quite keen to try out these legendary bikes from the sport's early days, so we jumped at the chance. Briggo adapted to his machine very well, even getting the long wheelbase Duggie into a slide as he leg-trailed in the corners. I wasn't quite as spectacular because I had trouble getting the bike to slide in the corners, but it was good fun. It gave me a better understanding of the early riders' skills at High Beech.

Later, I got a nice letter from Johnnie saying that we had raised £500 for the Speedway Riders' Benevolent Fund and £500 for local Canterbury charities. He also said that he especially liked the kilt I was wearing on top of my leathers and that it made him homesick for Scotland. He finished the letter in true Scottish style with, "Awa wi ye mon, Guid Luck and kind regards to a' the Clan. Yours, Johnnie H." A true showman indeed.

By the latter part of the season and with Tommy Jansson serving in the Swedish Army, Wimbledon slipped up by losing at home to Newport then drawing at home to Hackney. We finished in 12th place in the league; disappointing for the fans and the riders.

At the end of the season, we moved from Rugby to Abbots Langley in Hertfordshire where we rented a house from my Wimbledon fuel and oil mechanic, Ron Day.

23. The 1974 World Champions Troupe

My usual winter trips to Australia were about to take a different direction when Barry Briggs and Ivan Mauger asked me to join their 'World Champions Troupe' for their tour Down Under in the winter of 1974. We were a 'League of Nations' team, and joining the two World Champion Kiwis were Sweden's five-times World Champion, Ove Fundin, Scott Autrey (USA), Chris Pusey (England) and the lone Scot – me. The biggest scoop of all, however, was the inclusion of two Polish riders, Edward Jancarz and Zenon Plech. This was the time when the Iron Curtain was down and it was very difficult for Eastern Bloc sportsmen to travel outside of their borders. Through their reputations and negotiations, Barry and Ivan were allowed to take Zenon and Eddie on this worldwide trip, but on one condition. That was that they took an 'interpreter' along. This was agreed and Bernard Kowalski joined the party. Mr Kowalski was a big man, so he was promptly named 'Twiggie' after the famous stick-thin model.

Bernard was to be the Polish team manager and interpreter, but that made it a little difficult as the only language that he spoke other than Polish was German. That wasn't so helpful when we were travelling to New Zealand, Australia and California. Fortunately, the smattering of German picked up by Ivan and Barry on their weekend races on the Continent helped, but there are not many times you can use the phrase 'Zwei bier bitte' when touring Down Under.

Bernard soon settled in and became one of the boys, but I think that his main job, apart from his interpreter duties, was to keep an eye on his young Poles to make sure that having seen the joys of the western world, they did not defect in Christchurch or Las Vegas.

The idea of a having touring team of various nationalities was something that Barry Briggs and Ivan Mauger had been working on for over a year. It was an attractive idea because the public would get to see many top riders and World Champions all in the same meeting. It was attractive for the promoters too because they were able to book an entire show without having to negotiate with each rider individually. That made the promoting side of things a little bit easier. Also, all of the World Champions Troupe including our Polish friends could help promote the meetings on radio, television or by personal appearances during the tour. It was a win-win situation for the various promoters.

The Commonwealth Games were also due to open in Christchurch. Speedway's British Lions were also racing there and our 'Rest of the World' team with all those World Champions plus the competitors, teams and followers for the Games, New Zealand was fast becoming a very busy place to be. So busy in fact that Scott Autrey, who was flying from the USA, had his flight delayed in Los Angeles for 24 hours. He then had to wait several hours in Auckland before getting his connecting flight to Christchurch. No wonder he was tired when he arrived. Ove Fundin flew in from his home in Sweden, Garry Middleton arrived from Australia while Ula Olsen and young son Jacob, who later became a speedway rider, arrived from Denmark to join her husband Ole in 'The land of the long white cloud'.

Ivan, Chris, Zenon, Edward, Bernard and I flew out of Heathrow to Sydney in January 1974. The flight was a long and tiring one. It was approximately 36 hours, three airline dinners, two airline lunches and about five airline breakfasts later, we arrived in New Zealand.

Our journey included waiting at the airport in Sydney for three hours for our connecting flight to Christchurch and eventually we arrived there dog tired. There was no time to rest because meeting us at the airport was Raye Mauger, British journalist Peter Oakes and Templeton (Christchurch) promoter, Tony Nesbitt plus a full Maori 'Welcome Committee' performing their traditional Haka. I had a Scottish pipe band welcome in Los Angeles and now a Maori welcome in New Zealand. I was wondering what was next in store when I realised that the Maori were not there to welcome us, but to greet another overseas athletics team arriving for the Commonwealth Games. I brightened up a bit when I saw that one of the Maori ladies was wearing the kilt, I think she was known as 'Maori Queen of Scots'. (Sorry folks, I couldn't resist it.)

After the long flights and the welcoming party, we crashed into bed around 8.30pm. There was to be a televised practice session at Templeton Speedway at 9am the next morning before catching the 1.30pm flight to Palmerston North, so we needed some sleep.

The ship with our bikes and gear had been delayed in England owing to fuel strikes so we practiced on borrowed equipment. Zenon Plech wore my tartan helmet and boots so he became an 'Honorary Scotsman' for the trip. Ivan then arranged for six bikes to be sent to us from Christchurch, but mine was a real 'camel'. It was a former Graham Stapleton Jawa that he had raced in England and sold to a junior when he returned to New Zealand. We had had no time to check the bikes over before we raced. On this machine the frame was painted white and I remembered that at Wimbledon we had called it 'The white tornado'.

Unfortunately, it had been through some hard laps since its days at Plough Lane. The front fork springs were too soft and worn causing the front wheel to bounce and 'wash-out' on the corners. In one race, the engine sprocket came off along with the primary chain so I was heading straight for the fence, just like putting a car into neutral in a fast corner. Following practice, 'Twiggie' checked Zenon and Eddie's pulses. He also checked Chris Pusey's pulse, but walked away shaking his head. We never did find out why.

The first two New Zealand versus Rest of The World test matches were rained off, but when we eventually got going in Christchurch, the stadium was packed with over 13,000 spectators. The programmes sold out quickly. There were so many people in the stadium that 20 minutes after the scheduled start of the meeting, the announcer broadcast an appeal for those fans inside the stadium to crush a little closer to enable the thousands outside to get in. Eventually, the gates were closed with hundreds still outside. It was the biggest ever crowd at Templeton Speedway.

Ivan, Briggo and Jim Airey all stayed in Christchurch to ride at Templeton Speedway for the New Zealand Championship, which Ivan won for the first time, while the rest of our Troupe caught the 1.30pm flight to Palmerston North. Zenon, 'Steady Eddie' and Scott Autrey all rode well at Palmerston. Eddie won the International Best Pairs along with Kiwi Robin Adlington and Plechie won the second half grand final.

We also rode at Te Marua, which is 25 miles outside of Wellington in the North Island. 'Windy Wellington' it is called and we soon knew why when we were almost blown down the aircraft steps. The track there was 440 yards with a slight banking. Zenon Plech was the star performer here, breaking the track record in the process. The promoter, Kevin Baldwin, had worked hard on the publicity for this event. He was helped by former Wembley Lion of the early 1950s, Bruce Abernethy, so the stage was set for another bumper crowd. The crowds did roll up in their thousands, 15,000 fans. It was three times the normal gate at the track, so everyone was happy.

Zenon, Chris Pusey and Ole Olsen were the stars of the night bringing the normally quiet Wellington crowd to their feet cheering themselves hoarse. The flying Pole won the grand final after four pulsating laps.

Next day we were on the road again, bound for Palmerston North, some 100 miles north east of Wellington. This time we were travelling in five Mazda cars, each one with the name of a World Champion on the side. The cars were loaned to us by *5 Star Motors* of Palmerston North, the company where former Hackney and Coventry rider, Graeme Smith was their number one salesman. Palmerston North in the North Island of New Zealand was originally a Maori settlement in the forest and named "Papa-I-Oea" meaning "How beautiful it is". It was a beautiful part of the world. However, when we were there it was very, very quiet, so quiet indeed that in the evening the entertainment for Chris, Scott and myself was watching a couple of flies crawling across the table in the café and us betting which one would be first to reach the other side. Las Vegas it was not. Most of our spare time was spent either watching television or playing billiards. Ole Olsen's wife, Ula, joined in one of our big tournaments. Ula almost won the game and nearly beat us all with her trick shots, so she wasn't invited to play with us again.

On track, the New Zealand meetings were relatively injury free but off track was a different matter. After the meeting at Palmerston, Scott, Chris and I decided to walk to a local café for something to eat before checking back into our motel. As we were walking through the local park, Chris disappeared into the bushes. I thought that he had gone to 'spend a penny', or £1 as it is now, but he came rushing out and chased us, waving a huge cactus above his head. I didn't get out of the gate fast enough and was hit on the backside by this cactus. I collected a backside full of sharp cactus needles and that hurt. Unfortunately, I wasn't wearing my leathers so some of the long spikes embedded themselves in my tender Scottish skin. I tried unsuccessfully to remove the needles so we headed – I hobbled – to the café and found a quiet table in the corner. I then had to bend over the table with the Polka Dot Kid and the Sundance Kid pulling the needles out of my bare backside. Not a pretty sight. Fortunately, this was in the days before camera phones and speedway's ace photographer, Mike Patrick, was not on the trip otherwise the film could have been a hit on YouTube or Instagram. Luckily, the cactus wasn't poisonous but I still had to eat my meals standing up for a few days.

Between meetings we were well looked after by the Kiwis. Ivan and Briggo had planned to compete in a local motocross meeting in Christchurch on our free Sunday. However, the organising club, Corsair Motorcycle Club, also invited the rest of the troupe to compete as well. So what started as a quiet Sunday ride developed into a 'Speedway Riders Motocross Championship'. Our machines were supplied by Tommy McLeary, a former TT rider who owned the large *Tommy's Suzuki Centre* in Christchurch. Tommy was a lifelong friend of Briggo and his hospitality during our stay was overwhelming. He lent us some brand new 125cc and 250cc Suzuki motocross bikes and they were very fast.

Not having competed in a motocross, or 'scrambles' race before, I was given a new Suzuki to ride and was looking forward to the new experience. Zenon Plech and Eddie Jancarz were not so lucky as their 'minder', 'Twiggie' would not let them race in case they got injured and were unable to earn any speedway dollars to take home to Poland.

I lined up for my first race and charged off the line with all the others, but almost forgot that I had to change gear on this bike and had to turn right in the corners as well as left. I thought I was circulating fairly quickly when I went over a jump and saw a pair of wheels overtaking me at shoulder height. I looked up and there was Briggo, Barry Briggs, coming in to land after overtaking me in the air. The next big jump and another set of wheels were flying over my head, this time it was 'Stape', Graham Stapleton, and he was flying too. I later found out that both Briggo and Graham were experienced off road racers. When it came to motocross, they packed a lot more skill and experience than I did. Scott was also a star of off road riding, having raced motorcycles in his native California since he was 11 years old.

Chris was a top dog off road as British grass track champion, but he was also new to motocross. Ronnie Moore and Malcolm Brown were also riding so we almost had as many speedway riders competing as there were motocross riders.

I had ridden in the 125cc class and enjoyed the race so much that at the end of the race, I joined the starters for the next race, the 250cc event and so it went on. However, every time there was the black and white chequered helmet of Ivan Mauger in the same race. During that afternoon I was lining up for every race, 125cc race, 250cc race, Unlimited cc race , in fact, every time the local riders rode out to the start line, they would be joined by dust-covered Scotsman grinning from ear to ear. I had competed in six races non-stop and Ronnie Moore suggested that I should be given the 'endurance award' for stamina. It must be all that porridge and haggis I had been eating.

Once when I was just going to ride out of the pits I heard Briggo yelling "Get back in the pits, Haggis, this race is for club members only." The other riders were waiting at the start and I was just turning around to go back to the pits when the announcer shouted over the PA system "Where are you going Bert Harkins? We are waiting for you so that we can start this race." With such a pleasant invitation, I just waved to Briggo who was shaking his head and laughing his socks off and headed back to the start line. I don't think I won any races that day, but I had a lot of fun. By the next morning I could hardly move and felt that I had done 10 rounds with Muhammad Ali.

Pretty soon it was back to our own sport of turning left for a living. The famous Houston Astrodome in Texas was due to stage indoor speedway and Barry, Ivan, Zenon and Ove Fundin flew out to compete in America, leaving the rest of us to race in New Zealand.

On this tour, with lots of travelling to different towns in different countries, it could really upset your normal way of life – that is, if a speedway rider's life can ever be called 'normal'. On our travels, the three of us, Chris, Scott and myself, had been sharing motel rooms but despite being a seasoned long-distance traveller by now, Scott frequently jumped up in bed at night shouting something about an airplane crash or some other disaster. By the time everyone was awake and wondering what had happened, he was fast asleep again, oblivious to the turmoil he has caused. Chris meanwhile, was dreaming of English grass tracks and pints of Guinness. I was somewhere in the Scottish hills hunting the haggis.

142

Some of the Rest of the World team: Bernard Kowalski (accompanying the Polish riders), Edward Jancarz, Zenon Plech, Ivan Mauger, Bert, Chris Pusey, Scott Autrey.

One night, after we had returned to race in Australia, I surpassed even Scott's recurring nightmares. I awakened to imagine that I was in hospital and as I didn't like this dream I went back to sleep again. On awakening a second time, the hospital ward was still there and I realised that I had not been dreaming after all, I was actually lying in hospital in Sydney. The previous evening had been the Australia versus Rest of The World international at Liverpool. It had been a very close fought affair, but too close for my Edinburgh friend, Bill Landels and me. Apparently, coming out of the last corner in heat nine, our handlebars got hooked together and we collected the wooden safety fence in a big way. That crash put both Bill and I out of the meeting and into the local hospital for some bed and breakfast.

Bill and I had been team mates back in Edinburgh before he emigrated to Australia. Somehow we managed to knock one another off everywhere from Scotland to Sydney, not deliberately. It was just two Scotsmen chasing an extra Aussie Dollar or Scottish Bawbee.

Prior to my bone-crunching collision with 'Brickwall Bill' at Liverpool, Ivan Mauger had a bit of a shock in the pre-match parade. He thought that a girl had joined the Troupe. What happened was that I had donned my 'normal' pre-match outfit of kilt over my leathers and my tartan tammie (hat) for the parade. On the back straight, I stopped to try a practice start. The track was grippier than I had expected and the front wheel lifted high into the air as I zoomed past Ivan with my kilt over my head, my tartan tammie blowing off and then I ran into the safety fence because I could not see. Those Australian fans soon found out what a Scotsman wears under his kilt, but this time it was one piece leathers.

The Australasian part of our tour came to an end and The World Champions Troupe headed for California and a three-match USA versus Rest of The World test series with some more bumps and bruises ahead.

24. Broken bones and Boxing

Our 'World' team was now down to six riders because Ove had flown back to Sweden, so Martin Ashby was called up from England as replacement. By the time we all gathered at Costa Mesa, our team was looking a little second hand. Zenon had been nursing a foot injury and I had a broken rib and damaged shoulder from my coming together with Bill Landels at Liverpool the previous week.

We were due to race the three-match America versus Rest of The World series on Friday evening, Saturday evening and Sunday afternoon. There would be no time for rest and recuperation. Three tough matches and we did not know that the final result of the series would eventually depend on the very last race of the last match. Now that would have made good television.

The series produced some excellent racing and that tiny Costa Mesa track lived up to its nickname of 'Shinbone Alley'. The Americans were all experts on that small circuit, so we had our work cut out to try to beat them. Chris Pusey, Eddie Jancarz and Zenon Plech had never ridden there before, but the Polka Dot Kid looked good in practice. After being used to the big open spaces of the tracks in their native Poland and in Australia, Eddie and Zenon were not too keen on trying their luck on the 180 yard Californian track. However, once the meeting began, the boys adapted very well. Our other problem was that our Rest of The World team had only six riders and no reserve. There was nobody to replace me so that I could rest my injuries, I had to race, or at least try.

The first meeting was a beauty. Briggo and Ivan were in great form. We won, but took our fair share of knocks in the process. Martin Ashby arrived from England at 2am the next morning and had to practice before heat one of the second match. I dropped down to reserve for this one because I was struggling a lot with my injuries. The Americans were all flying and they beat us to level the score at one apiece. The dreaded jet lag from the long flights was catching up with us plus various damage to riders and machines so the stage was set for our decider the following day.

Most speedway countries race under FIM rules, but I soon rediscovered the joys of racing under American rules. Edward Jancarz was sidelined when he and Mike Caruso went into the fence. Eddie injured his arm and was out of action so I had to be ready to race again. American journalist, Steven Parker, writing in California's *Cycle News* magazine, wrote: "Danny Becker was troubled with a bad wrist injury all weekend and could not get his riding act together. Bert Harkins, one of the crowd's favourite riders also had his share of physical difficulties during the races. Harkins had suffered some hurt ribs and separated shoulder just two days before the American meetings but still managed a win over Steve Bast and Mike Caruso. Harkins is the friendliest of the foreign racers, and his colourful leathers and smooth style made him the most popular of the Europeans". Nice words from a respected journalist.

In my first race I was out in front and on the last lap, marshals were jumping around waving red flags at me. I knew from past experiences at Costa Mesa that a red flag does not necessarily mean 'Stop', so I kept on going. As I came round the pit turn, there was utter confusion. Zenon and Mike Caruso had crashed into the fence and there were bikes and bodies everywhere.

Officials were running across the track so I raised my arm to show that I was slowing down to avoid them. As I did so, Bill Cody came flying past me at full throttle, hooked the end of my handlebars and sent me tumbling off the back of my bike. My handlebars got caught on the push handle on Bill's rear mudguard, so he dragged my bike around the corner and across the finishing line. The fall aggravated my injuries and made me feel worse than ever. I felt even worse than that when the referee awarded 'Wild Bill' first place with me second while lying flat on the track. Mike Caruso was given third place even although he and Zenon were still trapped under their bikes. American rules? They were something else.

The scores see-sawed throughout the meeting until the penultimate race when Chris Pusey and Ivan Mauger put us into a slender lead. And then we came to the last race, the Series decider featuring the Rest of the World pairing of 'Cripples United', Zenon Plech hobbling around with a foot injury, and me with a damaged shoulder and broken ribs against the USA's top pair of 'Smiling' Sonny Nutter and Mike 'The Maestro' Bast. Tensions had been running high and a few heats earlier, Mike Bast had pipped Chris Pusey on the line only to be excluded for having two wheels over the white line and now, going into the final race of the series, it all depended on just four laps to decide the outcome.

The Rest of the World had to score at least two points to win the meeting. That may not sound too difficult but Bast and Nutter flew around the Costa Mesa bowl and we were short of bikes and fit bodies. Our World team all got together and Ivan loaned his bike, which was flying, to Zenon and I rode Johnny Fishback's machine, another flyer from the George Wenn stable. We had to make sure that the USA did not get a 5–1 or even a 4–2, so all of the team's hopes were pinned on Zenon and me.

We lined up for this important last heat decider with the atmosphere like a World Final run-off and the partisan American crowd cheering for their home made heroes. Mike Bast was off gate one, normally the best gate, and I was alongside him on gate two. But when the tapes flew up, I was able to outgun Mike to the corner, block him and get Zenon alongside me. Sonny Nutter was even faster and he drove around the outside of the three of us to take the lead. 'Sliding Sonny' was flying and Mike 'The Maestro' was last. So now we had to make sure that Mike did not pass either of us so we rode as closely as possible side by side for lap after lap. Mike tried everything he knew and got very frustrated. He was probably faster than both of us but when he tried to pass, he found himself running into my rear wheel or frame.

Zenon and I held on for that valuable two point win much to the delight of our buddies. As we stopped at the pits gate, neither of us were in a fit state to be 'given the bumps' by our team mates. Suddenly, an irate Mike Bast appeared, jumped off his bike and dragged me from my bike lifting me off my feet in a huge bear hug and yelled something about my on-track tactics. Not very nice when I had broken ribs. I was dangling in the air and frantically trying to get Mike to release his grip. I began trying to aim punches inside the opening of his full face helmet. I am not a violent person and very rarely get upset, but when faced with pain and the possibility of breaking even more ribs, I had to fight back.

Bert and Zenon Plech team-riding for the Rest of the World. Note the 22 inch rear wheels.

Beating the Americans for the Rest of the World. Bert leading (from left)
Danny Becker, Zenon Plech and Mike Bast.

Poor Mike had been so frustrated at being pinned back into last place by Zenon and me team riding against him that tempers boiled over and that ungentlemanly scuffle took place. At the trophy presentations several minutes later, I witnessed the most amazing incident I had ever seen in American speedway. As Mike Bast, the American Champion, led his USA team from the pits to the starting gate, he was loudly booed by his own fans. Mike gave a short speech over the microphone and criticised my riding in the last heat, saying "I have raced like a man in all three matches but he (meaning me) did not ride like a man in that last race." I guess that the art of 'team riding' had not reached Southern California.

The report in *Cycle News* outlined:

"Sonny Nutter won the event [that race] but Mike Bast had trouble getting by Bert Harkins who was riding slowly because of his injuries.[I was riding slowly, not because of my injuries but because Zenon and I had to stop Mike from passing either of us]. What happened after the event is disputed but the incident ended with Bast and Harkins being pulled off of each other. Bast got on the public address system after the race stating 'I ride like a man', giving the impression that Harkins doesn't. Harkins then took the microphone and thanked the Americans for their hospitality and said that he hoped he would be invited back soon.

The crowd cheered Harkins wildly, and just as wildly booed Mike Bast. It was a shame as Bast had been getting the cheers all weekend as he beat the Europeans. The incident embarrassed the American team and the crowd let Bast know just how they felt about it, although Harkins said that he had 'no hard feelings' while Bast stood and complained to Mauger about Harkins' riding. The weekend ended on a sour note, but the fans saw a lot of good action, fistfights notwithstanding. One will never forget the riding of Ivan Mauger his speed and his ability to seemingly know where the other riders were without even having to look. The crowds will also remember 'Bouncing' Bert Harkins and his bagpipe introduction on the first night of the series."

Yes, once again the Americans had laid on some bagpipes to welcome me, but this time it was a lone piper and not a full Pipe Band as at Los Angeles International Airport last time.

Once again, the normally partisan crowd gave Mike 'the bird' and booed their star man loudly. After the meeting dozens of fans came into the pits to apologise to me, saying "We are sorry, this is not the way we do it in America". There was even more controversy after the match with arguments between both teams and the AMA officials. On the aggregate score, it was America 163 Rest of The World 160, so the home team thought that they had won, but as it was a "Best-of-Three" series, we won by two matches to one and took the trophy.

It was all a heat-of-the-moment scuffle. Probably Mike had never finished in last place before and as it was normally all individual racing in California the concept of team riding and blocking was very alien. Anyway, it was a 'racing incident'. I thought no more about it, but was due for another big surprise when I got home.

Apart from the injuries and fisticuffs, the three meetings in three days had been fantastic and there was a final surprise for our Polish friends before we left America. Zenon Plech and Edddie Jancarz were presented with special red Bell Helmets jackets bearing their names from Bell Helmets and their team manager/interpreter/minder/policeman, Bernard Kowalski also got a Bell jacket, but it was just inscribed 'Twiggie'.

148

Not long after I arrived back in Britain, a nice letter of apology arrived from Mike Bast and I still have that letter. He wrote: "If the following words are put a bit awkwardly, please understand that this will not be the easiest letter I have ever begun to write. Over the past week since the World Champion Series ended in Costa Mesa, there has been time to calm down, let the tension fade away and reflect on 'our incident' and in this calm, relaxed and reflective mood, I want to apologise for my actions towards you at the conclusion of Sunday's event. We've both raced around the world, Bert and have both seen tempers and fists flare before. I'm not trying to excuse what happened, just stating basic facts, it will undoubtedly happen again somewhere, sometime- but I do not intend to be part of it. Bert, will you stretch your hand across the Atlantic halfway, shake mine, and let us meet as friendly rivals and rivalling friends at the next World Champions Series?

Good Luck with the Dons this year.

Sincerely,

Mike Bast"

A very nice apology which I was glad to accept. It takes a special kind of speedway rider to apologise, and Mike showed that he is that type of rider. I remained friends with Mike and had forgotten all about the incident when I returned to British speedway when, a couple of months later, another airmail letter arrived from America via the Speedway Control Board in London and this time it was not such good news. The letter was from Mr WA (Bill) Boyce, Director of Competition of the AMA, American Motorcycle Association.

He wrote: "Dear Bert, Reference to the International Speedway race meet sanction 6336, held March 17th 1974 at Orange County Fairgrounds, Costa Mesa, California. At the conclusion of event Number 20 you became involved in a scuffle with Mike Bast.

For your ungentlemanly like conduct, you are hereby fined $50.00 (50 US Dollars). Any rider upon whom a fine is imposed shall be deemed, suspended from all AMA competitions until the fine has been paid to either the referee or the Chairman of the AMA Congress, Ed Youngblood.

Sincerely,

WA Boyce.

Competitions Manager"

I was astounded. Being fined $50 for defending myself when I was already injured and I was certainly not the type of rider to get into a 'scuffle' as the letter said. I replied to Mr John McNulty of the SCB and also Mr Boyce at the AMA saying that it was heat-of-the-moment stuff on Mike's part and that I was the innocent party. I also explained that due to my broken ribs and shoulder injuries, I was unable to defend myself and that Mike had later sent me a letter apologising for his actions, so neither of us should be fined.

I also sent Bill Boyce a copy of the letter Mike had sent to me and asked him to rescind both of our fines and also that I did not want an "Ungentlemanly Conduct" stain on my record. Mr Boyce replied that the referee of the meeting, a Mr Hinshaw, requested that both Mike Bast and myself be fined $50 for 'Ungentlemanly Conduct' and reported that it was a 50/50 blame between Mike and me, so both of us would be fined the same amount. American

149

speedway rules once again. He then mentioned that the AMA had already received the $50 fine payment from Mike Bast and "Therefore, we will be looking forward to receiving the $50 fine from you". He then went on to say that the letter that Mike had sent to me was "A very nice letter that Mr Bast sent to you. I must write him a letter and commend him on this". I guess I could not win against the might of the AMA, but at least our Rest of the World team won the series, so that was $50 well spent.

This was not the first time I had had a run-in with the AMA. After an earlier trip to America, I had received a letter again from the AMA and again sent via the Speedway Control Board in London. This time it was a letter from the executive director of the AMA, a Mr Russell E March. In the letter to SCB Manager, John McNulty, he said that "Mr Bert Harkins, a Scottish rider entered a local speedway event in Gardena, California. Mr Harkins rode in that event which was not internationally sanctioned." Mr March went on to say that "We received no advanced notice from the ACU that this rider had been given permission to ride in the United States. Therefore, we are assuming that this man participated illegally so we felt that we should notify you of this". Gee, it was hard enough to make a living at speedway and here was the AMA trying to get my international licence taken away. Fortunately I was able to sort it out with the SCB and also make peace with the AMA.

And so the USA versus Rest of the World tour came to an end and we arrived back in London on 20 March 1974, battered, bruised but certainly not bowed.

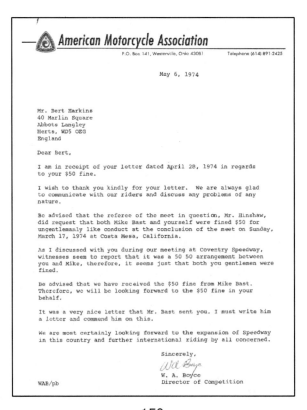

150

25. Wedding bells

Arriving back at Heathrow airport from Los Angeles, *Speedway Star's* Philip Rising was there to welcome us home. He told me that it had been secretly arranged that Barry Briggs would be the subject of the popular BBC television programme *This is your Life,* but Barry was not to know about it so to keep it very quiet. The idea was that at the Wimbledon practice session later that day, television presenter, Eamon Andrews would be dressed in white overalls as a mechanic and "ambush" Briggo with his famous 'Big Red Book'. Everyone was sworn to secrecy and invited along to the BBC studios to appear on the show. Unfortunately, while lifting my suitcase off of the luggage carousel at Heathrow, I had strained my back once again, it must have been that spare engine I had hidden in my hand luggage that did the damage, so when I got home I was flat on my back once again.

I had to miss the Wimbledon practice session and also hearing Eamon Andrews say those iconic words in his lilting Irish accent, "Barry Briggs, This is your Life". Briggo was caught unaware for a change and the programme which followed was a great advert for speedway. It shows how highly speedway was regarded as a major sport at that time and also how the name of Barry Briggs was known at all levels. I missed having a walk-on part on the show with rest of the Wimbledon team, my 10 seconds of television fame, but I was able to watch it at home as "The Grand Old Man of Speedway", Johnny Hoskins stole the show.

Despite Briggo leading the Dons, our 1974 season did not start too well and my own early form left a lot to be desired. We had the best stadium at Plough Lane with glass fronted grandstand and restaurant, tidy centre green with flower displays, good support and good crowds too. Wimbledon was the ideal place to show a potential sponsor in comfort what the sport was all about. Plough Lane became a Mecca for off duty London-based riders and with tight racing on that small, tricky track, it was an exciting place to be.

Our season improved as we went along and early in the year, I had another "Open Booking" to arrange. Edith and I decided to get married and looked for a suitable date in my busy diary. We thought it would be a good idea to get married on our joint birthdays, 15 April. Our birthdays were on the same day and the same month, but not the same year as Edith was younger than me. We checked the fixture list, but Wimbledon were at home to Oxford on that day, but decided that we could squeeze it in between meetings at Oxford and Wolverhampton so we settled on 20 April. Unbeknown to us at the time, in addition to having the same date for our birthdays, my home town of Glasgow was twinned with Edith's home town of Nuremberg in Germany.

Arrangements were made, invitations sent out, but there was still a lot of speedway racing going on. The night before the wedding, Friday, Wimbledon were racing at Wolverhampton where we went down 44–34 to the Ole Olsen-led Wolves so there was no last minute wedding present from the Dons. We may have lost at Wolverhampton, but we very nearly lost everything when barrelling down the M1 at high speed in the early hours of the Saturday morning after the meeting. Briggo was some way ahead of me in his Mercedes when I suddenly realized that the headlights I could see coming towards me and getting closer, were actually on my side of the motorway. It was a 'Ghost driver' heading north in the 'fast lane' of the southbound carriageway. Both the ghost driver and I must have been travelling at 70mph or more, so the closing speed of our cars was very high. Luckily we all managed to miss this crazy guy as he continued north on the wrong side of the road at high speed.

Next day, before the wedding, Briggo and June, Ivan and Raye Mauger, my best man, Norman Christie and I all gathered at Ron and Beryl Day's house in Garston near Watford. Ron was my fuel and oil man at Wimbledon, so we all met there before going on to the St Lawrence Church in Abbots Langley. By coincidence, the popular Saturday ITV sports programme, *Word of Sport* was playing on television when we got to Ron and Beryl's house and they were showing speedway. I can't remember what meeting it was, but Ivan and Barry were riding so we were all glued to the television watching the racing.

What we did not realise until Beryl reminded us was that time was getting on and we had to be at the church before Edith arrived. So, reluctantly with one eye on the television, we headed off for the church and just arrived a few minutes before the bride. Phew!

The wedding was an international affair with Edith's parents coming over from Germany, my mum, relatives and friends coming down from Scotland plus the two Kiwis, Ivan and Barry and *Speedway Star's* Phil Rising with the 'Happy Snapper', Mike Patrick. Mike was in action all day and evening, photographing guests and the specially-made wedding cake which featured model speedway riders and Scottish and German flags on top.

Unfortunately, after all his hard work, Mike later discovered much to his embarrassment that he had forgotten to put a film in his pre-digital days camera, so we had no photographs of the wedding other than those outside the church. Poor Mike has never lived this down.

No time for a honeymoon because we had just fitted the wedding in between speedway fixtures. That would have to wait as it was back to racing at Wimbledon two days later. I also changed my motto from 'Have bike will travel' to 'Have wife must travel'. There was also a very important fixture on the horizon, the World Team Cup qualifying round at Ipswich where Scotland would take on the might of England, New Zealand and Australia. Ireland, who had originally been nominated for this round could not raise a team, so with great relief north of the border, Scotland were reinstated.

England won the round ahead of Australia, but we finished third, 11 points ahead of New Zealand. This was to be our last World Team Cup event as although we finished ahead of the Kiwis, we were dropped from the WTC the following year to make way for the USA.

At that time, in the mid-1970s, recording records made by football teams were all the rage, not for their singing, but just for the idea of having singing footballers. London record producer, Karl Blore was a speedway fan and had purchased a Jawa bike from Terry Betts. Karl reckoned that speedway should also get into the act, make a record and try to get into the top twenty or *Top of the Pops*.

The idea was to get a group of riders together in the hope that they could sing in harmony then cut a record at the Decca Studious in London in the hope of bringing speedway to a whole new young audience. This so-called pop group was assembled and made a record under the name of *The Rivals*. The newly-written song to be recorded was called, appropriately, *Speedway* and featured an international assembly of voices from England, Norway, USA, New Zealand and, of course, Scotland.

A formal photo of Bert and Edith at the London Riders Awards Dinner in 1976.

For the record, this starry line-up consisted of Peter (brother of drummer Phil) Collins, Little Boy Blues brother, Nigel Boocock, Motown Martin Ashby, Scott (The Singing Cowboy) Autrey, Malcolm (The Voice) Brown, Dag (Elvis) Lovaas, (Elton John) Louis, Tuneful Terry Betts with full supporting (plaster) cast and The Loch Ness Trio from Scotland, George Hunter, Jimmy Mac ("When are you coming back?) McMillan and Bert Harkins. The flipside was called *Hoskins Rides Again*, a tribute to the Father of Speedway and star of Briggo's *This is your Life* programme, Johnnie Hoskins.

We all had to wear our racing leathers and team body colours for the publicity photos. Producer Karl put us all through our paces with various rehearsals throughout the day. To keep our voices lubricated, the record company supplied us with various alcoholic drinks, and as the day wore on, the combined voices and the laughter got louder and louder. Not only that, but during the slight breaks we did not realize that we could still be heard 'live' behind the glass in the control room.

We eventually got round to the serious business of recording the record and were all singing merrily away when a loud voice came over the speakers. "Stop, Stop!" It was Karl the producer and he went on to say "Can the Scottish voices turn it down a bit as you are drowning out everyone else." And so, Jimmy Mac, George and myself tried to sing quietly, but I think that it was a losing battle. The record was eventually released (actually I think that it escaped) and our good friend, DJ David Hamilton played it on his BBC Radio One programme, but after that, it sunk without trace. We did not manage to take the Hit Parade by storm, or appear on *Top of the Pops*, but we had some fun and gave speedway a little bit of promotion into the entertainment world. None of *The Rivals* went on to have a singing career so we all went back to being rivals on the track. Comments about the record still appear on various Facebook pages from time to time and there is a copy of the actual record in the World Speedway Riders' Association National Speedway Museum. It is locked away in a cupboard just in case anyone tries to play it.

Back in the speedway world, my season continued with riding for Wimbledon all around the country during the week and competing in weekend meetings in Germany, Austria and Italy. It was another busy season and things were going well. I was due to make another trip to Australia in the winter to ride at Liverpool Raceway in Sydney, but my year was about to come to an abrupt and painful end.

26. Speedway? What's that?
By Edith Harkins

Speedway! I heard that word for the first time in February 1971 when I came over to England to improve my English, which hitherto had only been commercial English for business letters and business communications. I had already been halfway round the world and decided that my English needed to improve and that England was the best place to do that.

I arrived at Heathrow and was picked up by Pat Williams who told me on the way back to the house that her husband Freddie was twice a World Champion in speedway. Champion? I was bemused, that meant mushroom to me so I was rather puzzled.

After about an hour's drive we arrived at a very nice country house in Hertfordshire, which was the abode of the Williams family with a swimming pool, horses, stables, trampoline and table tennis. Seeing all these things I was looking forward to a good time. I was to be their au pair, helping Pat and looking after the children.

1971 was the year Britain went decimal, and when travelling by bus to my English lessons in St Albans it was quite funny to see the conductors struggle with giving change with this new decimal system. I remember that there was also a bus strike at the time and I did a good bit of walking.

I found out about speedway in more detail, since Freddie (Mr Williams to me then) was the team manager of the Wembley Lions and Pat (Mrs Williams to me then) was singing the praises of this most marvellous fellow, who was on his way back from Australia to ride for the Wembley Lions.

I soon met this 'funny character', who was living in Glasgow and came down to Wembley every weekend for his home meetings and was of course invited to stay at the house, since it was a very long drive home for him. Fred and Pat were very hospitable and the house was rather spacious.

In no time I got to know Bert and his funny jokes as brooms and other things were strategically placed outside my door and fell on top of me as I opened it. This went on for a while and one day I decided to get my own back and the opportunity presented itself very soon. It was a lovely summer, the weather was brilliant and one day Bert just stood a bit too close to the edge of the swimming pool and a little push sent him splashing in. Well, he never came up and it was then that I realised that he could not swim, so I had to dive in and rescue him. But that was not the end of his funny jokes.

I can clearly remember my first speedway meeting at Wembley and I could not believe my eyes. It was a huge stadium and out came the riders looking rather small from the stands and marching to this tune to the starting gate. The atmosphere and the noise were rather inspiring, but the racing itself was too nerve wracking for my liking. Afterwards everybody met in the bar, but Bert took an age to appear, and when he did he was surrounded by lots of fans. This scenario never changed as I went more often to watch him.

Bert inherited his friendly manner from his mother Jean, who was a very lovely, hospitable person. On one occasion, when Wembley were going to race in Glasgow, the announcer indicated that any fan making it up to Glasgow was most welcome to visit Bert at his home.

The announcer gave out the address. Unbelievably, several carloads of fans turned up o Bert's parents' doorstep before the meeting and were invited in. To my utter amazement, Bert's mother produced countless cups of tea and biscuits, and made everyone feel very welcome.

Bert's mother was always worried about him racing speedway, and even when he was riding very well, she would ask him to give up speedway and get a proper job.

Anyway, Pat Williams was very much into match-making because she kept telling me to go and see the world and either go to visit their friends in South Africa or go with Bert to Australia in the next winter season. Although I did not have any plans to do that, somehow it worked out that way and by the beginning of November that year I found myself on a plane leaving Heathrow to Sydney. Since it was a very cheap ticket with Pakistan Airlines I had to change planes several times. On the same plane were Phil Crump and Jim Ryman and once I talked to them I thought that my English lessons were a waste of time, since I found their Australian accent hard to understand. However, we had a jolly good look around Karachi where we were stranded first, and as Pakistan were at loggerheads with India we had to fly all the way round India to Dacca (East Pakistan and now Bangladesh) where the antiaircraft guns were already lined up on the runway. The next stop was Manilla where again we were stranded.

After several days when I finally landed in Sydney. There was, of course, no sign of Bert, who was racing that evening. However all turned out well and looking back now we had a jolly easy life. Lots of water skiing, with the Swedes driving the boat and trying to make me crash, Anders Michanek went in tighter and tighter circles and went faster and faster. There were Bar-B-Qs and parties and, of course, the weather was great and life was good. I got various jobs and kept busy while Bert was flying all over the place to race.

In his spare time Bert loved to sunbathe. He would turn as red as a beetroot and the next day he was white again. But Bert being Bert he never gave up. Amazingly enough so far he has never had any skin trouble.

When the season ended I decided to stay on in Australia, as I was keen to see not only speedway tracks but some more sights of this interesting country. However, after a few months immigration caught up with me and wanted to deport me. I went back home and would have settled for a life in Germany, but Bert had other ideas so after a few months I found myself back in Australia via America. And so began my life with Bert travelling around the world for many years. Even after he finished racing and we had our business we often combined business with pleasure and had many interesting and varied trips and holidays.

We got married in April 1974. After consultation with Bert's speedway diary we were not able to marry on our birthdays – which happen to be the same day – but a few days later. My matron of honour was Raye Mauger who Bert immediately renamed my Mattress of Honour. Raye sang beautifully at our wedding which was a relatively modest affair, by today's standards, in Watford. We spent our honeymoon of one day in the Holiday Inn at Heathrow, since we did not know where else to go and Bert had racing commitments.

Shortly after that we bought our first house. In true style Bert inspected the garage first and as it was to his satisfaction he decided that it would be 'fine'. He did not seem to be too interested in the rest of the house. He was riding for Wimbledon at the time. I used to sit next to June Briggs and if Bert was not doing well she would joke for me to run down to the starting gate and wave the mortgage papers at him.

Six months later Bert had his dreadful accident in a second half race in Wimbledon when Reg Luckhurst ran into his back and he dislocated 5 vertebrae. Luckily Bert wore a back protector which saved him from the worst. He was lying in St. Georges Hospital in Tooting for a month where he had to lie completely flat on his back. He then was transferred to Stanmore Orthopaedic Hospital where he stayed another two months flat on his back. Freddie Williams was a great help then, as he organised some assistance from the Speedway Riders Benevolent Fund. Although I was working at the time it helped enormously with the bills as I travelled to the hospital every day.

At first Bert was not interested at all how his bike was, but as he improved slowly he started to enquire about his bike. The bike was in a sorry state and to this day I can only marvel at the miracle that he is still able to walk. Although it must be said that he is in discomfort and pain with his back nearly every day. But he never complains about it.

Since I was never that keen on speedway, this accident did not improve my feelings for the sport. Bert had to wear a made to measure corset for quite some time to help his back. And of course this was when his back troubles started. There are times when he completely seizes up and cannot move. Once such occasion was Barry Briggs' television appearance on *This is your Life.* Bert would have loved to be there, but he had just come back from a trip and was in great pain.

Looking back many of the meetings are just a blur to me, as I was always extremely nervous and for a while started chain smoking to get over my worries. However this lifestyle definitely beat a 9 to 5 working day. We met many interesting people on the way, and did many things we would otherwise not have been able to. And of course Bert loved it.

At the time I worked at Ovaltine nearby in Kings Langley for the Head of Research and Development. My boss was very nice to me because I often left early to go to the speedway meetings and I must have been the first person to work 'Flexitime'. I got a big send off when we went for the season to California, but when we came back at the end of 1976 I got my old job back.

For me personally 1976 was probably the best speedway year. Bert decided to race for one season in California, so we packed our bags and headed west. The perpetual sunshine and easy lifestyle was certainly very seductive. We had a great time and were able to do a lot of sightseeing as well. We stayed in a trailer with all mod cons at Ken Maely's ranch out in Corona. Every day we just knew that the weather was going to be good, it was great.

Every morning I would ride down on a little Honda monkey bike motorcycle to the main road where all the mailboxes were and collect the mail. Ken also had a couple of 'guard geese' which people had to be careful of when they were visiting, they were very intimidating. The sign on the main gate read: "Beware of the geese, Trespassers will be goosed". In fact funny signs were all over the place. The one by the swimming pool said: "Welcome to our swimming ool, You will notice that there is no P in Pool, Please leave it that way".

When we came back from Bakersfield after the races at night or rather early in the morning, it used to be lovely. All was quiet, the air was balmy and there was not a lot of smog, which we could see sometimes looking towards Los Angeles on the horizon.

Left: Edith presenting a trophy to DeWayne Keeter at Ascot Park in California. Chris Agajamian, the Ascot Park promoter, is on the left.

Below: Edith presenting a trophy to Mike Bast at Ascot Park. (Note the cardboard hand protectors on the bike, to protect the rider from lumps of clay from the track.)

Bert, Edith and four times World Champion Hans Neilsen at Oxford. The cheque was for Hans winning the World Championship while wearing Scott goggles.

In those days all around the ranch were Avocado farms and Orange groves, but now it is all build on and we don't recognise the place.

I worked at Ken's making Harley Davidson seats and stitching saddle covers. This was quite hard on my hands trying to stretch the covers over the saddle and the foam. Ken had lots of irons in the fire, so to speak, because he was a very shrewd businessman. Everybody who stayed on the ranch had to do some job – mostly unpaid to earn their keep – except for me and Bert. Once there were a couple of Australians staying and after a while when they wanted to leave Ken asked them for some help with a little job. They put up a huge barn and did not get away for some time. Ken's wife Judy did the bookkeeping for him and kept house, which was a big job, because there were always racers and friends coming and going. Judy Maely and I went on a Macrame course together and when we came back to England I was busily knotting away producing flower pot hangers and had parties 'Tupperware style'. Looking back in my diary I did very well, because I sold them also to shops in the area.

Our friends Norman and Karen from Glasgow came to visit us in Corona and we had a great time. We even managed to get a ride with their Greyhound bus tickets to visit the impressive Grand Canyon after they went home.

At the end of the season we decided to take a boat back to England from New York. So we travelled across America by Amtrak train and for a bit of extra drama we also had a derailment outside Denver. Actually the trains were so slow that we could imagine some Western Outlaws riding alongside the train as in the Hollywood movies.

Once we boarded our Russian ship, the Mikhail Lermontov – which later on sunk between the North and South Island of New Zealand – in New York heading for Tilbury we were introduced to the advantages of Communism. Everything was free, Russian Balalaika lessons, Russian Dancing lessons, Tombolas (everybody won something) and Russian language classes. One evening we were asked onto the Captain's table and were plied with Russian Champagne, Russian Wine and Russian Vodka. Bert was merrily knocking everything back like a trooper and since he never drank at all I was quite surprised to see him getting up after dinner and walking back to our cabin without a wobble. There he sat on the bed, smiled at me, keeled over and was out for the count. It was so funny. The amazing thing was that he never had a hangover the next day. There was a sad ending to the trip though, since somebody jumped into the pool (probably after an evening at the Captain's table), but there was no water in it, as it was November and too cold for a swim. Therefore we made an unscheduled stop in Le Havre where a hearse awaited the coffin.

A year later we ended up in South Africa which was also a very good trip. Apartheid was still in place and we stayed in the middle of Johannesburg in an area called Hillbrow in a high rise on the 50th floor. The boys used to run up the stairs to keep fit which was quite a feat, as the air there is much thinner. From what we hear the place is now not safe anymore, but in those days it was.

We met up with friends of Freddie's and Pat's and also with Bert's pals Alex Hughson and Roni Ferguson from Scotland. Somehow whichever country we went to there were friends and we never felt alone. Even when we went on a round trip to Japan we met up with Jimmy Ogisu who took us to his house outside Tokyo. This was a great honour, as the Japanese very rarely take anybody to their home. This was just a few months before the Fukushima disaster.

We were able to take a trip around South Africa in our sponsored car and saw a lot of this beautiful place. We went with Nigel Close and Benny Rourke and the boys had an ostrich race and although the locals showed them how to do it, none of them stayed on for long. At New Year Benny got very drunk and very homesick and subsequently went home early. We were visiting Gold Mines, Diamond Mines, went up Table Mountain in Cape Town, went along the coast to Port Elizabeth, Durban and back to Jo'burg, where we got rather a nasty surprise, but I expect Bert will write all about that.

Once again on our return from South Africa I got my job back at Ovaltine. They had a staff shop and I used to have to stock up with Malted Drinks, Chocolate and Ovaltine as Bert just loved that. He used to eat spoonsful of it. Actually he still does.

Once Bert had a bad crash and to this day someone maintains that I came down to the track and told Bert off for crashing. I am still angry about this. Friends were with me and utterly dispute this.

The very next day at home we played squash. During the game all of a sudden Bert went white as a sheet and slid down the wall and collapsed. He probably had concussion at the time and did not realise it. Getting Bert to a doctor was a near impossible undertaking. We never played the game again.

In June 1978 Nig Close had a very bad accident and ended up in Edinburgh Hospital. There we met his parents Hazel and Derrick and after that we became lifelong friends. As Derrick was always working at his garage, Hazel and I had many holidays together driving up to Scotland and also to Austria. She is great company and we always had a good laugh and a 'grand time', as they say in Yorkshire.

When Bert's speedway career neared the end we had to decide what we could do for a living. We opened a shop and sold motorcycle accessories and clothing for street bikes and off road. This worked well since I could look after the shop when Bert was still riding for Edinburgh. On the day we opened for business the first person coming through the door was a Gypsy women who wanted to sell me something, I think it was a bit of lace. As I was also in the business of selling I sent her packing.

Bert also made me take a motorcycle test, because he maintained I would know at least what I was talking about to the customers. He then purchased a Yamaha 125 for me which I used to ride to work on every day from Watford to Berkhamsted in all weathers. I must say I enjoyed it quite a lot and one day while he was away I bought a Yamaha 400. He was very surprised when he came back home and saw me on a bigger bike.

After a few years we enlarged the business and became wholesale only. We were very fortunate to have several franchises and were the sole importers for the Italian Plastics company Acerbis, who make bolt on parts for all off road motorcycles from tanks to handguards and Scott goggles, accessories and clothing, who had offices in Switzerland and Sun Valley in Idaho. We then got more staff and were able to travel more again and often combined business trips with a holiday. Our holidays were always something special, we went skiing, trail riding in California, hiking in Alaska and Canada, watching the motorcycle rally in Peru with Acerbis and going to Antarctica on a cruise with our friends Alex and Evelyn from Scotland.

However, when Bert talks about his past he very rarely mentions that we worked together and had a very successful business for 30 years. He always talks about his speedway days. It is something he wanted to do and achieved it despite all the odds. As he always says it took him 10 years to become an overnight success. He now rides a motorcycle which is much too tall for him and he can only reach the ground on tiptoes. To get on he sometimes takes a flying leap which looks very funny.

It could also not have been easy for him wearing glasses. He used to have special ones when they got knocked the lens would pop out. Once in Oxford the entire track staff were on their hands and knees in the first corner looking for one lens that had dropped out. Miraculously they even found it.

Despite injuries and setbacks I can honestly say that Bert has never lost his sense of humour and to this day he makes me laugh, and has me in stitches on a regular basis. He has never changed and still has this sense of adventure and happy go lucky attitude.

Before we got married Bert did tell me that he had a little girl from a relationship in Edinburgh in 1967, but had lost touch with her. As the years went by and internet became an everyday tool I was sure that she would turn up one day, as people are often trying to find their roots. And sure enough she did get in touch. Her name is Karyn. So in 2010 we went to meet her in Holland where she lives with her husband and a little girl. Looking at her we immediately decided that a DNA test was totally superfluous. She is just like Bert in many ways with a sense of fun and despite never growing up with Bert her mannerisms are just the same. Well it's all in the genes. We have a very good relationship with her and have holidays with them on a regular basis. They are in touch every day and make up for lost time. She has brought a new dimension to our lives and I am very fond of her and her family. I could continue with lots more stories, but do not want to take over Bert's book!

27. Bedpans and broomsticks

By the beginning of October 1974, the Wimbledon track at Plough Lane had taken a bit of a beating over the previous four weeks between bad weather and stock car racing but on the night of 17 October my season and almost my career ended in the mud and sawdust of the third bend. It was the Dons' last team meeting and the season was due to end the following week with the Favre-Leuba Laurels individual meeting. That evening, we had beaten our near neighbours and rivals, Hackney 51–27 in a London Derby Challenge match where I had scored eight points in my first three rides, dropping a point the Hawks' Barry Thomas. At the interval, the Dons riders were very happy when the Wimbledon Supporters Club presented each rider with a cheque for £15, a valuable sum in those days of two valve Jawas and petrol at 11p per litre.

In the second half Supporters Club Trophy, I was leading my heat when I slid off on the greasy third bend, just a simple slide off where the rider usually gets up and walks away. My Wimbledon team mate, Trevor Hedge managed to miss me when I fell, but as I was just starting to sit up, another fellow Don, Reg Luckhurst ran straight into my back. Apart from speedway, Reg was a top grass track rider and a Country & Western singer who had made a couple of records. On that evening, I think that he was probably distracted by rehearsing his latest song and did not see me through his shale-splattered goggles as he flew down the back straight. On that slippery surface, Reg could not avoid me and I caught the full impact of his machine on my back. The crash bent his front forks under his frame and it was very fortunate that I was wearing a back protector at the time. This was not a high-tech back protector like those on the market now, but a foam one used by the horse racing jockeys. It was good enough to absorb some of the impact of the crash.

It was a sad end to Wimbledon's season with both Reg and myself taken to the local St George's Hospital by ambulance along with junior, Ian Silk who had fallen in an earlier race. Reg had a bruised knee and had been hit in an unmentionable place. I don't know if it affected his singing, but he was allowed home later that night. My injuries were rather more serious. The doctors did not want to move me. The stretcher was one of the canvas ones. The ambulance men pulled the poles out of either side and I was left lying on a trolley with the Wimbledon shale still on the canvas below my back.

Various surgeons checked me out and I had so many X-rays that I thought I was in an X-rated movie. I was put into the Edward Wilson Ward (I wondered if they had a Ray Wilson Ward) and the doctors gave their verdict. I had dislodged five vertebrae and they could operate to repair the damage, but without a 100 per cent guarantee of success. Or I could opt to lie flat on my back without moving left or right for 12 weeks and everything may go back into place. I did not want the gamble of an operation, so I accepted the 'offer' of spending three months flat on my back. Three months is a long time to have to lie on your back without moving, but when I thought of some of my other injured friends in wheelchairs, it did not sound so bad.

I was well looked after in St George's with at least nine doctors and specialists checking me over from time-to-time. Within a few days, the 'Get Well' cards and messages began arriving from fans and every day the postman struggled in with an ever-larger mail delivery. The most frustrating time was on the week after I had had my accident. On the Thursday evening I could hear the sound of the bikes drifting over from The Laurels meeting at Wimbledon as I lay in my bed and wished that I could have been there. I had even asked team manager, Cyril Maidment to turn up the volume on the loud speakers so that I could fill in a programme, but that didn't work.

The other thing I could hear from my upside-down position was the sound of the big jets flying overhead. The sound of those great engines always gave me itchy feet and I knew that I should have been on one of them heading for Australia when the European season ended, but this year, it wasn't to be. I comforted myself by saying that I could do with a rest after racing almost 12 months of the year since my debut season in Australia in the winter of 1967–68, but I found it hard to convince myself that this was the case.

After The Laurels meeting was finished that evening, Ivan Mauger popped in to see me. It was 11pm and well after visiting hours, but I had the nurses well trained and they let him in. Poor Ivan looked so tired after his long string of meetings that I almost struggled out of bed and offered it to him for the night. It was very nice of Ivan to take the time to call in during his busy schedule, but he didn't stay as he thought that my Scottish Bed & Breakfast prices were far too high.

Another welcome visitor was my former Edinburgh promoter, Ian Hoskins. Ian came into the ward looking very serious indeed having feared the worst, but once he knew that I could wiggle my toes and move my arms, he relaxed. We had a good old chinwag about my novice days at Old Meadowbank in Edinburgh and the history and future of Scottish speedway.

As the weeks went by I passed the time by counting the cracks in the ward ceiling, I wasn't in much pain, so I tried to return to writing my columns for *Speedway Star* and *Speedway Express*. This proved more difficult than I thought as my Biro pen kept running out by being used upside down. I persevered and my 'Speedway World of Bert Harkins' column was changed to 'The Upside Down Speedway World of Bert Harkins'. Those caption writers at *Speedway Star* had a weird sense of humour!

Another difficulty I had was trying to drink while lying flat on my back. This problem was solved by Wimbledon's number one fan, Mrs Dorothy Charles-Batson, who supplied me with a box of drinking straws which hinged in the middle, a simple but worthwhile invention.

Probably the biggest problem with not being able to get out of bed was the daily 'Battle of the Bedpan'. It is extremely difficult to perform those bodily functions while lying flat on your back, but I won't elaborate just in case you are having your dinner whilst reading this chapter. Only to say that because I could not sit up, the nurses slid a flat inflatable bed pan under my backside and then blew it up with a bicycle pump. Very high tech, but it worked.

Edith and I were living in Leavesden Green near Watford at the time and she was driving from Hertfordshire to Wimbledon in South London to visit me every day, clocking up some 400 miles per week back and forward through the busy London traffic. It was a tiring journey for Edith, but I think that I was more worried about all those extra miles of wear and tear being put onto my car. The doctors agreed that when possible I would be transferred to a more specialist hospital, The Royal Orthopaedic Hospital at Stanmore in Middlesex. It was nearer home and that would save Edith from those long journeys through London every day.

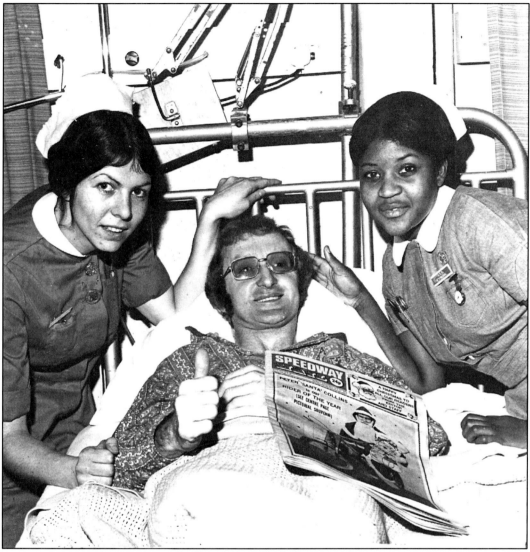

Bert in hospital after his serious back injury at Wimbledon in October 1974, with two of the nurses who cared for him.

On Thursday 14 November, just over three weeks since my accident and still flat on my back, I was transferred by ambulance to The Royal Orthopaedic Hospital in Stanmore and I settled down to my new life in Ward One. The orthopaedic specialist who treated me was a Mr Bendall, a worrying name for a bone doctor. The weeks went by, but I never got bored during that time as there was always something happening or plenty of visitors to see me.

The speedway fans were amazing with the postman struggling with over 300 cards including one from Eddie Jancarz and Zenon Plech's team manager / minder Bernard 'Twiggie' Kowalski in Poland.

George, the pits marshal at Wimbledon had lent me a portable television which helped to pass the time. I remember that an Irishman called Paddy was admitted to Ward One to have a new hip fitted and he made the classic remark, "What time is the Nine O' Clock News on tonight, Jock?" I think that he did that on purpose, but more about Paddy later.

Another fellow patient in Ward One was Solomon, a young man from Saudi Arabia. Solomon had broken his neck in a car crash in his home country and had been flown to the UK for specialist treatment. He was also lying flat on his back, but he had a bolt through his temple to stretch his vertebrae, similar to the gadget young Tony Briggs had on his head after his crash at Coventry some years later. Solomon had a mirror above his head so that he could see what was going on in the ward, so we managed to communicate that way. He was also due to stay in Stanmore for several months. His sister Delilah had flown over from Saudi to be with him. With daily visits to the hospital, she and Edith soon became friends. At one stage, Delilah had to fly back to Saudi Arabia for a week before returning to the UK. This time she had brought a present, it was a brass camel with a rug on its back. "Here", she said to Edith, "give this to Bert and tell him to ride this instead of a motorcycle." It was a lovely gesture, but it wasn't going to stop me from eventually riding my speedway bike again.

The days and the weeks passed by and I was still lying there in the same position. I guess you could say that it was not the first time Bert Harkins had been 'flat out'. The doctors were still a bit worried and kept testing the reflexes in my legs and when I heard that there was to be a London Speedway Honours Ball in January, I made it my aim to be out of the hospital and be fit enough to attend. I mentioned the event to the doctor and asked "Doctor, will I be able to dance when I get out of hospital?" The doctor graciously replied, "Yes you will, Mr Harkins". "Gee, that's great" I replied, "I couldn't dance a step before I came in here."

It was decided that I would be fitted with a special corset and allowed to get out of bed and into a wheelchair in time for Christmas. I had to get fitted for this made-to-measure corset and time dragged by as I had one fitting, then a week later another fitting until finally the corset arrived on 20 December, nine weeks after my crash. It arrived and the nurses raised me up gently to fit the contraption, but after lying flat on my back for over two months, I was so dizzy that they had to lower me down again. Eventually, the nurses managed to sit me upright, but the room was spinning and I felt sick. This was not as easy as I thought it would be. The corset consisted of a wide body belt type of corset with straps and steel rods coming out of either side with padded cradles which sat under my armpits to keep my back straight. Quite a contraption. That first day, they got me up in a wheelchair, but only for half an hour and that was enough. I needed seat belts in that wheelchair because the room was still spinning. I had to get back to bed and lie down again.

Next day, I managed to spend two and a half hours in the wheelchair before I felt nauseous and by the Sunday I managed to take my first steps since the accident supported by a nurse at either side. I was wobbling and my legs felt like jelly – or soggy porridge for a Scot – but with the nurses at my side it was a good incentive to start walking. By coincidence, my new Saudi friend, Solomon, was also taking his first steps that day and that was the first time we had seen each other face-to-face.

By Christmas morning, the doctors decided that if I wore the corset and someone helped me then I could go home for the day so Freddie Williams and his brother-in-law, Ned,

166

wheeled me out of the hospital, lifted me into their car and drove me home. My mum had come down from Glasgow so we all had a nice Christmas dinner and I stayed at home overnight before going back into Stanmore the following day, Boxing Day to complete the rest of my 'Sentence'.

Hogmanay came and went in Ward One and I was unable to toast in the New Year with my new Irish friend, Paddy, because he had been released a few days earlier with a brand new hip fitted.

By early January, some 13 weeks since the 'incident' the doctors decided that they would let me go and allow me to recuperate at home. Hallelujah!

Two weeks later, on 18 January 1975 and fitted with my new straight-jacket corset, I was able to make my first public appearance since October when Edith and I went along to the London Speedway Honours Ball. Despite what the doctors had said, I was still unable to dance. My British Lions mate, Chris Pusey was there from the 'Far North' as he had shared the title of the 'Most thrilling visitor to London' award along with Terry Betts. I picked up the 'London team rider of the Year' trophy so as least I had something to show for my previous season other than bedsores and bedpans. Other awards went to Ted Hubbard who won the 'Top London Junior' trophy; 'The Most Improved Junior' award was shared by Steve Lomas and Dave Morton with team mate, Laurie Etheridge accepting Dave's trophy in his absence and Hackney's Norwegian star, Dag Lovaas won the 'Mr London' trophy which was accepted by Hackney's Barry Thomas on Dag's behalf.

January rolled into February and on into March and I was still wearing my corset and attending Stanmore Orthopaedic Hospital on a regular basis, but still hoping to be able to ride again. The new 1975 speedway season came around and started without me, much to my disappointment, but Wimbledon were doing OK without me. Eventually, I was able to do without my corset and in April Doctor Thompson gave me the all clear to return to the saddle.

I made my comeback at Wimbledon on 17 April, six months after that tough night at Plough Lane. Everything went very well in that first meeting with the Dons beating Exeter 40–38 – that old moto, 'Happiness is 40–38' – and I scored 7 paid 8 in my first three rides, dropping a point to Exeter's Flying Falcon, American, Scott Autrey. After that early burst of power, I was still not race-fit and I tired and trailed in last in my final two races. Perhaps I had returned to where I had left off before my injury, or perhaps it was just that the other riders were keeping out of my way to avoid causing me any more injuries. Who knows? But at least I could say "Bert's back," in more ways than one.

Throughout my long hospitalisation my spirits (not whisky) had been kept up by the many speedway folk and friends who visited me or wrote to me in hospital. That was most welcome, but there was one blot on the landscape.

As I mentioned earlier, Edith was driving 400 miles a week to visit me when I was in hospital so when I was still in Ward One, I wrote one of my 'upside down' letters to the Speedway Riders' Benevolent Fund in London to ask for some financial assistance and explaining the circumstances. I also told the SRBF that I did not like having to write to ask for help and that I was not begging for charity. Speedway fans always gave generously to the track collections and still do and I said that I thought that the purpose of the Benevolent Fund was to help injured riders.

I was told by the Ben Fund that I should ask George Burrows Ltd., the speedway riders' insurance company (we paid into that each week and a sum was deducted from our points money) for an loan advance of £100 on the money I would be paid later when I would be eventually signed off as fit to race again. This was insurance money I had already paid into and nothing to do with the SRBF.

I was really shocked and angry about this and told the SRBF that I did not know how much more serious an injured rider had to be to receive any help from them. It wasn't as if I was an outpatient at the hospital, the doctors were estimating that I would be there for three months, so surely that would qualify a rider for some kind of help. This was a long-time injury scenario and we were just living on our savings. I also mentioned in my letter that my insurance money should be nothing to do with deciding if the SRBF would help or not. At that time I had been in hospital for eight weeks and eventually the Ben Fund sent me £40, a meagre sum for such a long term injury. I don't usually get angry, but I wrote back asking them if this was some kind of a joke. It was probably not the wisest thing to do but I had to vent my pent-up feelings and frustration.

My former Wembley team manager and double World Champion, Freddie Williams came to my rescue by contacting the Fund personally. He gave them a few home truths and he succeeded in getting a £100 payment from the fund.

Fortunately, today's injured riders do not have to go through such embarrassment when they get injured. The modern Speedway Riders' Benevolent Fund is run so very much better by former FIM referee, Paul Ackroyd and any injured riders are contacted immediately and offered assistance. Back in the1970s, I thought that the Ben Fund seemed to be like a secret society. I thought that it was difficult to find anything out about their finances, but now everything is transparent and the fans can rely on the money they donate being given to help the injured riders.

Enjoying a grass track outing in Kent.

Riding in Kempten in West Germany.

Left: Speaking at the Wimbledon Dinner Dance in 1973, with Edith listening.

Below: With my team mates at the 1974 Wimbledon Dinner Dance; from left: Roger Johns, Trevor Hedge, Graham Stapleton, Barry Briggs, Reg Luckhurst, Bert and Neil Cameron.

170

28. Two comebacks

The 1975 season rolled on and my injuries healed as I began trying to make up for lost time with Wimbledon. I was still racing in Germany and Austria from time-to-time, so the more I raced, the more my fitness improved.

Apart from my Wimbledon duties there was another important fixture on the horizon, the qualifying round of the World Team Cup at Reading in July where Scotland would take on the might of England, Australia and New Zealand. Scotland were the underdogs because the other three teams had their 'big hitters' in their side, but we Scots could usually rise to the occasion when we pulled on that Saltire body colour of Scotland. The Kiwis may have had two world champions with Briggo and Mauger, England were so strong that Malcolm Simmons was only in the reserve berth and they had 'World Cup Willie', Ray Wilson with Peter Collins and DJ, Dave Jessup. The Scots had Jim McMillan, George Hunter, Bobby Beaton and me with Brian Collins at reserve. We all had international experience, were riding well and aimed to qualify for the Final in Norden in Germany. Of course, the other three teams had the same idea.

In addition to trying to reach the World Final, the Scots were fighting for our very existence in FIM events. We had already almost lost our World Team Cup place to Ireland and were still in danger of being dropped from the Cup, so we had a lot to play for.

But, once again, as Scotland's most famous poet, Robert Burns wrote "The best laid plans o' mice and men gang aft a-gley" which more or less means that no matter how carefully you plan something, it can all go wrong, and go wrong it certainly did.

Only 10 days before the World Team Cup, I was riding in the London Riders' Championship at Hackney when, in my second race, the Hawks' Mike Broadbank rode into my left leg and broke it again, shades of déjà vu of my clash with Rick Woods in California. That was the end of my evening's racing and also the end of my dreams of riding for Scotland in the World Team Cup.

It was a Friday night and the ambulance whisked me off to the nearby Hackney Hospital, a pretty dull and drab place at that time. I was taken down to have some X-rays on my leg and when they came back, the duty doctor looked at the X-ray plate and said – I still remember his exact words – "It is only slightly broken so we will put him in the ward and the doctor will see him on Monday". Monday! This was only Friday night, I was in a lot of pain and didn't think I could last over the weekend.

The X-rays showed that the steel pin which was put into my leg when I broke it at Indio Speedway in California was bent and it was holding the break apart. No wonder I did not feel too comfortable. If I had stayed until Monday, gangrene would probably have set in.

Edith came to the rescue again and said "Let's get Bert to Stanmore, they will look after him." My friends Alex Wood and Ron Day carried me out of Hackney Hospital, lowered me into their car and drove me back to Stanmore Orthopaedic. We arrived there at 2am and I was asked if I had been admitted at Hackney. Fortunately, I had been 'evacuated' from there before any paperwork could be completed, otherwise they may not have accepted me at Stanmore. The next part of my journey was quite dramatic. Here I was in the same hospital

I had left just a few months previously. I was wheeled into the same ward, Ward One. Not only that, but into the same bed that I had lain on for three months.

I have to admit that this was a low point for me. After I had damaged my back at Wimbledon and the doctors told me that I had to spend three months lying flat on my back, I mentally prepared myself to accept that. I knew that if I did as I was told, I would be fit again, so I just took each day as it came and did not get stressed at having such a long 'sentence'. This time it was more difficult because it almost felt like a continuation of my previous visit and I had to accept that 'Here I am again'.

I had been admitted to Stanmore at 2am on the Saturday night and the surgeon operated on my leg at 9am on the Sunday morning. If I had not been able to get out of Hackney, I would have been lying there over the whole weekend until Monday with a bent steel pin in my leg holding the break apart. I shudder when I think of that scenario.

This time, I was only in for a week until they plastered me up. They fitted me out with some crutches and led me to the door saying "Goodbye, Bert, no doubt we will see you again soon." One thing that had lifted my spirits despite being back in the same ward and the same bed, was when my Irish friend, Paddy surprisingly came back in to get his other hip replaced. He came down the ward, saw me lying there and said "Jesus, Jock, are ye still here?" Ah yes, no matter what life throws at you, there is always a sunny lining somewhere, so thanks for that, Paddy.

And so I missed riding for Scotland in the World Team Cup where England won with 37 points ahead of Australia on 24, New Zealand on 21 and Scotland 14. England were flying high that year and went on to win the Final in Norden ahead of the Soviet Union, Sweden and Poland in front of 20,000 fans.

And so I was out of action again, this time for six weeks. I had another battle with the Benevolent Fund to get some help which eventually came in the form of a cheque for £60.

I eventually made my second comeback of 1975 in September, after a long nine week layoff, with my first continental meetings at Felixdorf in Germany on the Saturday and Krems in Austria on the Sunday. Then it was back to Wimbledon for my first match back at Plough Lane. It was a challenge match against Newport and I had two wins and a second in my first three races, so I was back in the groove again. I even got to race for my beloved Scotland in an international challenge at the end of the season at Newcastle. England beat us 59–48 and I collected nine points.

It was now October and the season was coming to an end so two days later I was at Heathrow Airport and on my way back to sunny California for a couple of meetings at 'Shinbone Alley'. I was a glutton for punishment. The Californian season was also coming to a close so these last few meetings were a nice way to end the year and have a little holiday.

During this visit, Costa Mesa announcer/presenter, Larry Huffman offered Edith and me the chance to stay in his log cabin at Big Bear Lake, some 100 miles north east of Los Angeles. This sounded a great idea and I gladly accepted Larry's kind offer. Before handing me the keys to the cabin, Larry produced some A4 pages for me to sign as an agreement. The pages had such conditions as, "I will not sue the owner if I fall and break my leg". "I will not sue the owner if I get eaten by a bear" and many other legal clauses. "Hey, Larry", I said, "I don't need to sign this, we are friends and I would never sue you if anything goes wrong."

172

"Sorry, Bert", he replied. "This is America and we have to cover ourselves for everything." I signed the paperwork, but thought that it was all a bit strange. But now it has come here from the US and we have the same compensation culture here in the UK. It's a crazy world.

Apart from our weekend in Big Bear, where we did not see any bears, and visits to Bell Helmets, Troy Lee and Justice Bothers, plus the usual Disneyland and Knotts Berry Farm trips, we also went to the big Motorcycle Show in Las Vegas with Ken and Judy Maely.

Scott USA had a booth at the Motorcycle Show and I spent some time chatting to them about goggles, glasses and speedway and my difficulties on mixing the three together. I was tempted to ask them if they had anyone importing their Scott goggles to the UK, but I chickened out, I was too reticent to ask. On leaving the show, we were walking across the car park to Ken's van when I suddenly said "Hold on, I am going back in to talk to Scott".

That 'light bulb moment' had a major impact in the years to come as this conversation led to us becoming the sole UK importers for Scott goggles and accessories when we opened our business.

After that busy visit to California, it was back to Los Angeles Airport and back on the TWA big bird bound for Heathrow. A winter at home for the only second time in many years, or so I thought.

In the lead for Wimbledon against Reading Racers' Anders Michanek.

The Scotland team that raced against England twice in 1973, winning at Coatbridge and losing at Halifax. Back: Jimmy Gallagher, Bobby Beaton, Neil MacFarlane (team manager), Andy Meldrum, Charlie Monk (Honorary Scot); Front: Bert, Jim McMillan, George Hunter, Alistair Brady.

29. Israel

This time there was no Australian and New Zealand winter racing for me. The only other time I had missed my winter trip down under was when I spent my off-season 'holiday' in Stanmore Orthopaedic Hospital, but this winter it was going to be different.

I had already agreed with Harry Oxley that I would come to California to race in the new American League for the 1976 season, so it was 'Goodbye Wimbledon' and 'Goodbye British speedway' for a while. The American season was not due to start until the middle of April, but something else new and exciting was coming along before then and I was soon back in the saddle again.

World Champion Series organisers, Barry Briggs and Ivan Mauger along with Costa Mesa promoter, Harry Oxley and PACE Sports promoter, Allan Becker had been negotiating on taking speedway to Israel for the very first time to stage a USA versus Rest of The World series in the Holy Land. They asked me to join the tour as their sole UK – and Scottish – representative. Allan Becker had prior knowledge of staging other sports in Israel, but this was the first time for motorcycle racing.

As far as I know, this was the first time that any motorsport had been staged in Israel, so there were a lot of technical and legal obstacles to overcome. The idea was that Harry Oxley would bring his seven man team out from California along with bikes, fuel and even the starting gate. American track builder, Spike Frownfelter would build the tracks in Tel Aviv and Beer-Sheba and we would go racing.

The USA team was to be Bruce Penhall, Rick Woods, Sonny Nutter, Dubb Ferrel, Steve Bast, Scott Sivadge and Mike Caruso. Our Rest of The World team was Ove Fundin (Sweden), Barry Briggs (New Zealand), Oyvind Berg (Norway), Josef Angermuller (Germany), Frank Shuter (New Zealand), Bengt Larsson (Sweden) and Bert Harkins (Scotland); quite an international line-up.

The Israeli Customs officers were not too helpful to us when bringing in all this equipment and shoved import duty on the racing fuel which made it work out around £25 per gallon. The promoters, Briggo & Co. had to pay this just to get the show on the road.

When we arrived, it was raining for the first two days which upset the schedule and our first meeting was rained off. This was just as well as our bikes had been held up by Israeli customs and because Saturday was the Jewish Sabbath there was no work done on that day.

The tracks were basically athletics tracks, around 400 yards long and quite narrow. The local health & safety officials were not too impressed with what we intended to do, race 500cc motorcycles with no brakes on an athletics track so they insisted on having a double 'safety fence' to protect the local residents. The tracks already had a wire fence, but we then had to line the outside of the track with straw bales in front of the wire fence thus making it even narrower. Another problem we encountered, similar to when we did that charity meeting for the San Marco High School in California, was that our speedway tyres were tearing up the surface of the running track. Briggo then had another of his brainwaves. We cut all the knobbles off of our rear tyres and rode with bald tyres. It hurt me to see these new tyres being chopped around, but it seemed to do the trick and even made the bikes a little bit easier to ride. The only problem was that some tyres were not cut as deeply as others, so everyone wanted the bikes with that little bit of extra tread and grip on the tyre.

The straw bales caused some problems too and with the flying dust, I sometimes rode too close to the bales and heard someone yelling at the top of his voice "Oi, Oi, Oi!" It was Barry Briggs – I had almost run him into the bales. Worse was to come in my last race when, disorientated by the dust, I moved just a little too far out on the straight and my right footrest hooked the straw bales. The bike stopped dead and I did a 'Flying Scotsman' act over the handlebars. Briggo came to my aid again by finding my goggles and also the lens which had been knocked out of my glasses. I was pretty well knocked around, nothing was broken, just badly bruised. However, at least the injuries got me out of the job of loading the bikes and gear onto our lorry transporter for a whole week of our five match tour.

The race programmes were written in Hebrew, so we had to have a local as pits marshal to tell us when we had to go out to race. Briggo had recently been awarded an MBE in The Queen's Honours List and that confused the announcer who introduced him to the crowd as "Sir Barry Briggs" something that Briggo did not bother to correct.

The racing was always fast and furious. The Americans just did not want to be beaten and us Europeans did not want to lose to a country from 'the new world' so every race meeting was treated like a World Final. The rivalry between the two teams was hard but, when Germany's Josef Angermuller, 'Sepp', sustained a nasty leg injury America's Rick Woods came to the rescue. Using an old Red Indian – Native American – remedy, Rick peeled the outer skin from a cactus plant and bandaged it to Sepp's leg as a poultice. Josef was able to ride again in our next meeting.

Being in the Holy Land was quite thought-provoking, it was like walking through the Bible with all the biblical names. Between speedway meetings, we had some guided tours which made me think that I should have paid more attention when I attended the local Church Sunday School in Glasgow.

In the spare evenings, the Americans would noisily head into Tel Aviv to paint it red, or red, white and blue, but the Europeans were a little quieter and more subtle. Josef Angermuller would often head into town on his own and usually finished up being surrounded by Israeli girls on the dancefloor. Sepp was so popular with the local girls that the whole USA team wanted to go into town with him.

We travelled to meetings by a special bus and found out that most of the Israelis were on standby for the Army in case of trouble. Our bus driver had the rank of Major in the Army and explained that the bus he was driving could be quickly converted to carry troops or arms at a moment's notice. Fortunately, that did not happen on our trip and we were quite safe.

We also had some time to spend on the beach, which suited our surf-loving Californians. Ove Fundin preferred to visit the local museums and art galleries instead. 'Bruce's Beach Boys' were always out to have some fun, but it almost backfired when they tried to trick their star man, Rick Woods. Rick was fast asleep on his bed when the others tied a cord around his big toe. They then opened the taps and left the water running in the washbasin with the idea that Rick would subconsciously hear the running water and want to go to the toilet. It worked OK, but when Rick jumped out of bed and fell flat on the floor, he was not amused and chased the Americans down the corridor aiming Kung Fu kicks at them.

On track, the two teams were quite evenly matched with the scores at two wins all going into the last match in which our Rest of The World team won by a narrow two point score. The first, and it now looks like being the only, Israeli Open Championship was won by Norwegian, Oyvind Berg with Ove Fundin second and Bruce Penhall third. Oyvind's win may never be equalled as there are no plans for speedway to return to Israel in the future.

It was a successful two week tour with good crowds. Speedway racing had been a bit of a novelty for the Israelis and it was doubtful if speedway would ever return to the Holy Land. At least the 14 riders who took part in this experiment could say 'I was there'.

When the trip was over, we all flew back to our various homes in the USA and across Europe. Fortunately it had been a short tour because I when I flew back into Heathrow Airport, I was only home for a week before returning to Heathrow and jetting off again, this time to Los Angeles and the new American Speedway League.

Photo: An example of the Israeli newspaper coverage of the meetings, with a photo of Bert in action at Tel Aviv.

USA versus the Rest of the World – the teams line up together. Rest of the World: Edward Jancarz (Poland), Martin Ashby (England), Chris Pusey (England), Barry Briggs (New Zealand), Bert Harkins (Scotland), Zenon Plech (Poland), Ivan Mauger (New Zealand; USA: Scott Autrey, Danny Becker, Bill Cody, Steve Bast, Sonny Nutter, Mike Caruso, Mike Bast.

At the start in a USA versus Rest of the World meeting.
From left: Zenon Plech, Scott Autrey, Bert, Bill Cody.

30. A star-spangled Haggis

Sitting in a TWA Boeing jet, somewhere between London and Los Angeles in April 1976, I got that feeling again: 'What are you doing this time, Harkins?' For a seasoned speedway rider-cum-traveller, I was still prone to make some unusual decisions, and this was the result of one of them. I was forsaking British speedway and on my way to California with my wife, Edith, to join the new American National Speedway League.

Ever since my first racing trip to America in 1969, when I was the first British League rider to race at Costa mesa I had the notion of spending one full season on the speedway tracks of California, and this time I was eventually succumbing to Harry Oxley's invitation to race in California. Previously each time I came back home to race in the UK and try to reach the World Final.

So why I was feeling a little doubtful during that flight to the States? Owing to a dispute between the American Motorcycle Association, which governs all motorcycle racing in the United States, and the Speedway Racing Association, which sanctions speedway racing in California, my international licence could have been in jeopardy. Also, it was not clear which of the five teams I would join. All in all, not a good start to a new season.

It did not seem quite right to be leaving Britain in the springtime when the racing there was beginning to awaken after the winter. Previous American trips were sandwiched between speedway meetings in Britain and Australia and were always enjoyable. This time I was on my way, and the thought of a full season in California began to excite me. With five tracks, Costa Mesa, Irwindale, Ventura, Bakersfield and San Bernadino all fielding teams in the new league, it could be a bumper season.

I knew that the racing technique in the USA was quite different from elsewhere. Sonny Nutter, the sage of American speedway once said "There is speedway and there is American speedway, and that is a whole new ballgame."

Speedway had come to America in the 1930s and, as in Britain, pulled in huge crowds before the War. Clark Gable and several other Hollywood stars became avid fans and, in 1933, the California Highway Patrol – the State Traffic Police – staged the National Short Track Championship in the Los Angeles Coliseum.

It was won by Cordy Milne and, after touring Australia with his brother Jack in 1935, they headed for England where they put their names in speedway history in a big way. Jack and Cordy still had many of their old trophies, so many that some were stashed away in cardboard boxes and stored in the garage. Jack was instrumental in the return of speedway to California in 1968 and, with co-promoter, Harry Oxley, ran the show at the exciting Orange County Fairgrounds in Costa Mesa and at Ventura. Jack enjoyed talking about 'the old days' but was more concerned to put on a good show for the fans who flocked to his tracks than boasting of his World Championship and other successes. He had a reputation as a golfer and had shown another former World Champion, Barry Briggs, the quickest way around a golf course.

America, as we know it in Britain, is the land of big cars, skyscrapers and spaghetti-like freeways, where everything is larger-than-life compared to the rest of the world. Everything, that is, except speedway tracks.

In Britain, tracks vary between 280 to around 440 yards long, in Australia, up to 600 and 700 yards long, but in California, the tracks averaged around 180 yards. So small that after riding four laps, I returned to the pits and felt inclined to ride another four laps in the opposite direction to unwind.

The promoters reckoned that the smaller tracks produced more exciting racing, and they were right. Throughout America, almost every town has a Fairground where the annual state or county fair is held. Many of these have small horse show rings where rodeos and cattle shows are staged. These can be easily converted into speedway tracks. Since its revival in the late 1960s, American – or rather Californian speedway – had been purely on an individual basis with scratch and handicap events.

There was no team racing except for the annual USA versus Rest of the World matches which took place when Ivan Mauger and Barry Briggs brought their team of travelling all-stars across the Atlantic. These needle matches were very popular with the American fans and always produced exciting racing and close results because, no matter how strong the Rest of the World team was, the Yanks' expertise on their small tracks counteracted the world team's experience.

For eight seasons, speedway racing boomed in California, and, although the crowds had not dropped, Harry Oxley thought that the time was ripe for change. It was decided to form a league and introduce team racing for the first time since pre-war days, when they had teams like the Glendale Ghosts.

The promoters of the five tracks got together and 'drafted' their teams. Thus Ventura Sharks would be captained by Sonny Nutter, Orange County Eagles of Costa Mesa by Rick Woods, Bakersfield Bandits by Jeff Sexton, San Bernadino Sizzlers by Larry Shaw and the Los Angeles Sprockets from Irwindale by national American champion, Mike Bast. The American National League had been born, but as expected, it had some growing pains.

My thoughts of the wisdom in leaving a good career in British League were suddenly interrupted by the air hostess announcing that we were now approaching Los Angeles. I rubbed the sleep from my eyes and peered out of the window onto the clouds beneath us.

Suddenly, the plane broke through the layer of yellow smog and, there twinkling in all its glory, was Los Angeles, City of Angels. We landed and, as we taxied up to the International Terminal, the captain concluded his little speech of welcome by adding "Now that the safest part of your journey is over, please drive home safely". I wondered if he was an American speedway fan in disguise.

Promoter Harry Oxley and his wife Marilyn collected us from the airport along with New Zealander, Frank Shuter, who had arrived on an earlier flight. It was not until we were whizzing down the Santa Ana Freeway to Harry's Spanish-style home at San Clemente that I learned that I had been allocated to Bakersfield, 150 miles north of Los Angeles.

I must admit that I was not too enthusiastic about the whole set-up because, during a visit to the States the previous November, I had made a verbal agreement that I would ride for Costa Mesa. I had nothing against Bakersfield, but I was 'known' at Costa Mesa so it would be slightly easier to obtain sponsors there. Another little problem was that Bakersfield was the furthest track from where I wanted to be based; not that distance is ever any object, but American speedway did not then pay travelling expenses to the riders, and that hits a Scotsman where it hurts – in the sporran.

Nevertheless, my stay with the Bandits was very enjoyable and we had a good, solid team which was helped immensely by a great promoter, Marshall 'Digger' Helm. 'Digger' as he was known, got his nickname because he was the local undertaker and indeed, the Bakersfield programme is the only one in the world in which I have seen an advert for the local cemetery, Greenlawns. Digger had always managed to spring a surprise or two, and he had another one in store this time.

Prior to the opening of the 1976 season, press conferences had been held and the concept of team racing explained. It was decided not to have the teams use body colours or helmet covers as in Britain then, but to supply each member with a made-to-measure set of leathers in his team colours. The leathers had the rider's name and number on the back, and the helmets would also be painted in team colours with the rider's number. Los Angeles' colours were blue and yellow, Ventura black, red and yellow, San Bernadino white, blue and red, Orange County orange (of course) and Bakersfield – purple. I had never heard of a team using purple as its colours but, knowing Digger's occupation, I can see why it was his favourite colour.

Now I was about to become a purple star-spangled haggis.

The sideways circus

The slick presentation made speedway the most exciting motor sport in California. Take Costa Mesa for example. The track was small and superbly floodlit and the spectators were close to the action. It was just like watching a race in your living room.

The individual programme opened with the handicap races. Six heats, with six riders per race and the first three qualifying for the semi-finals. Three semi-finals and the top two from each race transfer to the final, or 'Main Event'. After the semi-finals, the scratch heats followed, with four riders in each race. Four scratch heats with the first and second rider qualifying for the semi-final in the second half of the programme. A short interval allowed the fans to visit the beer and hot dog stands, then on with the show. Usually, a couple of special match races took place between some of the crowd's favourite riders, then it was onto the 'biff-and-bang' racing of the second division (junior) riders including the appropriately named "Tumbleweed", Pat Walton, so called because every week he would tumble along the track like the tumbleweed from a Western movie.

They had four scratch heats with the winners progressing to the final and often a few rather hairy handicap races. The meeting progressed with the semi-finals and consolation races, then wound up with the 'Main Events' of the handicap and scratch races, and presentation of trophies. All in all, a great night's entertainment which sent the fans home eagerly looking forward to the next meeting.

The new team racing formula gave the fans 12 heats of team racing with heat 13 a 'nominated riders' race for the top two in each team, similar to the heat 15 in British league meetings today. There were to be no drawn matches in the American League so, if the scores were level after heat 13, a deciding match-race took place between the next highest scorer from each team.

After the interval, the second half comprised about 12 heats of handicap events for first and second division riders. No one dared leave the stadium before the final race just in case they missed something. With such tight corners on the little tracks, the riders had to put their bikes into a slide on the straight and 'back-it-in' to the corners almost rear wheel first. No wonder I called it the 'sideways circus'.

So, the stage was set for the five team league, with such colourful names as Sharks, Sizzlers, Sprockets, Bandits and Eagles. Ventura opened the season with a nail-biting match against San Bernadino. Although light rain was falling, the meeting went ahead as planned. At the end of the nominated riders heat, the scores were tied 36–36. A run-off was held in heat 14, but due to a misunderstanding, both teams fielded two riders and the resulting 3–3 kept the scores level. Another 'decider' was held and the Sizzlers won by one point.

The next night, Wednesday, the rain persisted and San Bernadino had to cancel their first meeting. Irwindale's opening meeting was also threatened by rain, but by 4pm on race day, the rain stopped, the wind began to blow the clouds away and the sun came out. The track still had a lot of water, but after soaking it up with 100 tons of decomposed granite, and binding and tyre-packing the surface, the track was ready to race on. The visiting Orange County Eagles put up a great show before losing by two points, 43–41. But the victory cost Los Angeles the services of the experienced Mike Konle who fell and broke his wrist.

Costa Mesa's opening night saw 10,000 fans jammed into the Orange County Fairground stadium. As the riders were paid a percentage of the gate money, the huge crowd was welcomed by everyone. Bakersfield Bandits were the visitors, but we were unable to topple the Eagles that night. We were four points down going into the nominated riders race, but Bill Cody and Alan Christian took another 5–I to make the final score 43–35 to the Eagles.

The next evening at Bakersfield, we had a real battle on our hands against Sonny Nutter and his Ventura Sharks. The scores seesawed throughout the match and, with it tied after heat 13, another decider was required. This time, Ventura's Randy Marsh took the win over Dubb Ferrell to give the Sharks that narrow, one point victory. 'Jaws' had claimed another victim. So, the opening week of the season had San Bernadino and the Los Angeles Sprockets at the top of the league, and our Bakersfield Bandits firmly at the bottom. We were the only team to have raced two matches and we lost both of them.

The handicap final of that first Bakersfield meeting was dominated by two riders who had not signed for a team in the pre-season draft. Local rider Dan Toomey won the handicap main event, with Jim Gresham in second place. Both riders were riding for the Bandits a few weeks later. Jim was the elder brother of Steve Gresham who had a successful career in the British League.

The five league teams were all evenly matched, and last heat deciders took place almost every match. Throughout April and May, San Bernadino and the LA Sprockets swapped the top spot in the league. The Sizzlers, named after a chain of steak houses in California, slipped when the Sprockets outrode them on the fast Irwindale track and won by a gigantic 26 points. Most teams had difficulties when racing the Sprockets on their home track, mainly because of the longer straights and extra traction on the turns. Mike Bast was almost unbeatable around Irwindale and a young Bruce Penhall provided excellent back up to him.

Later, San Bernadino climbed back to the top with a 42–36 win at Ventura despite a fine 14 points from the Sharks' Scott Sivadge. In the second half of that meeting, 19 year old flat track racer, Steve Fortune of Anaheim, made his debut on a speedway track. Steve had raced a 750cc Yamaha in Class C events at Ascot Park. He celebrated his first speedway meeting by winning his handicap final. Soon, Steve was signed by Irwindale. He had a neat van with the logo on the side which read, "Wheels of Fortune"

On a hot evening on 12 May, the LA Sprockets came to San Bernadino, hoping for a win to put them back in top spot. Bruce Penhall notched a great 14 points from five rides and Mike Bast collected 10, but it was not enough to stop San Bernadino winning 42–36. Big Jim Fishback, the 'Iron Man' of the league, led the Sizzlers scoring with 11 points. Fishback, nicknamed, 'The Animal' by the adoring San Bernadino fans, was one of the State's top desert racers and had a reputation for being indestructible. A sort of 'Million Dollar Man' on wheels. Big Jim's exploits in the desert races were legendary.

In a desert race he once collided with a water truck while travelling at high speed. He just picked his bike up, pulled the forks straight, and carried on with the race. Rumour has it that the water truck did not get away so lightly. On speedway tracks Jim was equally tough. To watch him swooping around the fence in a handicap race, trying to overtake the other five riders all at once, was an awesome sight. He used the deeper dirt by the fence to gain extra traction and only his strength kept him on the bike when he was bouncing around the boards.

One particular night, he overdid his 'Wall-of-Death' antics and was catapulted over the low fence and onto the terracing. For a few minutes, the crowd was silent, then Jim climbed back over the fence and walked back to the pits unhurt. Flying over the safety fence was nothing new for Jim. In the 1975 US National Championship, at the Los Angeles Coliseum, he was involved in a truly frightening crash in which he flew over the fence and landed in the third row of the grandstand. The impact broke three seats and a spectator's leg – and the safety fence – but Jim walked away from it all uninjured.

Spectacular action was the name of the game in California and such hair-raising antics were not unusual among the Americans who went sideways for a living.

Strangers on the shore

The riders were generally in favour of the switch to team racing, although the second halves of the league matches were still all handicap racing. Six riders, with the 'backmarker' starting 50 yards behind, made for some hectic and exciting racing on a 180 yard track. No wonder the adverts told the fans to 'bring someone to hold on to'.

Rick Woods, captain of the Orange County Eagles, supported the idea of each team racing only twice a week. Previously, riders had raced five nights a week in scratch and handicap races at each track. It became very easy to bear a grudge against someone who ran into you the night before. As Rick said "The problem with the old-style individual racing was that by Friday night, you had not forgotten the guy who knocked you down at Irwindale on the Thursday night."

So, the riders supported team racing, but what about the fans? They had been used to seeing all the top riders every week, now they saw only some riders every few weeks. A non-league individual race meeting comprised of at least 25 events of scratch and handicap racing using 36 first division riders and 16 second division riders. Also, four reserves were on 'stand-by'. It was quite a long programme to run through, but usually ran like clockwork and was over in two hours.

During the close season, Harry Oxley had advertised in British speedway publications for six British League riders to come over and race in the new American National League, expecting a flood of top first division stars to head for California. This caused a few ripples on both sides of the Atlantic, but owing to the vagueness of the proposed contract, the expected reaction did not materialise. In the end, I was the only rider who took the gamble and 'defected' from the British League. Two other former British League riders, Eddie Reeves and Frank Shuter, joined the league, so I was not the only 'foreigner' racing in America. Former Kings Lynn and Hackney star, Eddie Reeves, was already based in California where his actress wife was making a movie. 'Fast Eddie' was eagerly signed by Oxley for the Orange County Eagles. New Zealander Frank Shuter joined the Los Angeles Sprockets.

Frank had, since his retirement from British speedway, been working in Israel so, when the Rest of the World team arrived in Tel Aviv for the series against America in March, he was quickly recruited as rider, guide and chauffeur to our World team. During our stay in Israel, Frank Shuter talked to Harry Oxley and Barry Briggs before finally deciding to try the American League. The Americans had already lost Mike Caruso, who headed to Britain to ride for Hull at the end of the series in Israel, and Mark Cherry who had signed for Birmingham. Mark, however, cut short his stay with the Brummies and returned to California for the beginning of the American League in mid-April.

Frank Shuter and I stayed at Harry Oxley's home near the beach for a few days until we got ourselves organised. Frank had purchased a Jawa from Barry Briggs and also Barry's Chevrolet station wagon which June Briggs had affectionately named 'La Bomba'.

Briggo's Empire was a large one. We collected his car from the home of film maker, Bruce Brown, and the Jawa from the home of former rider, Johnnie Roccio. John was the elder brother of Ernie Roccio, the young American who rode for Wimbledon in the 1950s and lost his life in a crash at West Ham.

There were a hundred and one things to do before the season opened, including driving over to ABC Leathers to be measured for our team leathers. Clarice Amberg and her staff worked really hard and had the completed leathers ready for us in only two days.

Another slight problem was that the Be-Be Jawa was minus a clutch, so that meant another chase around before we located one at the workshop of expatriate Englishman, George Wenn. Londoner George and his wife Freda were well-known in Californian speedway. They often accommodated European riders when they dropped by on their way to Disneyland, or to race at Costa Mesa. Freda's steak pies and Yorkshire pudding were famous throughout Californian speedway.

During these trips up and down the various Los Angeles Freeways we got to know 'La Bomba' very well and could guess why June Briggs chose such an appropriate name. As Barry had truthfully said in Tel Aviv, the car was fully carpeted, had an automatic gearbox and even a radio which worked, but what he didn't say was that the tyres were bald, the brakes almost non-existent and at anything below 25 mph, the engine cut out. This made traffic driving difficult and the engine tended to blow billows of smoke out of the exhaust.

As Bakersfield raced on a Saturday night, and Irwindale was a Thursday night track, Frank was the first into action. Further problems had beset the American teams when the former double United States Champion, and six times Californian Champion, Steve Bast, was in dispute over his team allocation.

Prior to leaving for Israel where he rode for the USA against the Rest of the World, Steve and his brother Mike, were allocated to the same league team. This decision was later reversed, as it was thought imprudent to have both brothers in the same line-up, so Steve was allocated elsewhere. Unhappy with this, Steve announced that he would not compete in the new league and headed to Northern California where he planned to race on the AMA-sanctioned tracks at Reno and Sacramento.

Unfortunately, Steve – the elder of the two Bast brothers – had to announce his retirement from the sport. Troubled by a weak heart which was aggravated by the nervous tension of speedway racing, Steve took his doctor's advice and decided to call it a day, for one season at least.

The launching of the new American National League was hampered by rainy weather and San Bernadino's first meeting was rained off. When I expressed surprise that California should get so much rain in the middle of April, I was advised to "make the most of it, as there will be no more rain until the end of the summer." That advice proved completely correct and for the following months, the sun shone relentlessly every day.

Over at Costa Mesa, Eddie Reeves had problems of his own. As he had not intended racing when he came to the States, he had no equipment. So it was beg or borrow to be ready for the new season. Jack Milne arranged a machine for Eddie, but with riding a strange bike and tackling stranger tracks, the former Hackney skipper found it tough. To ride the small Californian tracks a rider must forget all he has learned in British speedway, just 'gas it' flat out all the way and not forget to throw the bike sideways halfway down the straight.

My debut at Bakersfield was a bit of a disaster. My bikes had not arrived yet, so Digger Helm arranged for me to borrow a spare Jawa from a local rider's sponsor. The bike looked smart, all chrome and shiny, but unfortunately, the machine must have had a head-on confrontation with the safety fence. The frame was bent so much that the front wheel almost touched the frame.

I was in for another surprise when I rode it. The forks had such strong springs that there was no 'damping' effect at all and the wheel just slid away in the corners. The owner explained that his rider liked the heavier springs, as it "did not bounce so much when he did a wheelie". Well, I rode this camel, but between getting huge wheelies on the straights and then being unable to turn the beastie in the corners, I had a most embarrassing evening.

Frank Shuter and 'La Bomba' moved from San Clemente, the home of former American President Richard Nixon, to a motel nearer his home track at Irwindale. Edith and I moved out to the Ken Maely Ranch at Corona, some 50 miles south of Los Angeles where we lived in a large motorhome-styled trailer with all mod cons. Ken was one of the best-known characters in American motorcycle racing and made steel shoes for speedway, half mile and mile flat track racers. He later manufactured his own 500cc speedway engine, the 'Maely' so he was a man of many parts.

Ken 'The hot shoe man' was always in attendance in the pits with his fully equipped workshop van and frequently carried out running repairs for the riders. Anything from welding a steel shoe, to welding a broken frame. He was quite a guy and he helped me to 'get on the road' for the new season.

To get around in this country where nobody walked, I bought an old second hand Dodge van with 24,000 miles on the clock to transport my bikes. This was nothing like the immaculate motorhome-type vans used by the Californian riders, this was just a basic van with no extras. Ken sprayed painted it a fetching shade of blue and I was all set to take on the world.

One memorable incident with our 'Desperate Dodge' was when Ed Justice Junior, son of the co-owner of Justice Brothers, Ed Senior (obviously) invited us to Magic Castle, the Academy of Magical Arts in Hollywood one evening. Justice Brothers manufactured a large range of lubrication and maintenance products for cars and motorcycles and sponsored Speedway riders such as 'Wild Bill' Cody, Mike Bast and many others including Ivan Mauger and Ole Olsen plus drag racing cars, speedboats and JB Products were involved in all types of racing on land and in water.

Entry to Magic Castle is by membership to magicians only. Ed Jnr was an accomplished magician and a member, he was able to invite Edith and me along as his guests. The Magic Castle is a very smart private club and, as you drive up to the entrance, there is valet parking where white-gloved attendants will take your car and park it for you, very nice.

Magic Castle really is a magical place and Ed Jnr gave us a great time there. When you enter the foyer reception area, you are surrounded by a huge bookcase covering all four walls. There are no doors in sight so Ed walked up to the model Owl which was perched in the bookcase, said the magic words of "open sesame" and the bookcase parted to allow us to walk into the rest of the house. We walked past 'Irma' who is playing the magic piano. Irma is invisible but the piano keys move up and down and the cocktail drink with a straw that a waitress puts on the top of the piano for Irma, starts to do down as if Irma is drinking it through the straw finishing the drink with a loud 'Burp'. There are various rooms and visiting magicians are performing close-up magic tricks everywhere we went.

We also had a drink at the 'bar' where we perched on high tools and chatted away merrily while having a drink. I was talking to Ed for quite some time when I had the feeling that something was not quite right. I then noticed that my chin was almost on the top of the bar and that is when I realised that the bar stool I was sitting on was very slowly disappearing into the floor and I was ever-so-slowly getting lower and lower. I was very slow to catch on to what was happening and we all had a laugh about my predicament.

When we left, the valet parking attendants returned the car to us and, as we waited at the entrance, our vehicle was driven back to us. Imagine the scene. A queue of Cadillacs, Mercedes, Ford Mustangs and other exotic cars are driven back to their proud owners who wait patiently in the queue. Then a pall of smoke appears and an old blue Dodge van emerges from it. I sneak into the driver's seat while all around are trying to see who owns this apparition and we escape back onto the freeway for home.

186

Back to the speedway and in addition to Eddie Reeves, Frank Shuter and myself, a few other foreigners came to race in California. Marshall Pugh, the curly red-head who had raced speedway in Majorca under the guidance of Reg Luckhurst and Ian Hoskins, suddenly appeared and rode in a few second division races before packing up and heading for England.

From New Guinea, of all places, came Australians, Kevin MacDonald and Garnett Thistlewhaite, the latter giving the American announcers a few tongue-tied moments. Both rode very well in the second division and by the end of the season, Kevin had signed for Irwindale and was improving all the time. Kevin and Garnett had discovered speedway when former Sheffield captain and Australian Champion, Jim Airey, had taken a group of riders from Sydney over to New Guinea in an effort to establish the sport there. Their enthusiasm for speedway brought them to America but their main ambition was to race in Britain.

Kevin was involved in a slight controversy one night at Costa Mesa when he tangled with the promoter's son, Brad Oxley, who was later to sign for Wimbledon. Kevin Mac won the Handicap Race but when the results were announced, the referee had excluded him for running into Brad, which brought a few choice words from the guy from 'Down Under', especially as riders were rarely disqualified for bodily contact on the small Californian tracks.

Meanwhile 'La Bomba', with all its little peculiarities, had become just too much for Frank's nerves, not to mention the local Highway Patrol who were convinced that it was adding more than its fair share to Los Angeles' smog and pollution problems. Frank and La Bomba parted company and he acquired another, slightly newer, station wagon and began to relax again.

Both 'Europeans', as the Americans named anyone from outside their own continent, ran into various problems in adapting to the American style of racing and Eddie Reeves slipped down to reserve. In the American National League, only the six team members had programmed rides. The reserve was only on standby to ride at the captain's discretion. There were no official team managers, so the captain made any alterations necessary, a difficult role, as the captain cannot watch every race. So Eddie faded from the Californian speedway scene to be replaced by an up-an-coming local rider.

Frank had his troubles too, mainly caused by a communication gap between himself and his promoter. He was not getting along well with his team mates and, when a team practice was held without notifying him, Frank reckoned that things had come to a head.

Other problems arose owing to misunderstandings over bookings. In America, a rider did not get a weekly booking slip to notify him of his forthcoming commitments. He has to telephone the Speedway Racing Association where a tape recording gives the riding numbers – not names – of who is racing where each evening. Unfortunately, the tape was not infallible.

By mid-May, Frank had had enough of American speedway. He packed up his gear and headed for San Jose in Northern California. On his way, he stopped at Mike Bast's home in Canyon Country to explain his decision. Mike persuaded Frank to give it another try and ride for the Sprockets at Ventura that evening, so Frank agreed. He was riding well and liked the small Ventura track until he sustained a badly cut leg in a handicap crash. He did not realise the seriousness of the injury at first and kept riding, but a stay in hospital was necessary to cure the wound. On release from hospital, with a painful leg from Southern Californian speedway, Frank decided that he would be better off financially elsewhere. He headed north from Los Angeles. And so, there was only one European left in American Speedway – me.

The Bakersfield Bandits, with promoter Digger Helm made up as
'The old man of the mountains' sitting in front of Bert.

Bert leading for the Bandits, with team mate Dubb Ferrell just behind him.

31. A Bakersfield Bandit

As the long, hot summer progressed, our Saturday afternoon drives to Bakersfield were becoming more and more uncomfortable. Some of my American friends, on hearing I had been allocated to Bakersfield, held up their hands in mock horror and gleefully told me exaggerated tales of the travellers who had perished in the heat while trying to reach Bakersfield – an apt name, I might add. Unknown to my American friends, I had served part of my speedway apprenticeship racing in the humid heat of Australia, so the 100 degree plus of dry heat of Bakersfield was almost bearable. Even so, an air conditioned van was worth its weight in gold just for the drive to Bakersfield alone but my van was a cheapie and had no air conditioning.

The Interstate Highway 5, the Golden State Freeway, headed north out of Los Angeles and slowly climbed 4,000 feet over a range of mountains, down the other side, known as 'The Grapevine' and along a flat, hot, open prairie to Bakersfield. The long climb up over the mountains was the scene of many cars stranded by the roadside with steam gushing from their over-heated radiators like erupting volcanoes. My old Dodge van also had some problems. I always had to carry a few gallon cans of water to quench its thirst on the way.

In California, vans were the thing. Whereas a few years before I arrived, young Americans would invest all their money in souped-up Hot Rod cars, in 1976, popularity swung in favour of specially customized vans. The number of modifications and accessories were endless. All the speedway riders had their own ideas incorporated into their vehicles. Many vans had beautiful murals and paintings on the outside, anything from an action painting of a speedway rider, to a fantastic, colourful sunset over the ocean. The interiors were something else. Most were fully carpeted with separate sections for the bikes, leathers and tools. American vans were a little longer and wider than the ones we used then in Britain. They had power steering, quadraphonic sound, refrigerators and air conditioning – a must for the long, hot trips in summer. An 'extra' which many riders had, was 'automatic cruise control'. This device, when set at the desired cruising speed, maintained that speed uphill and downhill for as long as you wanted. You could almost fall asleep and let these vans drive themselves.

All these 'extras', including CB radio, made driving easier in America, but my old Dodge van had none of these items. The only air conditioning it had were the holes in the floor, but even they blew hot air when we were driving to Bakersfield. If the drive up to Bakersfield was hot, and it usually reached 105 degrees and more, there was no real respite when evening came. Sometimes it would cool down to 95 degrees and on a few occasions, it would be a 'chilly' 85 degrees at night. Unfortunately the 'Nicki Pedersen Blower' to blow cool air in our faces had not yet been invented.

Bakersfield was well-known for its Country & Western music and singers Merle Haggard and Buck Owens. The speedway track was situated in the Kern County Fairgrounds, home of the county fair, horse shows and rodeos. So, with its rows of stables, the western influence and aroma was not too far away.

After unloading the bikes, it was a good idea to have a shower to freshen up before the serious business of racing began. As the shower building was a few hundred yards away

189

from the track, a towel was unnecessary. By the time I walked back to the pits in my shorts, the hot night air had dried me. Dressing room facilities and showers at some tracks were non-existent. Most riders changed in their vans, which gave the multi-purpose vehicle another use.

Another unusual item was that after racing in the league match, riders had to change from their team leathers and helmets into their personal sponsor-covered leathers and custom-painted helmets for the handicap races in the second half. Failure to change leathers could result in a fine. The idea was to split the two sections of the programme and distinguish between team racing and individual handicap racing. Many fans got confused in their attempts to identify the riders during team racing as they were used to seeing their favourites wearing their sponsors' colours. It was also uncomfortable for the riders. Trying to remove sweat soaked leathers and T-shirt, climbing into another set, then going racing again, was not very easy on a hot evening.

The heat affected not only the riders but the bikes too. Tyre pressures had to be carefully checked after each race. With the combination of the hard, slick tracks made of decomposed granite, the spinning rear wheels and the very hot air temperature, tyre pressures could increase considerably during a race. When using the fat four inches wide tyre, most riders used a very low tyre pressure, of around five or six pounds per square inch. But during a race, this pressure could increase by two or three pounds. So between refuelling the bikes, checking tyres, spark plugs and carburettor jets and changing leathers, there was always plenty to do between races.

At Bakersfield we decided to wear our own custom-painted helmets in the team racing, because all the riders in each team had begun to look alike. This helped ease the rider-identification problem slightly especially because I was the only one with a tartan-painted helmet. All tracks, with the exception of Bakersfield, had their pre-season practice sessions to allow for team selection and track knowledge. When the Bandits eventually had their first home meeting we were promptly beaten by Ventura.

Promoter Digger Helm and Captain Jeff Sexton reckoned that a team practice session was badly needed. It was arranged that we would spend the following Friday evening in practice on the Bakersfield track, then we would be fighting fit for the match the next day. Digger treated the team, plus wives and mechanics, to a slap-up meal in a local restaurant with a Scottish-sounding name, The *Tam o' Shanter*. I was pleased to see that the waitresses all wore mini-kilts. But I never worked out why the insignia of the restaurant was a drawing of an American Footballer, complete with crash helmet, shoulder pads and rugby-style football.

Digger and Theda Helm went to great lengths to look after the Bandits. Digger was the only promoter who travelled with his team to every match, home and away. Often, teams would arrive at Bakersfield without a manager, but wherever the Bandits travelled, Digger was there. This made for a close-knit team and helped build team spirit too.

Digger's hospitality did not end there. After the practice, he booked the team into the Bakersfield Hilton Hotel. Next day, after checking the bikes over, we all headed for the Kern River to watch the Drag Boat Championships. It is similar to car drag racing, except that it is on water with high-powered speed boats and very, very fast. After such a relaxing time, the team buckled down and hit a winning streak which lasted for most of the season. Already a few matches behind, the Bandits had a lot of ground to make up to overtake the leaders, so every match was doubly important.

One of the 'fringe benefits' of riding for Bakersfield was the Kern County River. After the long hot drive from Los Angeles, and the equally hot Saturday evening's racing, few riders felt like driving home overnight. Once the racing was over, everyone headed out of town to the Kern River, where there was a National Park and campground.

The National Parks in America have all the facilities with showers, barbeque fireplaces and picnic tables. Most of the vans were equipped with beds, so we could just drive our vans into a parking bay and bed down for the night. It was so hot that we didn't need a van – just dump a sleeping bag on the grass and snooze under the stars. It wasn't a five star hotel, it was a thousand star hotel.

In the mornings, we had open-air breakfasts, then walked up-river to come floating down the river in huge tractor inner tubes. Nice cool relaxing Sundays. Some river travellers were really organised. They came floating down towing another tube with an ice-box full of drinks, so they did not get thirsty on their journey down river.

That was one big advantage that Bakersfield had over my old club, Wimbledon. I mean, can you imagine sleeping on Wimbledon Common after racing at Plough Lane? Or floating down the Thames on an inner tube?

Injuries, injuries everywhere

The risk of injury is always present with a sport such as speedway. American speedway had always been noted for its spectacular crashes, but in a majority of these accidents, the riders walked away just with bruises – until league racing began. Perhaps it was everyone trying to do his best for his team and over-riding themselves, or perhaps it was just a bad season. Whatever the reason, the injured riders list grew longer each week. It was like playing 'Russian Roulette' with four bullets instead of one.

The LA Sprockets had lost Wayne Lewis and Mike Konle with broken wrists, but managed to sign one of the top riders from Northern California, Norm Denny of Sacramento. 'Stormin Norman' was a big success with his new team, but following a pile-up at Bakersfield, returned to Sacramento to recuperate.

San Bernadino were still top of the league, despite the retirement of Ed Williams. The track at the Orange Show Fairgrounds in San Bernadino was fairly new, so the surface caused a few complaints early in the season. Occasionally, loose stones would work their way to the surface, as the track had been built on the sight of the old city rubbish dump.

Promoter John La Douceux called in the 'Man-for-all-tracks', Spike Frownfelter and, after a lot of hard work by the track staff, there were no more complaints. Spike normally prepared the Costa Mesa track for Harry Oxley and he was even flown to Israel to prepare the circuits there for the USA versus Rest of the World series.

San Bernadino's unbeaten home record tumbled when the in-form Bakersfield Bandits hit town in June, and that, coupled with a home-and away victory over the LA Sprockets, put 'Digger Helm's Wrecking Crew' on top of the league. After such a promising start, San Bernadino were running into injury problems. Billy Meister broke his ankle in a collision with

Dubb Ferrell at Bakersfield. Larry Shaw broke his tail-bone when he looped his wife's trail bike when riding in the desert and 'Big Jim' Fishback proved that he was not indestructible by breaking his leg at Costa Mesa.

And so it went on. The injury list for all teams mounted weekly and more and more second division riders had the opportunity to join a league team. The less experienced replacements were often involved in hair-rising pile-ups. In the handicap events, which had a mixture of riders of varying experience and ability, problems often arose.

As the 'backmarkers' caught up with those who had started from the gate, there could be quite a traffic jam with six riders fighting for one patch of track. On the smooth, slick tracks, overtaking could be quite difficult. It was not a matter of waiting for someone to make a mistake, more forcing your way through by whatever means were available like a two-wheeled version of stock car racing.

Generally, the Californian tracks had, apart from their size, one big difference from those in other parts of the world. In Britain, the dirt is graded down from the fence to the inside between races. In California, the dirt is left to pile up against the fence and the inside of the track is scraped down to a hard, slick surface. The spinning rear tyres leave a polished band of black rubber around the inside, known as a 'blue groove'. And when there is a layer of dirt on the outside, that's known as the 'cushion'. Ah yes, it is another language in the States.

Under FIM rules, riders in Europe could only use rear wheels and tyres of the 3.50 x 19 inch variety, but in America, anything went. Basically, two different sizes of rear wheel and tyre were used. The fat 4.00 (4 inches wide) x 19 inch Carlisle tyre or the larger 22 inch wheel with a Barum tyre. Riders using the fat Carlisle tyre stick rigidly to the inside white line (or pole), while those using the narrower, but larger 22 inch wheel, try to blast around the outside in the dirt. If this sounds confusing, don't worry, it is. If a rider changes the size of their rear wheel, they also have to change the size of the sprocket. In the end, the tracks were very predictable and gear ratios and tyres presented no real problem.

Coming back to the handicap races, it was not unusual to see a high speed 'freight train' of riders all trying to overtake each other 'on the pole' and using what Sonny Nutter described as 'The Buzz-Saw Technique' on each other. This was shoving your front wheel against your opponent's left leg and letting the tyre wear a groove in his leathers. Often, in the pits, there were 'heated discussions' when some of the faster riders failed to pass the front-markers. Many an up-and-coming rider was advised not to 'park it' in the middle of the corner. So when those riders are eventually given a team ride, they often tried just a bit too hard and yet another statistic was added to the injury list.

If there are a lot of crashes in American speedway, it is not because they are poor riders. On the contrary, they are all first class all-round motorcyclists with a lot of confidence and machine control. America is the 'Land of plenty' and the dry, warm climate of Southern California makes it ideal motorcycle country. Some kids learned to ride motorcycles almost before they could walk, and the opportunities to progress and develop in motorcycle sport were almost endless.

There were children's desert races, moto cross and junior speedway. They raced 200cc Triumph Tiger Cubs and Hondas in miniature frames on the normal speedway tracks. Even many high schools had their own moto cross teams and inter-school championships.

Many riders were experienced motorcycle racers before they even began speedway at the age of 16, and had already collected dozens of trophies, awards and newspaper headlines. Although there is no cycle speedway in the USA, one of the fastest growing sports when I was there was bicycle moto cross. The kids wore helmets, moto cross jerseys and face guards, just like miniature Roger de Costers. The bicycles were fitted with telescopic front forks and rear suspension.

The sport was so popular that famous names like Yamaha and Kawasaki were marketing their own special bicycles. It was quite amusing to see the kids come away from their meetings. Little guys, struggling to carry trophies which were twice their size and proud fathers wheeling the bicycles back to a special trailer behind their car.

The depth of talent in America for speedway and moto cross, was amazing, but to realise their true potential, the riders had to ride in Europe, like Scott Autrey and American moto cross star, Brad Lackey. Other Californian riders came over to Europe after I had left the USA and had a lot of success both in British League racing and in winning World Championships. This had just been the beginning.

The speedway thrills and spills continued each week without fail and the small tracks dished up excitement aplenty. While British fans may not have regarded it as 'pure' speedway racing, they would have found speedway in California the most exciting spectacle they had seen. Jerry Fairchild, who was involved with speedway in California since its early pre-war days, would, I am sure, testify to the unpredictability of American racing. Jerry, who sponsored Dubb Ferrell on the special fuel-injected Fairchild machine, was hanging over the pit fence at San Bernadino one night, watching a second division handicap race when a multi-rider pile up occurred. Mike Bendy hit the wall hard, and his bike flew over the low fence and whistled past Jerry's shoulder before landing with a crunch in the pits. Jerry calmly watched it pass, then turned around to continue watching. He had seen it all in American speedway, so nothing could disturb him, not even a low-flying Jawa.

Talking of low-flying Jawas, I met one of those UFOs at Costa Mesa one night. I was bashing around the outside of Mark Cherry and Phil Moon in a handicap race when the two riders collided. Mark's bike took off like an unmanned rocket before returning to earth and landed on my handlebars. It was one of the few occasions when all six riders in a handicap race crashed at the same time. There were some bent motorcycles after that little melee, but luckily nobody was injured and everyone took part in the re-run.

Yet another case of a speedway bike having a mind of its own occurred at Ventura, when 'Wild' Bill Cody's throttle decided that it did not want to shut off at the end of the straight. Bill tried to 'lay it down', but the bike spun around into the path of Mike Bast. Mike hit the rider-less Jawa and the impact knocked it back onto its wheels again. Still revving flat out, Cody's Jawa charged the pit gate like a bull. It hit the gate head-on, bounced back then hit it again, the gate burst open, knocking Jack Milne out of the way. With countless riders and officials scattering in different directions, the angry Jawa scythed a path through the large pit area and headed straight for the ambulance and track-grader pick-up truck which were parked only a few feet apart.

With its handlebars bouncing from side to side, the Jawa miraculously roared between the two vehicles without even touching them and carried on its crazy dance towards the speedway office. Luckily, it fell on its side before reaching the wall and was caught. With the cut-outs used today, this could not happen. The following week, Jack Milne had made a small grandstand in the pits for the riders, to keep them away from the fence.

Teams were sometimes finding it difficult to field a full squad of riders, because of injuries and, at one stage, second division rider, Ron Rose, found himself 'guesting' for three different teams in the same week. That will sound familiar to British fans. If a team turned up a man short, they would borrow Ron, thereby coining a new nickname, Ron 'Rent-a-Rider' Rose.

The American promoters realised that the guest riders would further confuse the fans and lead to the problems we had experienced in the British League, so they brought in a rider replacement system. It could only be used to cover the injury of one of the team's top three scorers and he could only be replaced, once per rider, by the team members who had lower averages than him.

Up in sunny Bakersfield, the injury bug was not biting too hard. We had lost Santa Ana fireman, Dave Galvin, from our early season team and Don Cullum who, after coming back from injury, crashed again, and was out for the season. Replacements were signed in the form of local rider, Dan 'sock-it' Toomey, and Jim Gresham.

Injuries were not confined to riders alone, spectators could get into the act too. Irwindale had two distinct racing lines. The inside was always smooth and slick but like an American version of Exeter, the quickest way around, was out in the deep dirt at the fence. Most weeks, the dirt piled against the fence like a banking and, by the end of the night's racing, it could be halfway up the low safety fence. Racing there, with everyone using the larger and less predictable 22 inch tyre, was always fast, exciting and sometimes pretty wild. It was quite a sight to watch a six-rider handicap field in action, with everyone trying to ride wider than his opponents.

Robin Hood, an alias used by a second division rider to gain extra rides, was involved in a rather nasty situation when he crashed heavily in a handicap event at Irwindale. He came off very hard and it was obvious that he was not lying on the track as part of his 'Robin Hood' act. His leathers were Lincoln Green and designed similar to the Robin of Sherwood Forest's outfit. The race was not stopped. The riders completed another two laps, spraying dirt on the prostrate rider and the track officials who were trying to help him. It was a dangerous situation, but one which was, unfortunately, not uncommon then in American speedway.

At the end of the race, the ambulance was brought onto the track and Robin was taken to hospital with a broken shoulder and collarbone among his injuries. Fortunately, an ambulance must always be in attendance before racing can commence. This rule was enforced in other countries too, but surprisingly, not in Britain at that time. The next race, the handicap fun event, was held up for some time, until a replacement ambulance arrived, which unfortunately, was soon put into action. In the main event, the riders went down like skittles. Somehow Mike Bast, coming from the 50 yards backmark, stayed upright. Guy Waterson and Bakersfield's Dan Toomey fell and, as Bandit Brian Short went down, his bike took off and, using the dirt banked up against the fence, as a launching pad, it cleared the low wall, injuring several spectators.

Dan suffered concussion and 'Thumper' Short sustained a badly broken right leg. The track looked like a battlefield, arid the meeting was abandoned as Brian and Dan lay on the track, waiting for yet another ambulance. It was a bitter blow for the popular 'Thumper' as well as to the Bakersfield team. Brian had been improving all season and his partnership with Bandit's captain, Jeff Sexton, made them the highest scoring pairing in the league.

He was also riding well enough to have qualified for his first US National Championship. But now Thumper faced having his leg in plaster for several months. Dan Toomey missed a few meetings and was back in the saddle very quickly. Dave Sims of Ventura was another who missed 'The National' because of injury. Fellow Ventura Shark, Dean York, was already out for the season with a broken leg when Dave was involved in an awful crash during a handicap race at his home track. His arm was trapped by the spinning rear wheel and he damaged his wrist and tendons badly. Luckily, Gene Wood's sponsor, a plastic surgeon, was in the crowd. He was able to assist Dave and telephone ahead to the hospital with the required information for an emergency operation.

If the first year of the American National League carried many more serious injuries than ever before, thankfully, there were other crashes which even had their humorous moments. Like second division junior, Jim 'Crashwall' Rogan, who earned his name by trying to eat the fence (or crashwall) at various tracks. 'Crashwall', a product of the Jerry Fairchild stable, fell off harmlessly at San Bernadino one night. In true American style, he left his bike and sprinted for the wall before the other riders came around. He leapt over the fence, but what he failed to notice was that because the dirt was piled against the fence on the track side, making the wall only about two feet high, the drop to the tarmac on the spectators' side was about six feet. Jim got quite a shock as he disappeared over the top. I guess there is a lot of truth in the saying 'Look before you leap'.

Another of Jerry's protégées, Brian Buffington, got that sinking feeling one night at Ventura when his rear wheel suddenly dropped out. Brian had changed gear and, in his rush, had forgotten to tighten the rear wheel. But if American speedway is dangerous, there are other off-track pastimes which can also be hazardous to one's health. Motorcycle riding is an extremely popular recreation in the USA and the climate on the West Coast is ideal for trail riding, desert riding or just plain old touring.

I spent a few days with friends who live at Lake Tahoe, Nevada, 8,000 feet up in the Sierra Mountains. It is a popular vacation resort for water skiing and Mountain Biking in the summer and snow skiing in the winter, not to mention the inevitable Nevada gambling. However, I had not come for the gambling – there was enough of that when we were racing – but to put in a couple of days of trail riding in the mountains and forests.

My host, Don Draper, an airline pilot, and his friend also named Don, who owned a barber's shop quickly became known as 'Don-the-Air' and 'Don-the-Hair' plus Ken Maely, 'The hot shoe man'. Before setting off, 'Don-the-Air' handed me a bright orange jacket to wear. "What is that for?" I asked. He replied: "It's the deer hunting season and the hunters sometimes shoot at whatever moves and ask questions later." Suddenly, I lost interest in going riding in those parts. Fortunately, no-one took any pot-shots at us and we enjoyed riding along the trails without bullet holes appearing in our jackets.

Yes, America could be thrilling, exciting, even tragic, but the speedway was always entertaining.

"Parlez vous American?"

Texas Tim got the holeshot from the pole. He was hanging-in there, doing his own thing down the back shute when he missed the blue groove, hit the whoop-de-doo on the berm, did a doughnut on the cushion and collected the crashwall.

Did you follow that? It is just plain American, and roughly translated it tells you how the aforementioned Tim got the best start from the inside gate and was merrily riding down the back straight, when he overshot the normal line for the corner. Whereupon he hit the bumps on the banked dirt, spun round in a circle of 180 degrees in the dirt, then proceeded to run into the safety fence. Easy, isn't it?

American motorcycle journalism is very colourful and picturesque, but it takes the average 'foreigner' a little time to work it all out. It is not just the language which I had to learn when arriving in the States on speedway business, there were other little differences too. The pits had to be cleared of early arrivals by 6pm and all riders and mechanics had to form a queue to 'sign-in' at a booth outside of the pit gate. Licences were handed over to be returned at the end of the meeting. If, however, a rider has been a naughty boy, the referee withheld the licence until he had a few words with the offender. Mechanics, as well as riders, had to have licences. The annual licence fee for First Division was $40, Second Division $30 and Third Division (beginners) $20. Upon signing-in, the rider paid his $5 entry fee and insurance, had his hand stamped with an indelible ink marker which did not wash off for a week, and was free to enter the pit area. The signing-on booth closed 30 minutes before the start of a meeting. Any rider who has not signed-in by then had to report to the referee before being allowed to race.

Sponsorship played a big part in American speedway and most riders were heavily sponsored, with bikes, leathers and spares. The sponsor normally supplied the rider with a bike, tyres and all the equipment and took care of the mechanical side of things. In return, the rider split a percentage of his earnings with his sponsor, sometimes as much as five percent, depending on the arrangement between them. However, more riders were doing their own pre-race maintenance, but for some fortunate ones everything was done for them so they only had to turn up at a meeting and race.

But even in America, sponsors could be hard to find. Jeff Sexton's sponsor pulled out of racing and the Bakersfield captain had problems finding a replacement. To help his quest, written in bold letters across the chest of his leathers, Jeff had printed 'This space to let'.

As well as the changes in equipment and vans that I noticed on my first trips to America, the bikes have come the full circle too. In the early days of Californian Speedway, many riders rode 'flat track style' with very low handlebars and high seats and in the UK, we had high handlebars and low seats to help to control our 2-valve Japs and Jawas on the grippy tracks. Following training schools by Ivan Mauger and Barry Briggs, the local riders began using higher handlebars and changed their styles to suit but now modern riders have gone back to having low Motocross-style handlebars and high saddles, so once again, the wheel has turned the full circle.

Another 'hot set-up' which made its debut during the season was the 'electric-starter' for Jawas. As there were no official 'pushers' on the track staff, the mechanics had to push their own riders to get their machines started. Jeff Sexton's mechanic, Roger Hayden, got tired of all the effort. He built a portable starter with a 12 volt battery and car starter motor, with a socket at the end to fit the engine sprocket nut on the Jawa. The whole contraption was transported on a small wheel barrow, then connected to the Jawa. With a touch of the starter button, the engine roared into life. America truly was the land of labour saving devices.

The fans also had their comforts because in Californian speedway no-one stands; everyone has a seat. In addition to the covered main stand at tracks like Costa Mesa and Ventura, there are 'bleachers' all around the track. These scaffolding-like stands can be added to, when larger crowds are expected, but Costa Mesa, which can seat almost 10,000 fans, has reached its limit. To sit high in the bleachers, one must have a good head for heights.

There was no music played except for the American national anthem, but then who needs music when there are such lively announcers as 'Piccadilly Willis', Larry 'Motormouth' Huffman & company? The American national anthem reminds me of an embarrassing incident on a previous trip to the USA. It was one of the first USA versus Rest of the World matches at Costa Mesa and the teams lined up in front of the grandstand. The strains of *The Star Spangled Banner* filled the air, and the World team of Ivan Mauger, Barry Briggs, Jim Airey, George Hunter, Jim McMillan, Dave Gifford and myself all stood at attention facing the crowd. Unfortunately, no-one had told us that in America, you must face the flag and, as the stars and stripes were fluttering from a flag pole in the centre green, we were standing with our backs to the flag.

American racing rules were also a little strange at times, like the time I was leading a race for almost four laps at Bakersfield when my opponent rammed me, very hard and very deliberately. I bounced along the fence and just managed to keep control to finish third. I protested to the referee. I was told that, had I fallen off when the other rider hit me, I would have been awarded first place and the other guy relegated to third or fourth. However, as I had managed to stay in the saddle, it was not counted as foul riding. No wonder there were so many feuds on the track. Moral of the story? Don't get mad, get even.

The American referees came in for a lot of stick, even more so than their British counterparts, but one referee made a very strong, but necessary decision at Ventura during an individual meeting there. A first division rider arrived at the meeting in a rather glassy-eyed state and, after he had fallen in his first race, did not look fit enough to continue. The referee had a few words with him, and automatically withdrew him from his other races, despite protests from the rider. The official explained that it was for the rider's own safety and that of others in the meeting. No amount of arguing by the rider would alter his decision. The rider concerned had been one of the top young stars of American speedway a few years ago until hitting some drug problems. It was a great pity as he had a neat riding style and a lot of potential.

The announcers in American added much to the general atmosphere and excitement including a 'blow-by-blow' commentary in each race. The ultimate in entertainment was to watch Larry Huffman perform at Costa Mesa. He was the announcer, but had as big a following with the fans as most riders.

He began his act quietly, then suddenly jumped up on the table, and got the fans to yell along with him as he introduced "Wi-i-l-l-l-d Bi-i-l-l Cod-d-eee" .

It was like a miniature Wembley Roar. He whipped the fans into a frenzy as he threw his jacket into the air, did his famous Huffman Hop, a kind of mid-air scissors jump, and introduced Danny 'Berserko' Becker, 'Radical' Randy Marsh, Bruce 'The Fox' Penhall, "Bouncing Bert" Harkins and Michael Bast. The latter name produced a mixture of cheers and boos; although Mike Bast was the American number one, many fans disliked his consistent winning of almost every race.

Larry Huffman once suggested that Mike should be arrested for impersonating a computer, a nice tribute to his winning ways. Perhaps Larry's kind of showmanship would have been great on British tracks, and it would have been fun to see him try.

Interval attractions were also fun, but didn't take place every week, as the full programme was pushed through quickly and smoothly in little over two hours. In addition to the usual 'Miss Speedway' contests, they had a 'Miss Wet T-Shirt' contest, but I don't think that will ever catch on in Britain, as all the winners would get the flu.

Another guy who was always good for a gimmick was Rick Schwartz, brother of Ventura's Bobby. 'Rocket' Rick worked in the Hollywood Studios as a make-up artist, and produced some weird and wonderful costumes. When the Ventura Sharks visited Costa Mesa, the Ventura team had a mobile 'Jaws', who went around the track trying to eat home captain Rick Woods. Also, at various tracks we met up with some creatures from *Planet of the Apes*, which looked quite frightening in their costumes.

At Bakersfield, Rick glued a long droopy moustache on each of the Bandits and, during the parade, we looked like a band of Mexican bandits. Jeff Sexton liked his moustache so much that he kept it on while racing. With it being another hot night, I could not stand the extra heat generated by my whiskers, so off they came.

Rick's masterpiece was to make our promoter Digger up as 'The Old Man of the Mountains'. The make-up was so good that during a confidential team talk before the meeting at Ventura, I could not work out who this ugly man was trying to eavesdrop on our conversation. It was not until I noticed his purple gloves that I realised who it was.

Other interval attractions were the junior speedway events for riders aged 10 to 16. Each junior must be represented by a first division rider. Often the junior used the same design of leathers and helmet as his sponsor.

It was quite amusing to watch a race of miniature Bruce Penhalls and Dubb Ferrells buzzing around on their small bikes. Current junior champion was little Louis Cossuth riding a very fast Triumph Tiger Cub. Juniors could graduate to full 500 cc speedway on their 16th birthday, so there was always a steady stream of good, young riders. Brad Oxley was one of them. A few years in schoolboy moto cross, winning dozens of trophies, made the transition to 'sideways racing' quite easy.

During the close season Barry Briggs had put Brad and his own son Gary through an intensive all-day training session on the small Californian tracks. Brad then begun the new season in second division races, progressed to first division handicaps and by the end of the season, had earned the reserve berth at San Bernadino. Ironically, Brad scored one point in his first team meeting for the Sizzlers and helped them defeat Ventura, one of the teams owned by his dad, Harry. Brad later became a favourite at Wimbledon in the British League.

Most of the American stars are in the teens to early-20s age group but, as in everything, there are always exceptions. Riders like Irwin Moon, Grant Murray and Harland Bast – uncle of Steve and Mike – were all in their 40s and still sliding their motorcycles around with the young uns. Grant only took up speedway at the ripe young age of 42 and steadily improved. Irwin, like Harland, has real family ties in the sport as their sons also raced.

At the other end of the age-scale, was 16 year old Denis Sigalos of Fullerton, California. Young Denis came straight from high school to be signed by the injury hit San Bernadino team. Although having raced motorcycles since he was 13, Denis had only made his speedway debut a few months earlier. With encouragement and advice from Irwindale's Bruce Penhall, and further assistance from his new team mates, Denis began to get among the points. By the end of the season, he was mounted on a new 4-valve Jawa and showing tremendous potential. He went on to ride in Britain for Ipswich and Hull before retiring prematurely through injury.

On one of my earlier American trips I was asked to compete in a mini-bike match race at Costa Mesa against the then mini-bike champion, young Jeff Ward. Young? He was seven or eight years old and had all the gear: Bell Star helmet, one piece made-to-measure leathers, steel shoe and a cheeky up-turned nose. Jeff, despite his size, or lack of it, was the mini speedway champion of California. A real 'King of the Kids'.

The surprising thing was that this freckle-faced youngster was not an all-American boy. He was Scottish. His dad, Jack, had been a near-neighbour of mine in Glasgow before the family moved to Los Angeles when Jeff was four years old. It sure is a small world. Anyway, it was arranged that I would use a little Hodaka mini bike for the race, and much to my embarrassment, Jack Ward insisted that little Jeff would give me a 10-yard start.

As I rolled round to the gate on my mini-bike, I was thinking, 'This is crazy, it is too easy. I'll ride around for a couple of laps then wait for the poor wee fella and let him win'. The tapes were up and I was racing again, concentrating on scraping that wobbling mini-bike around the tight corners and forgetting all about waiting for my mini-opponent.

For two laps I pushed that little machine hard and then I was aware of another buzzing noise in my ears. There, sitting on my rear wheel, was that 'poor wee fella' flat out in a full-lock slide. He was incredible. He was throwing his bike into a big slide going into the turn and holding the throttle flat out all the way. I decided that I had better get a move on, or the kid would show me up. I dived into the corner, but Jeff came in even faster, he clipped my rear wheel and went flying over the handlebars.

So the match race to decide who was the true 'Flying Scotsman' ended with Jeff Ward picking himself up off the track and Bert Harkins taking a lot of ribbing for 'knocking the kid off'. By 1976, Jeff was one of the top motocrossers in California and went on to win the AMA Motocross Championship five times, the AMA Supercross Championship twice plus competing for USA in the Moto Cross des Nations seven times. After finishing his motorcycle career Jeff swopped over to car racing achieving second place in the famous Indy 500 race plus wins in truck and Rally racing. He even appeared in that cult Bruce Brown motorcycle movie, *On any Sunday* when he was 10 years old, performing a very long wheelie on his mini bike.

Jeff did not race speedway anymore and perhaps that was just as well for me, as he may have tried to get revenge for knocking him off in that controversial match race.

Making a start for Bakersfield – Bert is in the white helmet.

The Bakersfield Bandits versus San Bernadino Sizzlers
match programme with Bert on the cover.

Needless to say, I did not let myself be persuaded into any more minibike match races. As any good actor will say: 'Never perform with kids or animals as they are sure to steal the scene'. The same advice applies to speedway riders.

In those days of 'equal rights' it was not surprising to see the female influence creeping into speedway. One girl, Pam "Pinky" Bennet, raced in junior 200 cc speedway, wearing pink leathers decorated with hearts. 16 year old Bobbie Hunter was striving to make the grade in the senior speedway with a 500cc Jawa. Young Bobbie was a flat track racer of no mean ability and frequently beat most of the boys. She turned her hand to speedway and looked good. She persuaded her father to buy a Jawa which she raced at the second division-only track at Chula Vista, near San Diego. The track was an ideal training ground for the non-team riders where they ran Saturday night meetings throughout the summer. Chula Vista is right on the Mexican border, very close to Tijuana.

"Kung Fu speedway"

Mike Bast stayed on top of the individual league points averages all year, closely followed by his Irwindale team mate, Bruce Penhall, with Bakersfield's Dubb Ferrell and Jeff Sexton battling it out for third.

Four-valve engines were not too easily obtainable in America then, but nevertheless, there was quite a variety of different machinery around. Mike Bast was well equipped with two Weslakes; Bruce Penhall had a Weslake and a Neil Street Four-valve Jawa, before dropping the British engine and purchasing another Streetie special. Sonny Nutter tried a Weslake, but put it aside and used a standard Jawa which had been raced in Israel. This machine were exceptionally quick, and 'Sliding Sunny' came back to his old form in time for the USA National qualifying rounds.

Irwindale's Wayne Lewis was also using a British Weslake until a broken wrist halted his progress. America was not far behind in engine development. Jerry Fairchild had perfected his fuel-injected two-valve engine which Dubb Ferrell used with great success. Ed Schaffer, another local tuner, had Gene Woods on one of his new Drake Engineering Four-valvers and even sent an engine over to Scott Autrey in England. Even on the small Californian tracks, the Four-valve motors proved to have a slight advantage and when it came down to heat 13, the nominated riders race, in the league match, the Four-valvers of Mike Bast and Bruce Penhall were seldom beaten. Later, Ken Maely was to manufacture his own Maely Special engine which Mike Bast and others tested, but unfortunately it was not too successful.

One memorable occasion, shrouded in controversy, was a last heat decider at Bakersfield, when Bast and Penhall met Sexton and Ferrell. It looked an impossible situation, as Bakersfield needed a 5–1 to win the match and if they lost, Irwindale would go top of the league. In the rush for the first corner, Bruce Penhall fell and almost knocked off Mike Bast. Amid the confusion, the Bandits raced away with the 5–1 we desperately needed. As Ferrell and Sexton took the chequered flag ahead of Mike Bast, the referee was surrounded by angry Irwindale riders. Despite protests by Bruce Penhall that he had been knocked off by Dubb Ferrell, the result stood.

One of the funniest last heat deciders was when San Bernadino visited Bakersfield early in the season. After the customary heat 13, the scores were still tied, so Dubb Ferrell and Larry Shaw came out to settle the result with a match race. Ferrell led all the way until Shaw dived through the inside. The bikes collided and both riders fell, but they kept their engines running and were quickly back in the saddle, the race continued with Ferrell winning.

Another incident at Bakersfield happened when home rider Dan Toomey and Orange County's Mike Muntean tangled and fell on the fourth corner. Unlike Ferrell and Shaw, they did not remount and continue the race because, owing to a skirmish at Costa Mesa the previous evening, they still had a grievance with each other.

They jumped up, and in the middle of the third corner, began trading punches, oblivious to the other riders who continued for another two laps, narrowly missing them each time. The spectators were treated to a speedway race and boxing match all-in-one.

Tempers were frequently on a short fuse during tense racing on the little tracks. The enthusiastic atmosphere of the crowd and the closeness of the racing put a lot of riders on edge, and sometimes tempers flared over an on-track incident. Like the time Irwindale visited Costa Mesa and home captain Rick Woods was a bit upset by some of his opponents' riding tactics. The matter came to a head when Irwindale's Rob Morrison put Woods into the fence in a fast and furious heat nine.

The race continued with Rick standing fuming on the centre green and, as the riders returned to the pits, he stormed after the unfortunate Rob. Moments later, the Costa Mesa pits looked like a scene from a Kung Fu movie. Toolboxes were knocked over and helmets kicked around as Rick proceeded to demonstrate his skills in martial arts. I suppose it was thoughtful of Rick to remove his steel shoe before swinging those kicks, but in any other speedway country, his actions would have been looked on very seriously indeed.

Not that Rick was the only one at fault. One of his team mates was also pretty handy with Kung Fu kicks, and towards the end of the season, he was involved in a few 'conflicts' with other riders. Sometimes it looked to me as though Californian speedway was a cross between Kung Fu fighting and Roller Derby. But usually it ended up with everyone shaking hands and becoming friends again.

Bakersfield Speedway was the home of the annual Firecracker Derby and the Californian Championship, two of the most important individual events on the calendar. The Californian Championship dated back to 1968, when Sonny Nutter won the title. After that, it was almost the exclusive property of Steve Bast. Ever since the smiling Mr Nutter won it, Steve dominated the event, winning a record six Californian Championships.

In 1973 year Steve missed out but his brother Mike took top place and kept the title in the family. When Steve had to retire for a year owing to health problems, the way was open in 1976 for a new champion to be crowned. Home stars Dubb Ferrell and Jeff Sexton had been in great form at Bakersfield, but Mike Bast came through to win again.

In addition to his exploits in speedway, Mike built a reputation in films. He was another American all-round motorcyclist and was equally at home on anything with two wheels and an engine. The Hollywood film studios recognised Mike's talent as a stunt rider. In 1976 he completed his second film and was in great demand for television commercials.

Since he made a good living in America with his racing and film work it was unlikely he would ride in Britain. A pity, as he could have been quite a useful rider in British League. One thing the new American League proved was that Mike was not just a brilliant individual rider, but also a captain who tried to help his team on and off the track. His team partner admitted that he would not have scored as many points in league racing, had it not been for Mike's willingness to team-ride and help him.

Team racing was new for the Americans, so very few riders could ride smoothly together. Some, like the Brian Short–Jeff Sexton pairing had it worked out, but others thought that team racing meant trying to run your opponent into the fence, or knock him off.

There were some American riders, including Mike Bast, who would have welcomed the opportunity to race in Britain on a limited tour, say one or two months. The problem was that the Californian season ran parallel with the British one and the American promoters would be unwilling to lose their stars during their season. However, the Americans could not do themselves justice, during such a short stay, unless they added the experienced Scott Autrey, Steve Gresham and Mike Caruso, to their team. Later, of course, many of the Americans I rode against did come to the British League, and were very successful.

At that time, an American team of only Californian-based riders, would find it tough even against a British National League (second tier) team, owing to their lack of experience on European tracks. But the same squad of Americans, racing on their own fast, tea-cup sized tracks, could have challenged and beaten any visiting overseas team.

Most of the top American stars wanted to ride in the World Championship events in Europe but the dispute in 1976 between the American Motorcycle Association and the Californian Speedway Racing Association put paid to that idea. As the riders on the Southern Californian tracks were ineligible to race on tracks governed by the AMA in 1976, it was thought that the AMA would appoint Scott Autrey as the American to be seeded to the Inter-Continental Final at Wembley. Scott was the obvious choice, The AMA, however, had other ideas and decided to stage an American Round of the World Championship. At short notice, Scott along with fellow England-based Americans Steve Gresham and Mike Caruso, had to fly back to California to compete in the qualifying rounds. Two rounds were held in Northern California with only local riders competing against the British League Americans. The top Californian riders missed out owing to the licencing dispute.

It was a great pity that the AMA decided to hold qualifying rounds that were not a true representation of the strength of American speedway. Scott qualified to give America its first World Finalist since the early 1950s, but he had to fight a controversial tape exclusion which threatened his chances.

With respect to Northern Californian riders, it would have been disastrous if a local rider had won the round and qualified for Wembley. Many European observers would have doubted the wisdom of allocating a place to the USA and it would have done more harm than good to America's quest for another World Champion. Scott gave a great performance in his first World Final and kept the Stars and Stripes flying high.

If the trade of riders from America to Britain was rather small, there were always 'foreigners' dropping in to the Californian tracks to catch a whiff of the speedway atmosphere. Robin Addlington of Berwick dropped in on his way home to New Zealand. Robin was very keen to see American speedway live, so I took him with me to the Ventura track, very similar to the famous Costa Mesa circuit.

As Robin watched the spectacular show, his jaw dropped and he kept muttering "They must be crazy". Other visitors were former Crayford rider, Tony Armstrong, who came down from Canada, and former Cradley and Wimbledon favourite John Edwards who was working on the Indianapolis racing cars in the States.

Bob Chater, a track raker from Birmingham also viewed the scene with amazement, but thought that he would return someday and start a training school – for track rakers.

The funniest visit was when my Scottish friend, Norman Christie, arrived from Glasgow for a holiday with us at Ken Maely's Ranch. Always a bit of a character and, like many Scots, fiercely patriotic, Norman thought that he would surprise me and before the plane landed at LA International Airport he got changed and stepped off the plane wearing his tartan kilt.

Unfortunately, when Norman arrived, there was no-one there to greet him. I was working on my speedway bike 50 miles away, unaware of the details of his flight. The airmail letter which Norman had sent me (no emails, texts or mobile phones in those days) with his arrival time had not arrived so I was not there to pick him up.

By coincidence, the Scottish pop group The Bay City Rollers were due to land at LA that day and when the waiting teeny-boppers saw this guy in a kilt coming off the airplane, they thought that he was one of the group and rushed towards him. I received a phone call from Norman's girlfriend, Karen and moments later, and I was in my van, speeding down the Freeway at the regulation 55mph.

In the meantime, Norman was busy warding off the teenagers who had gathered at the airport to meet the Bay City Rollers. When I eventually found him he was busily signing autographs and tactfully answering embarrassing questions like 'Hey buddy, what d' ya wear under your skirt?' A dangerous question to ask a Scotsman. Nevertheless, he survived and during the next few weeks we toured around the speedway tracks and he quickly realised that it was not like any speedway he had ever seen in Scotland.

Who says it never rains in southern California?

The USA National Championship was the biggest event in the American speedway calendar; the big money individual event at the end of the regular season. Apart from a break in 1975 when it was held at the LA Coliseum, the National was always at the Costa Mesa circuit.

Despite the success of the event in the vast Coliseum Stadium, where one end was blocked off to form a D-shaped track, the meeting lacked something, the electric atmosphere of the small Costa Mesa bowl. It was not until a few weeks before the 1976 National that Harry Oxley announced it would be held at Costa Mesa instead of the Coliseum or the Anaheim Angels Baseball Stadium.

It was uncertain how to decide who would qualify for the final and how to go about it. In previous years, qualifying rounds have been held, but at one stage, it was proposed that the top 16 point scorers from the league averages be seeded direct to the National. This was later amended to seeding the top 10 riders with qualifying rounds to fill the other six places.

It was then decided to seed the top 10 point scorers, regardless of averages, because some riders had missed matches due to injury. Thus San Bernadino's Jim Fishback, who had been out with a broken ankle in mid-season, did not qualify in the top 10 even though his points average rated him around 6th place. Instead, former USA champion, Rick Woods, qualified owing to having a higher number of total points.

Qualifying rounds were hastily organised and each of the league tracks was allocated a championship meeting. Bakersfield's fell foul of a violent tropical storm which washed out their round and, the meeting was then allocated to Ventura. This gave their riders a second 'home' round while Bakersfield staged a meaningless 'open' meeting in its place.

I missed out on qualifying for the National despite a good meeting at Costa Mesa, but perhaps it is just as well, the American Championship for the Americans, Australian Championship for Australians and so on.

The tropical storm which hit Bakersfield was a wild one, just like something from Universal Studios or Disneyland. Arriving at Bakersfield, the weather was still hot and dry, but black clouds were gathering from the south and seemed to have followed us from LA. It seemed as though the storm may pass us by, so the riders unloaded their equipment and changed into their leathers. Just before the scheduled 8pm start, the evening sky got very black and a strong wind begun to blow. Knowledgeable weather prophets yelled 'That's it' and suddenly everyone was clearing the pits and loading their bikes into their vans. Having been brought up in British speedway, where wet meetings were not unusual. I hung around to wait for the official cancellation from the referee.

I should have followed the crowd when they rushed out of the pits because, minutes later, the wind whipped up and created a gigantic dust storm. Still no rain and very hot, but the pits and car park area only had a dirt surface. The ensuing sand storm made me feel like Lawrence of Arabia.

It was difficult to see more than a few yards ahead and the remaining riders who were trying to rescue their sand covered toolboxes had resorted to wearing goggles. Then torrential rains came, with flashes of lightning overhead and peals of thunder. The heavens really opened as I splashed back to the shelter of my van. The electrical storm was pretty frightening, especially because all the lights around the stadium kept flickering and going out. Everyone else was sheltering under the concrete grandstand, the only cover available. The speedway office, a small wooden hut in the car park, was a little island in the middle of a rising flood.

Then tragedy struck. One woman, intending to rush for the shelter of the grandstand was struck by lightning as she stepped from her car. Track officials rushed from the speedway office to assist her. Unfortunately, the ambulance, which was in another part of the Fairgrounds, had problems reaching the scene due to the traffic chaos. Despite their great efforts, the woman died on the way to hospital. Two women were also injured when lightning struck the car park, so all in all, it was a very black day for Bakersfield. By the time the storm had moved on, one hour later, reports of floods, fires and damage were coming in from all over Kern County.

Costa Mesa had also been washed out by sudden thunderstorms which flooded the track and car park the night before and the unusual wet weather upset the running of the fixture

List. Suddenly it was decided to cancel the remaining two weeks of league matches, and replace them with a Best Pairs tournament and a Four-Team Championship.

Bakersfield were still on top of the league, so we were awarded the title with Irwindale breathing down our necks in second spot. It was reasoned that, as the Bandits had a commanding points lead they were assured of victory, but the injury to Brian Short, one of the most improved riders in the league, and the late season return to form of the LA Sprockets could have altered that result in the final run-in.

'Digger' Helm was well pleased that his beloved Bandits had finished ahead of all the more fancied clubs, and we were also happy at being able to repay him for the help he had given us throughout the year. It had not always been plain sailing for the Bandits. We began the season as a close-knit team although riders who had always raced individually sometimes found it difficult to realise that they were part of a team. Perhaps the saying 'Familiarity breeds contempt' was true, because friction began to build up between team-mates.

The most difficult period for the Bandits was when Brian Short broke his leg late in the season. 'Thumper' was a key member of the team on-and-off the track. After his injury, the pressure really was on. His absence could not be covered by rider replacement because he was not one of the top three Bakersfield riders.

Tom Morley, son of former flat track and speedway rider Stu Morley, was brought in from the ranks of the second division and, although he rode very well, the Bandits missed Thumper's consistent home and away scoring.

Meanwhile, the LA Sprockets got their act together and, magnificently led by Mike Bast, were knocking spots off the opposition, especially at home. Riding on the longest track in the league, and with four riders using four-valve engines, the Sprockets were almost invincible at home.

In California, track measurements then varied from week to week, depending on where the white line, made of white plastic hose piping, was laid. When Bakersfield visited Irwindale in a crucial league match, the 'pole', or white line, had been moved and the straights were even longer than usual

Friction begun to also build up in the Bandits' camp. Every point in every match counted in our bid to stay at the top. We had been at the top for 14 weeks and did not want to slip now. Heated words were exchanged between team-mates, and the Bandits, once renowned for their team spirit and comradeship, were slipping back to becoming a team of individuals.

The climax for me was when I was unable to attend a Friday evening team practice session at Bakersfield, due to collecting 'Bay City Roller' Norman, from LA Airport. Practice sessions are very good, up to a point, but they tend to be rather wearing on the bikes and tyres. Besides, I could not leave my friend sitting on an airport bench all weekend until I returned from Bakersfield.

The next day I set off for Bakersfield, where we were due to entertain the LA Sprockets that evening. On arriving at the pit area in the Fairgrounds, I was rather surprised to find that the Bandits' side of the pits was completely filled with bikes. Normally, the opposing teams park on opposite sides of the pits, except for one Bandits' rider who preferred to park his machinery elsewhere in a Greta Garbo 'I want to be alone' style. It was this individual who had spread his two bikes and multitude of equipment plus deckchair, across the area where I normally pitted.

The reply I received when I asked him to make room for my machine, would have been quite funny, if it had not been so childish: "You didn't come to the practice, so I thought you were not on the team anymore." Ah well, it is nice to know that I was missed. Incidentally, the same rider missed a team practice a couple of weeks later. His excuse? His mechanic could not get time off work.

My strange friend also happened to be my team partner, so there was usually some dispute about starting positions. On one occasion, while trying to 'team ride' with him, my partner – I use that word loosely – executed a right hand turn and tried to run me into the concrete wall at Bakersfield. That, and a few other incidents, made me think that perhaps some of the boys were carrying their Bi-Centennial celebrations just a little too far. Maybe they had chased the British out in 1776, but trying to drive a Scotsman out in 1976 was a different story.

Even the highway patrol got into the act. One Wednesday evening I was driving my van to San Bernadino for a meeting when I was rudely interrupted by the wailing siren and flashing red lights of a motorcycle cop. Thinking that he was in a hurry to get to the races, I pulled over to let him pass but, to my surprise, he pulled in behind me. I assumed that he did not want my autograph, so I made a quick mental check of my driving technique over the past few miles. I knew that I hadn't been speeding; it took my van all its time to reach the 55mph limit. I knew I had halted at the stop sign coming off the freeway. I was surprised when he asked: "Do you have a permit to carry that motorcycle in your van?"

I explained that the bike was used only for speedway racing and could not be ridden on, or registered for, the road. He told me that there was a new law that all motorcycles used in 'closed course' competition must be registered and that a 'Transportation Permit' was required to carry them from track to track.

He then wrote me a ticket, although I told him I was only a visitor to his wonderful country but that cut no ice. The next day I bought the necessary permit and took it to San Bernadino County Court, thinking that all I had to do was show the document and leave as a free man.

The counter clerk took my permit then, after studying a huge law book, said "That will be $65 Mr Harkins. Are you going to pay now?"

I protested, but the only alternative was to attend court that afternoon and explain my case to the judge. The courtroom was packed with petty offenders and, after waiting a couple of hours, my turn came. The judge was certainly friendlier than the highway patrolman who had booked me. He waived the fine and let me go. Thereafter, all riders who were transporting their speedway or moto cross bikes in vans around the San Bernadino area kept the curtains drawn on the van windows to hide their motorcycles.

This racing over-exuberance was not confined to speedway racing, as I found out when I went along to see the United States Grand Prix Moto Cross at Carlsbad. Motocross is big business in American, so when all the top international riders came over to California, I went along to see them.

On a hot, sunny Sunday, Dutch dentist Gerrit Wolsjnk extracted a couple of painless wins, but world champion Roger de Coster had mechanical problems all afternoon. I had come to see fellow Scotsman, Vic Allan, who was riding the British CCM machine. The deep burble from the exhaust of the big four-stroke was a welcome change from all the screaming two-strokes. During one race, Vic was involved in a rough-and-tumble dice with American Harley Davidson rider, Rex Staton, which ended with both riders trading punches after a pile-up on a corner – shades of Dan Toomey and Mike Muntean at Bakersfield. Vic rode his damaged CCM back to the pits to retire from the race, while the ambulance helicopter whisked Rex off to hospital. It certainly didn't pay to upset a Scotsman.

After the meeting, I made my way to the pits, only to find that the armed security guard on the gate would not let me through with my Wimbledon Speedway pit pass. I wonder why?

Undaunted, I walked around the perimeter fence, found a quiet spot and, with some difficulty, climbed the high barbed wire fence. I managed to rip my shorts and T-shirt and cut my fingers in my efforts to get over this fence so with bleeding hands and torn pants, I headed happily to the CCM pits, congratulating myself on my 'great escape'; like Steve McQueen but without a motorcycle. Just as I opened my mouth so say "Howz it goin, Vic?" a large hand clamped on my shoulder. I turned around to see a black leather jacket and, looking upwards, I noticed that it was connected to a very large policeman, complete with white crash helmet, evil-looking sunglasses, and droopy Wyatt Earp moustache. He also had a pearl-handled revolver swinging from a holster on his hip in true cowboy style, so, when he spoke, I really took notice.

"OK Buddy, now you get outta here the same goddam way you got in." My injured hands did not feel like trying to scale the 'Stalag 15' fence again, but the gum-chewing policeman, with his hands on his six-gun seemed quite persuasive. I started babbling away in my broadest Scottish accent and by luck, Vic Allan noticed my troubles and came over to explain things to the confused cop. With my Glaswegian accent and Vic's Aberdonian one eventually, the policeman walked away muttering something about foreigners who cannot speak English.

At this motocross event at Carlsbad Raceway, I met up with the Scott Race Rep, Don McGee, or as he was named at the time, 'Don McGoggles'. He gave me some new Scott Model 87 OTG (Over-the-Glasses) goggles with spare lenses and tear-offs to try out. My first goggle sponsorship! These goggles had a deeper frame to fit over the top of spectacles, different to the "Monkey Masks" and even "Gas Goggles" I had used previously. They fitted very comfortably although the peripheral vision was slightly affected due to the deeper frame, but when you wear glasses when racing, you are aware of that slight problem.

32. Reflections on American speedway

It was a lot of fun for the fans. One of the nice things about being a speedway fan in California then is that the promoters really cared about you. From time to time, the tracks had 'Fan Appreciation Nights' when various members of the public got into the speedway free of charge. Like 'Student Nite', when students were admitted free and given free popcorn. Or 'Fox Nite,' the evening when all female fans (Foxes) could walk in without paying.

Or the 'Select Vans and Al Martinez Nite' at Costa Mesa, when the track's biggest sponsors gave out free T-shirts, caps, jackets, posters and other souvenirs to the fans.

The fans sometimes spotted a celebrity or movie star mingling with the crowd. Top European and American motorcycle racers dropped in when they have a race meeting in Southern California, and a few Hollywood people too. Robert Blake, star of the American television series *Barretta*, was a keen speedway fan and enjoyed most motorcycle sports. He was interviewed in the LA Coliseum during the stadium Moto Cross and said how much he was enjoying the racing. Then he added that it was not quite as good as Costa Mesa.

Robert Redford was another star believed to sneak into the Orange County Fairgrounds to watch the 'sideways circus' from time-to-time, and the original 'Clark Kent/Superman' was a keen spectator at Ventura and Costa Mesa. He seemed to spend most of his time waiting outside the telephone box to become Superman, so I never met him. Movie star, Ann Margaret one time girlfriend of Elvis Presley was supposed to have been at Costa Mesa the night I crashed at her feet, but I was too dazed to realise that she was there. 'Spot the Star' was an interesting game in California, but what the fans really came to see were the thrills and spills of speedway. They were never, ever disappointed.

Every weekend, the freeways out of LA were filled with thousands of vehicles heading for the mountains, the beaches or the desert, all within a couple of hours drive at most. Cars and trailers with boats, caravans and motorcycles, huge 'mobile homes' towing speed boats and trailbikes on a rack on the rear bumper or strapped across the front bumper were leaving town. Everywhere there were 'Recreational Vehicles' (RVs) towing everything from Volkswagen Beach Buggies, to the latest 'Fun Bike' for trail or desert riding or even small cars. Since Costa Mesa ran on a Friday evening, many fans went to the races before heading out of town, and allowed the freeway time to cool off a little. The Californians really knew how to make the most out of their long, hot, summers, but to be correct, we should change Albert Hammond's song from *It Never Rains in Sunny California* to 'It hardly ever rains in Southern California'.

Characters, American speedway was full of them, but I suppose it is only natural in such a large country. Where else do you have a former television star turned speedway rider? Or a 17 stone novice by the name of 'Tumbleweed' who needed three pushers to get his bike started? Or a rider who posed au naturale for the centrefold of a girlie magazine?

In the early 1960s, there was a very popular American television show called *Father knows best*, starring Robert Young. The series was also shown in Britain and the Anderson family became quite popular on both sides of the Atlantic. The series has long since departed from

British screens, but thanks to the miracle of video tape, the show still had a weekly spot on many American television channels in 1976.

Billy Gray, who played Bud, the teenage son of the Anderson family, was then in his 30s. It is quite a few years since he gave up performing in television studios and moved to the floodlights of the speedway track, but he still could not shake off that 'Bud Anderson' image.

Billy was a popular member of the Orange County Eagles at Costa Mesa and had many fans. However, many did not realise that the television series they watched every week were old repeats and were quite surprised when they came to the pits and saw that 'Bud' had grown up. Perhaps he should star in a new series with an American speedway theme. We could call it *Father knows Bast* – Mike, Steve and Harlan.

A star of another kind, but nevertheless a big star in every sense of the word, was Costa Mesa's favourite novice, 'Tumbleweed' Walton. Tumbleweed – real name Pat – earned his nickname by the number of times he bit the dust while trying to finish a race in his first season in 1975. The hefty and rather round Tumbleweed began in third division races at Costa Mesa. With his frequent bounces down the track, he really captured the crowd's support. When he appeared for his five-lap, six rider, novice handicap races, the cheers equalled anything that Bruce Penhall or Bill Cody's fans could raise.

Tumbleweed's first appearance on a speedway track was not as a rider, but as a gorilla (only in America)! He dressed up in a gorilla suit one night, pushed Jeff Sexton's bike onto the track and everyone thought that it was a remake of *King Kong*. In his first season Tumbleweed lived up to his name and never finished a race. He often had so much trouble that the fans would bet on which lap he would fall. Not daunted, he went on a crash diet before the next season and lost a few pounds. He had to be careful during his off-season training. In his normal large form, he was such a favourite with the crowd that Harry Oxley said that if he became a better and slimmer rider, he would drop him from the programme.

Tumbleweed did progress, and became a firm favourite with the crowds wherever he rode. His new custom-made leathers were designed to look like a pair of blue bib-and-brace overalls with a red shirt underneath. They were so effective that he looked like one of *The Beverley Hill Billies*. On the front of the leathers was 'Thanks Dad', appreciation for his father's encouragement and financial help in his speedway career.

His big moment of the year came in one of the novice handicap events at Costa Mesa. After starting from his usual position at the front of the field, the other five riders overtook him. During the next few laps, the others managed to crash or run into each other, leaving him to pick a path through the fallen bikes and cross the line to a standing ovation from his happy fans.

Living in Corona I had an American-size speedway track outside my door and knew that I could get out of bed, fuel and oil my Jawa and put in a few practice laps before breakfast. This was the case when I stayed at *Hot Shoe Manor*, alias the Ken Maely ranch. Edith and I had a big trailer home on Ken & Judy's ranch.

Ken was more than just an accomplished welder. On his ranch in the hills outside LA, he bulldozed a 200 yard speedway track in a canyon beside his house, erected a wooden safety fence, battery powered starting gates, and opened his own training school. Mike Bast and Sonny Nutter ran training schools there and the track was available for hire at other times.

Left: Ken Maely.

Right: The entrance to his ranch, which had a speedway training track.

Below: The LA Sprockets team from the 1976 American League, including a young Bruce Penhall.

Ken's son Mike made good use of the facilities and it was here that the prototype four-valve Maely engine was put through its paces for hours on end. In addition to the engine project, Ken also made his own speedway frames, saddles, steel shoes and more. With his wife Judy, they would post steel shoes, boots and other items to customers all over America. I suppose it was the original, 'Maely-Order' business.

There was another training school in operation in the Los Angeles area, but there were no speedway bikes at this one, only tape recorders and microphones. It was run by Larry Huffman for track announcers. The extrovert Mr Huffman set up his own school to teach his pupils the arts of speedway and sports commentating, radio broadcasting and even how to become a disc jockey. Well, having risen from a job as a supermarket checker, to his lofty position as speedway's top presenter, I reckon he was well qualified to pass on a few tips.

If enrolling in an announcer's training school did not appeal, then how about becoming a swimming pool cleaner? I suppose it is a job which is easy to 'fall into' as my Bakersfield team-mate, Brian Short could have told you. In his early days in speedway, Brian was also employed as a swimming pool cleaner and had the good fortune to have many show business customers in the Beverley Hills and Hollywood areas.

Brian was called to one of these Hollywood homes to clean the large outdoor pool. The owners, a well-known American pop group, were away on a European tour, leaving their butler and staff in charge of the house. What followed was a weekend-long party. Brian still cannot remember if he ever cleaned the pool.

The original *On any Sunday* movie by Bruce Brown still rates as one of the best, it not **the** best motorcycle movies ever made. A mixture of the fun and thrills of motorcycle racing and the dangerous side, all to a background of some feel-good music. Speedway racing was featured in the original filming when Bruce and his crew came to Costa Mesa to catch the action but unfortunately, being Friday evening racing, it didn't quite fit in with the movie's title of what motorcycle racers did on a Sunday. A great pity; perhaps I could have become a movie star a stunt double for Woody Allen or Michael Caine. (Not a lot of people know that.). Barry Briggs meanwhile became good friends with Bruce Brown and his Hollywood star and fellow motorcycle racer, Steve McQueen. He went on to buy Bruce's lovely house overlooking the harbour at Dana Point and Briggo also found time to teach Steve McQueen how to ride a Speedway bike. A handy topic of conversation to throw into the mix at a party!

At the end of the 1976 season, with another exciting American trip behind me, I was pleased that I had taken the opportunity of spending a full season in the States. My team, Bakersfield Bandits, won the first American League Championship and I survived the 'Lions versus Christians' season without bouncing down the track too often.

A major benefit of my season in the sun, and one that was to play a huge part in my post-Speedway life, was my first goggle sponsorship and meeting up with the people from Scott USA, the American Ski and Motocross goggle company, but more of that plus Troy Lee and Malcolm Smith later. I thoroughly enjoyed the sunshine of the Californian summer and the completely different speedway scene there. I guess I made the right decision after all, when I decided to pack my bags and race speedway – American style!

33. Trails of the unexpected

When that Californian League season ended, Edith and I decided to make the most of our trip home and instead of just hopping on a plane in Los Angeles and flying home, we booked the Amtrax train to take us right across America from Reno in Nevada to New York in the East and then we would head home to the UK by ship.

We had a few days to spare before our epic train journey and were invited to stay with our friends, Linda and Don Draper, at Lake Tahoe in Nevada with the offer of doing some trail riding there. That offer sounded too good to be true, and it was. I sold my Two-valve Jawa complete with tartan rear mudguard for $1,300 in California, then headed up to Lake Tahoe. Don was a TWA airline pilot and had a garage full of KTM motocross bikes – one of which belonged to Linda – so he loaned me a 490cc machine for our trail ride along with another guy called Don, who was a barber so they became 'Don the hair' and 'Don the air'.

They also lent me some riding gear which included a pair of ancient leather Motocross jeans which were so big that I could have wrapped them around my waist twice. But those extra inches on the waistband would prove a vital safety factor later that day.

The oversize Alpine Stars boots they gave me were so old and heavy that they felt like the 'concrete boots' worn by enemies of the Mafia when they went swimming. A faded Airtex Honda race shirt added to the outfit that made me look like a recycled Motocross Factory team rider from the 1950s. Luckily my own Bell helmet was new as I tended to test them personally and it was not wise to be wearing a second hand helmet. My borrowed outfit was topped off with a pair of well-worn gloves and a third hand set of Scott goggles. Mr Immaculate I was not. We loaded our bikes onto a pickup truck and headed to the desert to meet up with some of the guys from the local motorcycle shop. The boss had left a note on the shop door: 'Sorry, closed today – gone riding.'

We met the rest of the riders for this 'trail ride' at the edge of the desert near Mono Lake almost on the border between California and Nevada and that is when I realised that these guys took their off road riding very seriously indeed.

As they off-loaded their bikes from their trucks, there were brand new Honda, Yamaha and KTM motocross bikes and the riders had all the latest motocross gear and body armour even to the extent of having tear-offs and roll-offs on their goggles. These guys meant business. They made my off-road wardrobe look even scruffier than I had imagined, but they were not worried, they were just out to have a good time riding in the desert.

They blasted away in a cloud of white dust and wheelies as I tried to kick start my KTM into some kind of life. I followed on with some of the others at a more leisurely pace whilst trying to work out how these things called brakes and gears were used and how to get round a right hand corner. I soon gained confidence in this motocross bike which had a saddle so high that I began to get nose bleeds and I settled into my 'racing-rhythm' which was just fast enough to save oiling up the spark plug.

Experienced off-road riders learn to 'read' the trail ahead, things like stones and dirt in the desert must have come from somewhere and that is usually an old silver or gold mine or a dried up river bed –pity that no-one had thought to tell me that before we went riding.

I was charging along when I went careering over the edge of an old mineshaft in the classic 'Flying W' position, hands on the handlebars and feet up over shoulder height. When I crash-landed, it took me some time to clear the dust out of my throat, clean my goggles and glasses and fire up the old KTM to try to get out of that mineshaft. Fortunately, the two Dons had doubled back to see where I was and once they had stopped laughing, hauled me out. I guess they liked to take unwary foreigners on these trips to have a laugh at their misfortune, and I certainly filled the bill. We rode through canyons, along dry river beds and to Mono Lake where I had a head-on collision with a giant hare, a 'hare-raising' experience.

As the others blasted around the sand dunes, I decided to see how close to the lake I could ride, and that was another mistake. As I raced along the shoreline at a mind-boggling 45mph, the KTM suddenly ground to a halt as if the engine had seized, but it was not as simple as that. I had ridden straight into the soft quicksand at the edge of the lake, something else no-one told me about. The bike had sunk down to its rear wheel spindle. 'No worries', I thought, 'I will just sit on the back of the seat to get some traction and off we go.' Some hope! As I dropped the clutch, the KTM rear wheel spun and the bike sunk further into the quicksand up to the seat. I stepped off, put my hand under the seat to lift the bike out. The KTM did not move, but I promptly sank up to my boot tops in this bottomless pit.

By this time, the others had seen my frantic efforts as my wearying body tried to escape from this slow sinking feeling. I had visions of disappearing under the quicksand just like an explorer in those old 'B' movies of my schoolboy days.

My 'friends' gathered at the shoreline laughing as I sank into the goo until Don Draper realised that I was riding his bike. I was also in danger of losing my boots because I could not pull my feet out of this quagmire so a 'Save-the-Haggis' rescue operation quickly started. The two Dons found an old tree lying nearby and dragged it to the lake. They laid it across the quicksand and cautiously walked along it to pull me out. Then they formed a human chain to pull me and the motorcycle onto harder ground. I never had this problem in speedway. It certainly was a scary situation and I had visions of only my tartan-painted helmet being left visible on top of the quicksand like a memorial to a lost Haggis.

I had had enough 'fun' for one day, so we headed back towards the truck and civilization but my crashing days were not yet over. The trail back to where we left the vehicles wound around the side of a mountain and the shortcut we took was just wide enough for a 500 x 18 motocross tyre. At one stage, the trail was broken by a 'wash-out' and the only way to get across was to lift the front wheel and 'bunny hop' across. I managed to get the front wheel across, but did not quite make the rest of the manoeuvre and the bike toppled upside down over the washout. I toppled over too and this is where I was thankful that I was wearing these baggy motocross pants. As I fell over, the end of the KTM's handlebars went inside the waistband of my baggy jeans and caught under my belt, saving me from a quick trip down the mountain without my motorcycle. It took a lot of effort to haul me and the KTM back onto the trail, but we made it and I lived to tell the tale. Back at the truck, I was aching all over and my friends were aching too, but they were aching with laughter.

And so we returned to Don's place at Lake Tahoe and next day, Edith and I set off on our relaxing homeward-bound trip across America by train. Well it was relaxing until the train got derailed at Denver and we had to take the bus. Yes, you do get your kicks on Route 66.

34. Going home

1977 and arriving back in Britain after my season in sunny California, I was still a Wimbledon asset and was looking forward to returning to riding for the Dons, but another new venture was on the horizon. My original club, the Edinburgh Monarchs were returning to speedway and they wanted me to captain the new Monarchs.

Originally I had no intention of dropping down from the British League First Division and had planned to stay there for the rest of my career. However, the lure of returning to Scotland, and to the team where it had all started for me, was too much to resist. Once again, my heart ruled my head.

Somehow, in my speedway career, I never did quite get my commuting right when signing for a new team. When I first got into the Edinburgh team as reserve at Old Meadowbank, I was living in Glasgow, some 50 miles away. I went to Australia and when I came back Old Meadowbank had closed down to be rebuilt as the Commonwealth Games Stadium. Incidentally, that 'new' stadium is now being demolished again to make way for another new athletics stadium on the Meadowbank site. The Edinburgh Monarchs then moved to Coatbridge, a mere 15 miles from home. I went to Australia again and when I came back Coatbridge had closed and I was transferred to Wembley, a mere 400 miles from my home in Glasgow. Another couple of Australian trips, then Wembley closed down. Perhaps I should have stopped going to Australia in the winter and these tracks may have survived. Even in the season I spent racing in the American League, I rode for Bakersfield, the furthest track from where I was living in Corona. Other tracks to receive the 'Haggis kiss of death' treatment included Wimbledon, Cowdenbeath, Powderhall and Milton Keynes. Fortunately, both Sheffield and Edinburgh have survived having me in their teams. No wonder I never had a testimonial during my long career, I was the BSPA's human chess piece, being moved from club to club to suit their demands.

Now I was returning to the land of my birth. I was quite excited to be returning to captain the Monarchs, but just one wee problem. By this time, I had kept moving home south, first to Rugby and then to Hertfordshire, so after riding for Wembley when living in Scotland, I was now going to do it the other way around, living in Hertfordshire and riding for Edinburgh. It was lucky that I enjoyed travelling.

The news was that the Monarchs would be racing at the neat and tidy Powderhall Stadium in Edinburgh and that Mike Parker, who was the main architect of the Provincial League when it was launched in 1960, would be the promoter. That shrewd operator, Neil MacFarlane, would be team manager. The new Monarchs were boosted by the signing of Australian former Glasgow Tigers favourite, Charlie Monk, along with Jack 'The villain' Millen, Dave Trownson, Alan 'Doc' Bridgett – who later became a much sought-after track builder and curator – plus junior Alan Morrison at reserve. The best signing was to have Doctor Carlo Biagi as our official track doctor. We all felt better when Carlo was around.

The stadium was packed for our first home match of the season, a challenge match against our near neighbours, Berwick Bandits, who beat us 42–36. Berwick's Willie Templeton had the honour of winning the very first race on the new track. I remember it as being very grippy and so deep that my primary chain guard hit the dirt in the first turn.

The Powderhall circuit was a tricky one with tight bends, but I liked the shape and the surface improved.The track always produced good racing and I finished the season as the track record holder with 65.8 seconds. Other riders who joined the Monarchs later included former Boston star, Rob Hollingworth, Steve Lomas, local boy Benny Rourke, and all-action American Ivan Blacka. Edinburgh-born Brian Collins was riding at number one for Glasgow, but by 1978 he had been transferred back to his home town where he had begun his career in the mid-1960s.

Although I was riding for Edinburgh a 'home' track which was 400 miles from my home, the travelling was not too bad. Previously, when I had been racing for Wembley and living in Glasgow, I could judge how long the journey would take, almost to within half an hour. I don't envy the riders and mechanics who do the driving these days as road works, traffic jams and accidents make it almost impossible to estimate journey times.

I had secured a nice sponsorship deal with the 4-star King James Hotel just off Princes Street in Edinburgh, so I could have a comfortable night's sleep if I wasn't driving back overnight after a meeting. The King James even had a framed photograph in the hotel foyer of me wearing their body colour alongside photographs of other Scottish sportsmen and stars from the Scottish entertainment world. That gave speedway a little bit of extra promotion. It was good for both the rider – me – the hotel and speedway in general. When I eventually left the Monarchs to ride for Milton Keynes, Edinburgh-born Benny Rourke took over the sponsorship and kept that connection alive.

Sometimes on a Friday I would head up to Edinburgh on the train with my bike and gear in the guard's van. It was quite relaxing because I could have a meal on board on the way to Scotland. I would race in the meeting at Powderhall in the evening and then get the night sleeper train back to London afterwards. Not that I got much sleep with all that rattling and swinging down the tracks, but at least I could get a bit of rest en route. The train pulled into Kings Cross very early on the Saturday morning where Edith would be waiting with my car so we would load my Jawa onto the bike carrier and head off to drive to Germany for another race meeting the next day.

On our road trips to Edinburgh, we had also worked out a routine to save time on the long journey. Any time we stopped, for petrol or coffee or whatever, it took longer to reach our average speed again when we restarted, so the idea was to keep going if possible. I had an old diesel Mercedes at the time and it had a bench front seat instead of individual seats, so Edith and I worked out a plan. To save stopping to change drivers, I would slide gently to the left on this long seat while still steering the car. Edith would climb over from the back seat, slide into the driving position, swap feet on the accelerator pedal and we would carry on merrily heading north without missing a beat. Obviously we only did it when the road was very quiet, so that rules out trying to do the same now due to the heavy traffic these days.

Fuel stops were something to be thought about in trying to drive non-stop without having to waste too much time filling up on the way. Stops had to be factored in to these long trips. In the earlier Edinburgh days at Old Meadowbank and Coatbridge, then Monarch Wayne Briggs lived with his brother Barry in Southampton, so he travelled around 450 miles for a 'home' meeting. Wayne also had a Mercedes, but he had fitted an extra fuel tank in the boot so he was able to avoid any lengthy stops at the petrol stations.

Memories of my early days with Edinburgh come to mind and I explained in an earlier chapter that on our long trips south, in order to save time when we stopped at the motorway services, George Hunter would fill up the car with petrol while Alex Hughson and I ran across to the cafe to order our food. George did everything so fast – both on and off the track – that he had filled up with petrol, eaten his meal and was on the way back to the car while Alex and I were just starting to eat. No wonder we got indigestion on these epic journeys with George.

The cars we were using did not have the same fuel consumption as they do now. Most of the trips were governed by how many miles to the gallon we could travel before we had to stop. Nowadays when I am driving long distances, it is governed by 'How many miles to the bladder' before I have to stop!

The Monarchs' first season at Powderhall went well with good crowds and good racing, but the injury bug kept hitting us hard. Charlie Monk was out for a month and Australian reserve, Mal Chambers, broke his femur. Disappointingly, as the new Edinburgh Monarchs we did not live up to expectations and, by the end of the season, we finished in the lower end of the league. I had the consolation of ending the season as the Powderhall track record holder, but I would have been happier seeing us challenging for the league title.

Scottish Championship at Blantyre on 14 August 1977, which Bert won. Left to right: Benny Rourke, Phil Kynman, Jack Millen and Bert.

Edinburgh won the Scottish Cup, beating Glasgow. Jacqueline Beaton presented the cup at Blantyre on 23 October 1977.
Back: Peter Waite, Alan 'Doc' Bridgett, Neil MacFarlane (team manager), Colin Farquharson, Steve MacDermot; front: Dave Trownson and Bert. Bert scored maximums in both legs.

35. Under African skies

By the winter of 1977, another 'Have bike will travel' tour was on the horizon. This time it would not be to Australia, but to South Africa.

I had only visited South Africa once and that was a non-riding visit when my ship, *The Fairsea*, stopped in Cape Town on my way to Australia. I remembered that it had been a very beautiful country with a lovely climate. I had also heard stories from Trevor Redmond and Freddie Williams about their exciting racing trips to that country in the days when there were quite a few top riders hailing from South Africa. Riders such as Henry Long, who rode for Belle Vue, Birmingham's Doug Serrurier, Wembley's Fred Lang and Edinburgh's Roy Bester plus many others. TR (Trevor Redmond) loved to tell the tale of when they were camping in the African bush and at night, he would creep up outside Olle Nygren's tent and roar like a hungry lion. Poor Varg-Olle was so scared that he would not come out of his tent until the others persuaded him that it was all clear. I am not sure if the Swede knew that the 'Lion' was really TR, but I am certain that Olle got his revenge with stunts of his own.

A young American touring team had visited South Africa in 1972 with current US Champion Rick Woods, Scott Autrey, Sumner McKnight and Mike Caruso setting the tracks alight with their spectacular skills. The American team manager was the flamboyant Alan Seymour III, but he soon ran into trouble as first Sumner McKnight suffered back and thigh injuries, then Mike Caruso had to fly home with an ankle injury. However, the Americans certainly left their mark on the speedway tracks of South Africa.

My own visit to South Africa was due to turn out to be a very memorable trip in more ways than one. For the vist I was being joined by Teeside's Silver Helmet holder Nigel Close and Glasgow Tiger Benny Rourke, both on their first ever racing trip overseas. We were due to have a series of meetings around the country with our home base being the Wembley (a very famous name!) Stadium in Johannesburg run by an English-born promoter. We shall just call him 'Mack the knife'. We also had meetings in Cape Town where former South Africa star, Buddy Fuller, was the promoter. There was also a contract in place to run the South African Individual Championship at the end of the season at Wembley Stadium with live coverage on South African television. The winter season ahead looked very promising.

My Edinburgh buddies, Alex Hughson and Roni Ferguson, and former Wembley Lion, Peter Prinsloo, were already in South Africa preparing the tracks. Alex and Roni had previously run speedway in Rhodesia, so had plenty of experience and expertise. Our base was Ponte City in Johannesburg. It was a brand new 55 storey tower block of apartments with a restaurant, pizza parlour and swimming pool on the ground floor, very nice.

The 55 floor cylindrical Ponte City had been built in 1975 and was the tallest apartment tower in Africa. We were on the 36th floor with panoramic views over Johannesburg. We often ran up the stairs to keep fit, but it was difficult because of the thin air at 6,000 feet high altitude in Johannesburg. However, it did help us to acclimatise. I had even carried my spare engine up to the 36th floor so that I could work on it in our apartment, not a typical workshop but handy if I wanted to have a quick cup of tea.

We had arrived at Jan Smuts Airport in Johannesburg on a Thursday afternoon, but sudden heavy thunderstorms washed out our first meeting which had been due to take place at the Wembley Stadium on Saturday. This was a bit of good fortune as our bikes, which had come by sea, were being held at Customs in Cape Town, around 1,000 miles away. I had brought a spare engine with me in my hand luggage (honest!), but that wasn't much good without the rest of the bike. At the Jan Smuts International Airport (later renamed the OR Tambo International Airport after the ANC [African National Congress] President, the Afrikaner customs officer took a liking to my engine and refused to let it into the country. I spent two days with various SA customs agents before I was allowed to bring my Jawa engine into the country. My sporran became a lot lighter after paying the import duty.

With some spare time on our hands until the bikes arrived from Cape Town, we decided to check out the local area. We spent some time wandering around the giant international hotel and shopping complex called the Carlton Centre. Our first day in Johannesburg certainly went with a bang as, not long after leaving the Centre, a bomb went off there injuring 19 people but fortunately we were all back at our hotel relaxing by the swimming pool when the explosion occurred. This was at the time of apartheid ('Apartness' in Afrikaans) so there was some unrest in the country. For us visitors, it was unusual to see signs on the benches at the bus stops reading 'Whites only' or 'Blacks and Coloureds Only'. It was all very strange to our European eyes. At that time, cricket and most other sports' national organisations boycotted South Africa. Perhaps some people thought that we should have been part of that boycott too, but we were only some young speedway riders in a minority sport, and we went ahead with our trip.

Still waiting for the bikes to clear customs, we paid a visit to the Simmer & Jack Gold Mine which dated back to 1886 and was still in use. John Jack was a Scot from Glasgow who owned the mine in the early days so it just shows that where there is gold, there is a Scotsman nearby. To go underground we had to be kitted out with miner's hard hats, overalls and wellington boots. I remember that Nig Close reckoned that it would be a good idea to have one of those lamps on our helmets on some of the tracks at home where the lighting was not too good. There were no free gold bars, but we did have our photographs taken with some, but had to hand them back.

Eventually our bikes arrived and it was all systems go to get ready for our first meeting at Wembley. Meetings in South Africa comprised of speedway, sprint cars and flat track racing. The flat trackers used Honda, Yamaha, BSA and Bultaco machines, six riders per race, six laps but with an eight lap trophy final. Fortunately, in the speedway races we did only four laps and even that was quite hard work in the thin air of Johannesburg on the 360 meter Wembley track.

We finally got underway on 2 December 1977 with Wembley's 30th Anniversary Championship. The rain kept coming down every time the flat track riders came out, but the track held up well and Peter Prinsloo won the Grand Final ahead of me, Nig Close and Benny Rourke.

Peter broke South African Arthur Bruin's track record at Wembley and Scottish Junior Champion, Benny Rourke, collected the track record when we raced at the Mahem Stadium in Pretoria so all was going well for the tourists. The opening meeting in Pretoria was run on

220

the current Grand Prix formula of heats, semi-finals and a Grand Final. Benny went through his first four rides undefeated with 12 points, then lost to Peter Prinsloo in the Trophy Final. This time I was knocked out at the semi-final stage. The final was won by Peter ahead of Benny Rourke, Nig Close and Arthur Bruins.

We were kept busy with meetings and publicity events, but still found time to do some sightseeing in this beautiful country. The South Africans had been generous to us because apart from our sponsored accommodation at Ponte City, the local Ford agency, Grosvenor Motors of Parktown North had sponsored Peter Prinsloo and myself with a new Ford Escort each plus a Ford pickup truck to Nigel and Benny for carrying the bikes and equipment. We also tried to help the local South African riders at Wembley with riding and mechanical tips. Rhodesian born Denzil Kent later came to Britain to ride for Glasgow and other clubs. He looked like a really good prospect, but retired too early and returned to live in South Africa.

In addition to Wembley and Pretoria, we also got a booking to race at Buddy Fuller's Goodwood track 1,000 miles away in Cape Town. Flying was too expensive for us and travel by coach was too long and tiring so we settled on travelling by train. The South African 'Blue Train' was the jewel in the SA Railways crown, a bit like an African version of The Orient Express, but this too was out of our budget. We settled on taking the normal tourist train which would take longer and be a bit more spartan, but that didn't matter. It was another adventure to see some more of the country en route so Nig, Benny, Alex Hughson, Roni Ferguson and me booked into a carriage with bench seats which folded into beds. It was comfortable enough except that we had to be careful because if we were in the top bunk and the window was open, there was a danger of sliding out of the bunk and straight out of the window when the train rounded a corner. It was just like the films when someone is being buried at sea.

There was no air conditioning - apart from opening the window and letting the even hotter air come in - so it was a hot and sticky journey. Eventually, a few hours outside of Cape Town, our train pulled into Bloemfontain station and stopped for a while. The announcements were all in Afrikaans so we did not understand them as we piled out of the train and onto the platform to stretch our legs. It had been a really long hot journey and we were all stripped to the waist and dressed only in shorts as we wandered along the empty platform. Then we had a huge shock. A whistle sounded and the train started to chug away back out of the station. We were still there on the platform waving and yelling like mad. The train disappeared out of the station and we were left there in the silence on our own with whatever clothes we had on, and this only amounted to a pair of shorts each. As we were wondering what to do next, another problem came along in the form of a large Afrikaner policeman who began shouting at us in Afrikaans. We couldn't understand him and he pointed to a notice which said that walking around without a shirt on is an offence which carried a hefty fine or even arrest.

We panicked and spluttered out that we had been on that train and it had left without us and our shirts, money and passports were all on that train. We were stuck, had no other clothes and no idea of how we could get to Cape Town. The policeman did not sound too sympathetic as he continued to berate us in Afrikaans. We didn't understand a word he was saying, but he sure sounded very serious. Just as we were thinking the worst and that we would be arrested for indecent exposure and that Buddy Fuller would not have his British tourists racing in Cape Town , we heard a train and, turning around, here was our overnight home coming back to pick us up. We ran towards our carriage, waved to the policeman, who still did not seem amused, and scrambled aboard the train before it could leave again without us. Only later did we find out that the train was not abandoning us at the station, it had merely shunted out to fill up with water before returning to the station. Phew, that was a close call. We eventually made it to Cape Town and promoter, Buddy Fuller was happy with the extra fans that the 'foreigners' pulled in.

Over the Christmas period, there was no speedway because Wembley closed down for the holidays. I thought it was strange because I thought that this would be the time when everyone was off work and had some spare time to come and watch speedway. But no, over Christmas, there was no bike or car racing at Wembley.

With some unexpected time on our hands, we decided to do some more sightseeing so Edith, Nigel, Benny and I headed off in our Grosvenor Motors sponsored car to drive down to Cape Town, then along the Garden Route and the coast to Port Elizabeth, through the Transkei, Durban and back to Johannesburg. Transkei was interesting because it was nominally a separate state and we had to have our passports stamped at the entry post. However, when we were leaving, there was no-one at the Border to stamp our exit visas, so technically, we are all still in Transkei. Nelson Mandela was born in Mvezo, but Transkei as a separate state is no longer on the map as in 1994 it became part of the Eastern Cape.

On our travels we visited an ostrich farm which specialized in the 'sport' of ostrich racing so this was something we had to try. Nig Close, Benny Rourke and I lined up on board these long-legged birds, the feathered kind, and off we went. There were no handlebars to hang onto, so I held on grimly to the poor ostrich's neck. As I slowly began to slide off down the bird's feathers, I nearly strangled it by trying to hang on. It survived and so did I.

We were away over Christmas and poor Benny, on his first ever trip overseas, got quite homesick for Scotland when the New Year celebrations came around. That was only natural, all Scots get nostalgic around Hogmanay and begin thinking of home and having a 'wee dram' to see in the New Year.

Later, when we got back to Johannesburg, we had yet another shock. Wembley Speedway had closed down and we were stranded in South Africa without return tickets to get home.

36. There's a Rainbow round my shoulder

As the shock of having no more speedway sunk in, we realised that the promoter still owed us the contract money for our fares and he had gone to ground to avoid us. We managed to arrange a meeting with him at his house one evening to try to sort out the finances because he would also suffer from the Speedway's closure. As we walked through his garage to reach the entrance to the house, we noticed on the walls a collection of A4 size photographs of each of us tourists which had been printed in the programme. Nothing wrong with that we thought? Well, each photograph had bullet holes in them. We had been used for target practice.

We gathered around the kitchen table to try to sort out what had gone wrong and where our money had gone. What had begun as a business-like discussion soon got quite heated. We slowly discovered that there was no money in the pot and that we would not be paid. As our voices raised and tempers began to boil over, the promoter calmly opened a drawer in the kitchen table, pulled out a revolver, laid it on the table and said "This meeting is now closed, boys."

We quietly filed back out into the street with our tails between our legs and decided to return to our Ponte City apartment to discuss our next move. On the down side, Wembley had closed and was being sold off to property developers so we had no track and no income. One glimmer of hope on the horizon was that South African Television still wanted to film the SA Championship, so that was a plus. The problem now was that we had a television contract to run the National Championship, we had the riders, but we did not have a track to run it on.

Meanwhile, we had the impression that the promoter, whom we called, 'Mack the Knife' (it should have been 'Mack the Gun'), was going to leave Johannesburg and disappear into the African night. Our plan was to stake out his house to make sure that did not happen.

Away from speedway, the promoter's business was with breakdown trucks and recovery vehicles. He had a large tow-truck with suitcases on it parked in his driveway. We set up our surveillance operation outside his house that evening and I am sure that the SAS would have been proud of us. We hid behind trees and even up in the trees just to keep watch on his front door. At the same time, we became aware of someone else hanging around watching the house as well. We found out that he was from Grosvenor Motors who had sponsored us with the Ford cars. He had heard that Wembley had closed, but we had forgotten to tell him that we were driving around the country over Christmas, so he thought he had lost his cars. Fortunately, we were able to convince him that all was well and the cars would be returned later, so he was quite relieved.

Suddenly, the tow-truck started up and headed onto the road. It was like the tapes going up in a race. We still had the two sponsored cars; everyone rushed to their allocated vehicles, jumped in and gave chase. If we got separated in traffic, someone would jump out of the leading car and wait at the corner to direct the second car in the direction of the pursuit, like a Keystone Cops film. Our target then noticed that he was being followed so speeded up, put on his yellow flashing lights and drove through red traffic lights so we lost him.

223

The riders at a Sponsors' Cocktail Party before the South African Championship.

Left: Roni Ferguson with the South African Championship Trophy. It had been borrowed from a jewellers for the event and had to be returned to them afterwards. Bert got a smaller trophy for winning the event.

The riders parade before the South African Championship.

Back at base, we decided to concentrate our energies into trying to find a way to run the South African Championship for television and raise some money there. Our next move was to form what we called 'The Syndicate' to run the event. The members were Alex Hughson, Roni Ferguson, Nigel Close, Benny Rourke and me. Doug Willoughby joined us later.

First of all, we had to find a track. Wembley, which had flourished in the heady days of South African speedway in the 1950s, was definitely finished. It was about to be demolished. We found an old neglected practice track at a place called Rainbow near Alberton in the southern suburbs of Johannesburg. It was completely run down with weeds growing through the track surface and no safety fence, but we decided that this was the only other track in the Jo'burg area so it was 'now or never' for The Syndicate so we drew up a business plan.

Our first priority was to try to get sponsorship to be able to run the meeting. Instead of one main sponsor for the championship, we decided to try to get individual sponsorship for each rider. We hired South African promotions man, Doug Willoughby, to help. Alex Hughson and Roni Ferguson put on their best suits - their only suits - to call on companies and give them our sponsorship proposals. Every morning, Doug would hit the telephone and give the big sell to prospective sponsors. He had the gift of the gab and because we had a very good

225

product to sell, the South African Speedway Championship with full television coverage, it was a very tempting offer.

Our campaign was going well. The South African companies were very publicity conscious and joined in with our television dreams. We managed to get each rider sponsored with prestigious brand names such as Wilkinson Sword (Benny Rourke), Cadbury (Arthur Bruins), Blaupunkt (Tommy Fox), Canon Cameras (Graham Long), SKF Bearings (Denis Brunton), Sealy Posturepedic Beds (Nig Close), Valvoline Oil (James Bruins), Grosvenor Motors (Boet Strydom), Fleishmans Motor Accessories (Danie Fourie) and Pantene (Brian Stephens). Peter Prinsloo was sponsored, appropriately enough, by the Rhodesian Tourist Board and I rode for our home base, Ponte City. Every sponsor received a full page advert in the programme and their rider wore a race jacket with their logo on the front, so there was plenty of television coverage for the sponsors. We also staged a press conference with television and newspaper reporters in a local hotel. All the riders lined up wearing their sponsor's body colours so there was plenty of pre-match publicity for the sponsors and for the South African Championship.

So far, so good, but Rainbow was just like a rundown field with no facilities so we set about building the pits, Nig Close made a wooden rostrum and we even went around the track on our hands and knees pulling out weeds. Perhaps we were forerunners of Ole Olsen's technology of building temporary speedway tracks.

There was no proper terracing or grandstand at Rainbow so 'Agent Willoughby' sprang into action again and rang around various companies to find some bleachers to act as a grandstand. Our smooth-talking salesman, Alex Hughson, then managed to get the company to lend the bleachers to us in return for some banner advertising on television. Job done.

The next part of the jigsaw was the trophies. We needed trophies to be presented to the top three on television at the end of the meeting and as usual, we did not have the money to buy them. Alex and Roni, again suited and booted, visited a few trophy shops in Johannesburg in the hope of some more sponsorship. At one shop, they saw a beautiful large silver trophy which would be ideal for the South African Championship. Somehow the silver-tongued duo managed to persuade the shop owner to lend us this large trophy on the basis that we would get television coverage for his company. We would return the trophy to the shop after the meeting and buy a smaller one for the winner.

The owner told them: "I don't know if I should be doing this as it is not good business practice, but I am going to trust you." We kept our word and after the Championship, the large silver trophy was back in his shop window once again.

Television coverage arranged, check, sponsors arranged, check, Grandstand arranged, check, trophies arranged check, pits area built and painted, check, riders booked, check, programmes printed check; our syndicate had done well getting everything into place for the biggest meeting of the South African season. However, there was still one big problem, we did not have a proper safety fence and could not run without one. There was no way that we could build a wooden fence around the track this size in time or financially, so thinking caps were put on once again.

It was Alex Hughson who came up with the brainwave. We would visit the local gold mines to see if they had some rolls of old rubber conveyer belt from the mine. We could fix that around the outside of the track and paint it white to be our safety fence. It was a great idea, so when the deal was done we collected the rolls of conveyer belt and began fixing it around the track. Then we hit another problem, we did not have enough conveyer belt to go around the whole circuit. With no more conveyer belt available, we decided to use the next best, and cheapest thing: corrugated cardboard. You can see that there were three Scots working on this project. Armed with some huge rolls of corrugated cardboard, we continued with building the safety fence. When it was all finished, we painted the whole fence white so the track made a good impression for television. It looked very professional.

Race day arrived and everything looked spic and span in the African sunshine. Sponsors welcomed, fans arriving, television cameras in place, bleachers grandstand erected, Grosvenor Motors sponsored cars for the parade lined up, colourful flags and banners everywhere and a beautiful white-painted safety fence; everything looked great for the cameras so what could go wrong? Well, we did have some problems during the meeting. Our tractor and water truck driver was a local African lad. We had asked him that when he was watering the track to stay well away from the corrugated cardboard fence. Unfortunately, during the meeting, he drove a little too close to the fence, the cardboard got soggy and started to wilt and sag. Some quick repairs with racer's duct tape and whitewash and we were back in action again.

The meeting went off very well, the track was rough but not too bad and I became the new South African Champion ahead of Nigel Close and Benny Rourke. I was presented with the large silver South African Championship trophy, but as we had agreed with the trophy shop, I handed it back in exchange for a smaller one. I guess I should have paid extra for the original one, but at least I still have the replica at home, and I was South African Champion.

Sponsorship and television money had paid for our costs in running the meeting and our fares back home. We had given away plenty of free tickets to swell the crowd for the television coverage, but we still charged entry for the other spectators. To ensure that there was no chance of any dispute, our wives and girlfriends were in charge of selling the tickets at the entry booths, so we had everything covered. Back at Alex Hughson's house in Alberton after the meeting, we emptied the cash boxes onto the floor to count our earnings. We felt like The Great Train Robbers counting their ill-gotten gains but our money was far from ill-gotten. We had all worked very hard to make this happen and to save our season from disaster. 'The Syndicate' had been a master class in improvisation, organisation and how to build a great speedway meeting out of nothing.

We had recouped the money owed to us by the previous promoter and hopefully put on a good show for the South African fans. However, unfortunately after we left, speedway racing in South Africa slipped back down under the radar again. At least we could say that we had 'Been there, done that and got the T-Shirt' and that we even had a 'Rainbow around our shoulders'.

Nigel Close and Bert in one of the South African Championship heats. Behind them is the cardboard safety fence which was made for the event.

Nigel Close, Bert and Benny Rourke on the rostrum for the South African Championship.

37. Knight rider

I stayed with Edinburgh for three enjoyable seasons and began thinking about what to do after 'life behind bars' (handlebars!). Edith had wanted to open a gift shop, but I had a better idea. Why not a motorcycle shop selling clothing and accessories, but not motorcycles? That way, Edith could run the business while I was away racing and we could use our knowledge and contacts in the motorcycle world to try to make it a success.

We located a small corner shop for rent. It was formerly a grocer's shop in the High Street of the Hertfordshire town of Berkhamsted, so this was the humble beginnings of our future business. The shop, which in the late 1800s had originally been a bicycle shop, was returning to two wheels again. We had to clean the place up and paint it, but when we were doing that, I crashed at Edinburgh and suffered a shoulder injury. So there was the amusing sight of Edith being at the top of a ladder painting the outside of the shop while I, with my arm in a sling, stayed on the ground holding the ladder. Fortunately, Julian and Simon Wigg's dad came along and did the sign-writing for us so that was a big help. We wanted to use my name on the shop, but as we were not selling motorcycles, we could not call it Bert Harkins Motorcycles, so we settled on Bert Harkins Racing instead. We sold gear for the road riding motorcyclist and covered motocross and speedway as well. There was no big fanfare opening, in fact our first customer was a little old lady who saw the sign Bert Harkins Racing. She thought it was a betting shop and came in to put money on a horse. I took her money then later told her that the horse had lost.

Our first products were Belstaff clothing, Bell helmets, Scott goggles and Malcolm Smith Racing Products (MSR) from California. Malcolm, along with Steve McQueen, was the star of the excellent Bruce Brown movie *On any Sunday* and had helped me when I raced in California. In the shop when we sold anything, it left a gap because we were not carrying much stock but, as the saying goes, "From little acorns..." and our supply of 'acorns' could not have been much smaller.

By the end of 1979, our off track business was growing, no thanks to me because I was always away racing somewhere, but Edith had done a very good job. I had been a full-time speedway rider for many years, but it was time for me to help out a bit more. Reluctantly, I put in a transfer request to Mike Parker.

Romantically, I had thought that I would finish my racing days in Edinburgh, where it had all started for me as a wobbling novice in the 1960s and finish it as a wobbling heat leader in the 80s, but this time my head overruled my heart. I needed to cut down on the long hours I spent travelling to home meetings. When Ron Wilson came along and wanted to sign me for his Milton Keynes Knights, a mere 30 miles or so from my home in Berkhamsted, I signed on the dotted line. I was sad to leave Scotland, but pleased to have a new challenge with the Bob Humphreys-led Buckinghamshire team. I was being 'down-graded' from a 'Monarch' to a 'Knight', but at least I didn't have to travel so far to put on my speedway suit of armour. The Groveway Stadium was neat and tidy with a café and bar along the home straight. The track was good although sometimes slick and bumpy, but our Australian skipper, Bob Humphreys, seemed to know the fastest way around it.

Above: Julian Wigg and Bert at the Wimbledon
press and practice day in 1977.
(JSC- Alf Weedon)

Left: Bert pictured during his last season with
Edinburgh.

230

The pits were at the top of a steep ramp leading to the track, very handy for starting the engine on the run down, but not so good if the rider's bike packed up and he had to push it back up that steep hill.

My season with the Knights started pretty well at Oxford in March where I picked up 11 points in the Inter-City Cup but the Cheetahs beat us 45-33. Another 9 paid 11 on my return to Edinburgh's Powderhall Stadium on my birthday of 15 April followed. I dropped a point to my former team mate George Hunter and his partner, Neil Collins. This bode well for the season, especially as I got my revenge by beating 'The Ladybank Express' when we met for the second time in heat 12. As often happens in our sport, just when you think that everything is going well, it all comes back to slap you in the face.

It was a cold night in Berwick when the Knights came to the border town. We struggled to hold onto the Bandits on their big fast track and I was soon in the wars again. Travelling flat out at the end of the fast back straight, my 4-valve Jawa seized solid and I was thrown over the handlebars and hit by the unfortunate Brett Saunders. He was close behind and I bounced down the track under a mass of bikes and spinning wheels. It brought back memories of my early debut at Costa Mesa where a similar thing had happened with American flat tracker, Don Hawley. However, this time I was travelling about 40mph faster than on the little Californian track, so the consequences were a bit harder to take. Brett was also injured in this crash which finished the night's racing for both of us. I was pretty well knocked around, although nothing seemed to be broken. My tartan-painted Bell Moto3 helmet suffered deep grooves completely from one side the other and across the front chin piece, caused, I believe, by the spinning clutch on my bike. Luckily, I was wearing a top quality full face helmet at the time so that certainly saved me from some more injuries. That damaged tartan helmet, along with some of my other Bell helmets, is now on display at the World Speedway Riders' Association National Speedway Museum.

That crash knocked me back physically and mechanically for a little while, but I soon got back in the groove and among the points again. Milton Keynes finished up as the strongest team in the league because we were near the bottom holding everyone else up.

By mid-October, with the nights drawing in and the weather getting colder, I remember one wet and very cold evening at the Groveway. As I was slowly riding down the back straight on my way to the starting gate, the track surface was glistening under the floodlights like polished ice and the cold wind chilled my fingers in my thin speedway gloves. The wintery night air brought clouds of condensation from my breath and my goggles and glasses were fogging up. 'What am I doing here?' I asked myself. I wished that I was somewhere in the sunshine of an Australian speedway season, but I soon came back to reality as the starting marshal waved us up to the tapes. The tapes flew up and the wind was even colder at speed, but at least it cleared the mist from my glasses. I could see where I was going on the slick and slippery track. I had always preferred grippy tracks, even if they were bumpy, but sometimes I struggled to get grip when the track was slick, so with winter setting in and my motorcycle accessories business growing, I decided that I had to reluctantly call it a day and hang up my tartan leathers and white boots.

I stayed in touch with Milton Keynes in the following seasons and was even the Knights team manager for a while, but I priced myself out of that job - I wanted a free programme!

But it wasn't all fun and games at Milton Keynes because, in 1982, we lost young 18 year old Australian, Brett Alderton in a track crash at Kings Lynn. I had raced with Brett's dad, Denis in Australia and young Brett had started riding motorcycles at 14 years old. When he moved onto 500cc speedway bikes, I thought that he looked quite natural with a smooth and safe style. When he came over and rode for Milton Keynes, his speedway future looked bright. Unfortunately, while guesting for Kings Lynn one evening in April, young Brett was fatally injured long before he was able to fulfil his potential. The following year, Milton Keynes also lost 23 year old Craig Featherby in a fatal track crash at Peterborough. Two young men taken from us far too soon.

38. Life after speedway

Away from the pressures of racing speedway and travelling thousands of miles each season, the BHR business was growing nicely. Because of my contract with Scott USA, we went more and more into the wholesale side supplying motorcycle shops throughout the UK and eventually closed the retail side of our business. In addition to the goggles, grips and gloves, Scott began making mountain bikes. We were the sole UK importers until Scott UK was set up to handle the bicycle and ski distribution directly so we could concentrate on the motorcycle side of the business.

We had moved to a warehouse and offices in Houghton Regis and then subsequently to larger premises in Luton. We also became the sole UK importers/distributors for other top products such as Premier Helmets from Italy, Thor Motocross gear from Sweden, Troy Lee Designs USA and Acerbis Plastics from Italy. In my racing days in California, Troy Lee was a very good motocross racer and the top helmet painter who did helmets for all the top motocross and Nascar racers. When I first knew Troy, he was working from a hangar on the local municipal airport in Corona. He made special Vacu-formed peaks for a variety of motocross crash helmets plus painting everything from motorcycle and car helmets to race cars and even police helicopters. Troy even painted a beautiful tartan helmet for me.

I used to bring boxes of Troy Lee peaks back with me in my luggage just to save freight charges, but as Troy's business grew and he added more lines of clothing and accessories, I had to start air-freighting the American products. Troy moved to larger modern office and warehouse premises in Corona and now has a huge range of products for motocross and mountain biking. He still paints helmets for, as his logo says "The world's fastest racers". In speedway, Troy sponsored Greg Hancock and Billy Hammill as TLD riders. They both rewarded him by becoming World Champions in the sport.

The Italian company, Acerbis, for whom we also became the sole UK distributors, was founded in 1973 by former off road racer, Franco Acerbis. It was set up to manufacture replacement plastic mudguards, fuel tanks, handguards and other bolt-on products for off road motorcycles. Franco originally got the idea for making replacement products for motocross bikes when he saw the Preston Petty plastic mudguards in California. His Acerbis company soon grew into manufacturing motocross, enduro and road clothing and helmets. More recently, the company has moved into Franco's other passion, football but his main passion is still motorcycle racing.

He organised and sponsored various off road motorcycle races in such exotic locations as Brazil, (International Six Days Enduro), Peru (The Incas Rally) and Nevada USA (Nevada Rally) to which, as their UK importers, we were invited along. The International Six-Days in Brazil in 2003 began along the beach in Fortaleza and into the mountains. The Acerbis hotel was right on that beach, a perfect location. James Easter from Travel Plus Tours was also among the support group because he had the unenviable job of organising travel for the British ACU riders and their backup teams to get to Brazil. However, everyone made it there with all their bikes and gear intact.

The first premises of Bert Harkins Racing.

The Nevada Rally began and ended at the fabulous Excalibur Hotel in Las Vegas. This was a huge hotel with an 'English castles' theme inside and out where Franco and 'King Arthur' cut the ribbon to start the Rally. It also had a speedway connection because former Swindon American rider, Sumner McKnight, was among almost 200 starters for the event.

The route was a tough one, this wasn't just a 'walk-in-the-park', but a full-blown desert race with check points along the way. The map of Nevada shows the large distances these riders had to cover off road. A lot of it was on the old Pony Express trails. From Las Vegas, they headed to Tonopah, Fallon, Winnemucca, Elko, Ely, Mesquite and back to finish with a couple of laps of the hotel's Knights' Jousting area in the basement of the Excalibur. This dirt track would have been ideal for an indoor speedway track. Sumner, who was riding a big 670cc Honda rode the first day and it was a tough one, didn't rehydrate properly in the hot desert sun and crashed big time in the last sandwash. He damaged his bike and himself. Several other riders did not finish the first day. That evening, Sumner's fellow Costa Mesa speedway rider, Ed Williams, rebuilt the damaged Honda in time for the following day's long stage in the heat and desert scrub. This second day was even tougher and Sumner was forced to retire because of his injuries and sheer exhaustion. The last time I saw him at the rally he was drinking a Bloody Mary and barely alive. He told me that he had to pull out of the race as he was peeing blood. Sumner was experienced in desert racing because he had ridden the Colorado 500 about 20 times, but this Nevada Rally was a real physical challenge. He retired from the race and I didn't see him again.

The Acerbis Incas Rally in Peru was another great experience. It was the first time that motorcycles had been allowed to ride close to the sacred site of Machu Picchu. It was an extremely tough rally, not just for the riders but for the support crews too. Cusco is 3,400 metres (11,200 feet) above sea level, so the air is very thin. This makes it hard to breathe so people are advised not to do anything strenuous until their bodies become acclimatized. Strenuous? It was exhausting for the riders. Even walking uphill was tiring; several of our party had to head back down to lower levers to recover. I am still amazed at how the riders coped. The hotels along the way supplied free cups of Coca Tea, (Mate de Coca) made from the leaves of the Coca plant. It helped us to breathe better in the high altitudes.

As if all that was not tough enough, the riders, working in two-man teams, had to ride to the Urubamba River, a head water to the Amazon, load their bikes onto rubber rafts then paddle downstream to the next checkpoint. The Urubamba is fast flowing and the bikes had to lie on their sides in the rubber dinghy while the riders paddled frantically and tried to keep away from the rocks. On arriving at the next stage of the Incas Rally, the riders, knee deep in the water, had to haul their bikes out of the rafts. They were then faced with a steep muddy bank to ride up to get away from the river. Having been lying flat, some of the bikes were hard to start, but when they did fire up, they found that as more and more riders tried to ride up the bank, it got wetter and muddier from the spinning rear wheels of the bikes that had just come out of the river. Eventually, riders had to form a human chain to pull one another up the hill and onto the narrow trail above.

After a hard day's riding, most competitors just wanted to grab a bite to eat and sleep, but the organisers had arranged for us to experience some Inca folk dancing and a traditional Inca meal. With long tables lined up in a large marquee, this traditional meal turned out to be called 'Cuy', the Peruvian speciality of roasted Guinea Pig with potatoes. I felt a bit sorry for that wee roasted beastie lying on my plate with its mouth still open so I moved it around and ate the potatoes instead. During the meal, riders, mostly the Italians, were quietly slipping out of the marquee at regular intervals. I thought that they must be visiting the rest rooms, but then I noticed that they did not seem to return. Eventually many of the tables were empty and I felt a bit embarrassed for our Inca hosts. In the end, we also sneaked out then someone told me what had happened. The various nationalities of riders were also finding Guinea Pig hard to take so they had slipped out and headed for an Italian restaurant just down the road. We wandered down to have a look and when I opened the door, the restaurant was jammed full of the riders and support crews from the marquee. It transpired that the owner of the Italian restaurant came from Bergamo, the same town as Franco Acerbis, so the service and food were first class.

One nice touch was when the parade of riders and support vehicles rode into a small village on the way to Machu Piccu. As we passed the local school, all the children were lined up along the side of the road to greet us. Franco Acerbis halted the convoy outside of the school and the children gave us juicy fruits to refresh us along the way. Franco also gave them presents of exercise books, pens and pencils for the school and, of course, Acerbis Incas Rally decals. He had visited that school some months earlier while doing a recce on the route for the rally and had promised the school that he would bring something back for the children. Well done, Franco.

Although Acerbis are mostly involved in Rally, Enduro and Motocross, they also sponsor young Italian speedway rider, Paco Castagna son of the legendary multi-Italian Champion, Armando Castagna who now heads the FIM Track Racing Commission, so they cover all disciplines of motorcycle sport.

Back home, our business was steadily growing and until we got some sales reps, I was mostly on the road calling on motorcycle dealers all over the country from Exeter to Inverness. My Mercedes van was stocked with the various BHR products we sold to the trade. My trips to visit the dealers in Scotland involved a week-long trip as far north as Inverness and even up to Thurso. The van would be stocked up with our best selling items to be sold from the van directly into the motorcycle dealers. What I did not have on the van we sent directly from the warehouse. I would normally leave Berkhamsted on the Sunday and drive north to Glasgow so that I could begin my calls first thing on Monday morning. It was always a busy week with lots of miles between calls, luckily my life in speedway prepared me for lots of driving. When I was in the north of Scotland, in places such as Aberdeen, I stayed with our friend Alex Wood - my former fuel and oil man in Edinburgh. I often tried to be back down in time to see some speedway at Edinburgh on a Friday night.

Although most of our business was in motocross and enduro, I still kept in touch with speedway, but I was now on the other side of the fence. Over the seasons, we sponsored various riders with Scott goggles and had a good run of World Champions including Hans Neilsen, Erik Gundersen, Per Jonsson, Jason Crump, Jan O Pedersen, Gary Havelock, Mark Loram and Simon Wigg in his early days. We sponsored the Scottish Open at Armadale in 2000 and also tried to help some of the young up-and-coming Scots such as James Grieves, Barry Campbell, Blair Scott and others. I knew from my own experience how difficult it was to break into speedway, so I thought that every little helps. I was Scotland team manager for the Scotland versus Young England series, which included a young Scott Nicholls. The Scotland team was all home-grown, but sadly those days have gone and we are struggling to find the new young Scots who could step up and wear the Saltire on the world stage. The lack of second half races has curtailed the progress of all British riders. The cost of the machinery is certainly high, but all this is relative.

Back in the late 1960s and into the 1970s, team riders had just one bike and probably a spare engine but the novices had to scrape around on whatever they could afford or buy the hand-me-down boots, leathers and bikes from the team riders. In modern speedway, even some juniors have two laydown machines, fresh tidy Kevlar suits covered in sponsors' logos, large tool chests on wheels and a new sign-written van at their disposal. The only way to progress in speedway is to race as often as possible, some tracks do offer practice facilities but speedway, like any sport, requires dedication if someone is going to progress.

Take my own situation. When I started out as a novice at Edinburgh in the mid-1960s, there were very few opportunities and it was a long, hard road to try to make the grade. It wasn't until I scrimped and saved and paid my own fare to race in Australia that I managed to make progress in my career so I owe a lot to Australian speedway.

After my retirement from speedway, I joined the Canadian television announcer and former Edinburgh presenter, Don Cummings in the commentary booth at Powderhall Stadium in Edinburgh for the televised Scotland versus England International. It was being covered live by STV, Scottish Television, so this was getting thrown in at the deep end. The stadium looked bright and clean and the red shale looked great on television. Don did the race commentary and I did the 'summing up'. The pre-meeting entertainment had parachutists jumping out of an aircraft and landing expertly on the centre green. The racing during the meeting was not too good with not much overtaking. To make matters worse, England hammered us 64–43. I guess my television debut did not go too well, so Kelvin Tatum and Nigel Pearson have nothing to worry about from me.

39. Close encounters of the speedway kind

I did eventually come out of retirement and ride speedway again. This was for Barry Briggs's Golden Greats meetings at Coventry and Edinburgh. The ever-enterprising Briggo had the brilliant idea of getting many of his old friends and rivals who had also retired back onto the track for a last farewell tour, World Champions such as Ove Fundin, Bjorn Knuttsen, Peter Collins and BB himself plus a galaxy of former stars. The fans flocked to see their old heroes back on the track one more time.

At the Edinburgh meeting at Powderhall in 1995, former Monarchs favourites Doug Templeton, George Hunter and Freddie Greenwell all rode. Briggo supplied the 2-valve Jawa bikes for all the riders so there was no choice, we just took what Tony Briggs gave us. Since the time when I had last ridden for the Monarchs at Powderhall, some 16 years earlier, the starting gate had been moved to the opposite side of the track.

Also, I had not sat on a speedway bike since finishing at Milton Keynes in 1980. I remember that in my first race I made the gate ahead of the others, round the first turn was fine but, as I charged down the back straight towards the third bend I thought 'What do I do now?' Fortunately, my previous 'turning left' experience kicked in and as the track was not too grippy for us 'Blast from the past' riders, I was able to slide into the corners and take the win. The Golden Greats may have just been thought of as a bit of fun, but when the riders got onto the bikes and pulled on their goggles, they put on their 'race face' and everyone was young again and wanted to win, especially Ove.

Between races, other former riders who were not racing in the meeting did a couple of parade laps riding Alan Hartley's immaculate chrome plated Jap, just dressed in their normal clothes and waving to the crowd. This went down very well with the fans as they were able to see former Monarchs riders such as Wayne Briggs, Jimmy Tannock and others close up and without helmets. The next day, I got a rather angry phone call from a referee who had watched the meeting and he said that Wayne and the others should not have been allowed to ride around the track on a speedway bike without a helmet and should not have worn outdoor clothes. I tried to explain to him that this was quite safe, they were only going around at walking pace and they were very experienced riders. I also tried to explain that this was for the fans' benefit and that everyone had enjoyed the meeting and voted it a great success. This kill-joy ref could not understand the promotional side of the game and signed off by saying that he did not agree with anyone riding a speedway bike without proper protection, even on a parade lap and that if it happened again, he would have to report us. I wished him good luck and goodbye because several thousand fans at Powderhall that night certainly did not agree with him.

Many a 'Close Encounter' took place at Poole when visiting riders stayed at Ken and Bridget Middleditch's "Speedway Hotel", Bailie House in Sturminster Marshall. This was in the days when young Neil and his brother, Steve would ride their bicycles down the stairs inside the big house. Bruce Cribb did the same at a party and I seem to remember him crashing into the sideboard at the bottom.

Many teams had the same experience, but usually after racing at Poole's Wimborne Road stadium, we would head back to Bailie House and reminisce as to where we went wrong against the Pirates while drinking our night-time Horlicks. The first time I stayed there with Edinburgh, I remember that we were all sitting around in the large living room chatting, the long drape curtains were not closed and I was suddenly aware of something outside the window in the dark. There was someone peering through the window and it was an old lady with a headscarf.

Ken said "Oh don't worry, that is only Ruth, a Poole supporter who likes to come along when there are riders staying", and with that, he opened the door and let Ruth in. She was pale and wearing a long grey coat and headscarf and had prominent large teeth and looked quite scary. She didn't talk but wandered around the room, eventually sitting on promoter Ian Hoskins' knee. Poor old 'Hossy' was mortified and didn't know what to do as Ruth began ruffling what hair Ian had left.

To Ian Hoskins's relief, Ruth continued around the room, passing her autograph book to each rider. Eventually, with everyone feeling like nervous wrecks, 'Ruth' took off her coat, her headscarf and her protruding joke teeth. We realised that it was Bridget Middleditch in disguise winding us all up.

Her disguise fooled everyone, and when a new, unsuspecting rider visited Bailie House, the riders who had been caught previously kept quiet and never gave away the secret. They then waited in anticipation as to how their team mate would handle 'Ruth'. 'Ruth' was speedway's best kept secret.

When Arnold Haley came down to Poole with Sheffield, he got the same treatment, but panicked and ran upstairs with Ruth chasing him and he jumped out of the window to escape. Happy days at Bailie House and R.I.P. Bridget ('Ruth'). Southern tours will never be the same again.

My life away from speedway was keeping me very busy driving all over the country to visit my motorcycle dealers but even that had its surprises. On one of my Scottish trips I was parked at the side of the main street in Tranent in Edinburgh when a pedestrian wandered past, looking at my van. He walked past the van then turned back, looked again and came up to my open driving side window. Pointing up at the side of the Mercedes which had my sign 'Bert Harkins Racing', he said, in his east coast Edinburgh accent, "Is yon the same Bert Harkins that used tae ride fur Edinburry Monarchs?" Modest as ever I said "Yes, yes, that is me" to which he replied, "Och, that's great, can ye do me a big favour?" "Of course", I said, reaching for a pen to sign my autograph for him and then he said, "Can ye lend me 50p fur a drink?" That really took me by surprise, but as I was laughing so much and rummaging in my pockets for some coins he added "Och, just make it a pound as ah huv spent a lot o' money watching you racing!" I had met up with the local drunk and he had been a fan of mine, so I guess that must have been what started him on his drinking.

Close encounters came in other ways as well. Just a few years ago, Edith and I were travelling into London by train. We were sitting in the seats with a table in the middle and the man sitting opposite did not say a word during the whole journey. Even when the train stopped for 10 minutes outside of Euston Station he remained quiet but, as the train eventually limped into Euston and we were getting off, he turned and said, "Bert Harkins, you were my favourite rider at Wembley". My 'mystery guest' turned out to be Mark Lewisohn who is the world authority on The Beatles and has written widely about The Fab Four. It transpired that, as a teenager, Mark had been a red hot Wembley fan and he even had a photo of the two of us together taken outside of the Wembley pits at the time. He was also one of the many visitors who came to see me when I was spending that three months flat on my back in Stanmore Orthopaedic Hospital.

Mark and I live a few miles apart in Berkhamsted and Edith and I have since become good friends with Mark and his wife, Anita, so, as the saying goes, "It's a small world". Another 'small world' situation occurred at a party in 2017. I met another person called, 'Mark' this time it was Mark Frey, and he produced a Wembley programme because he too had been a Wembley Lions fan back in the 1970s. The two Marks and I all live within a few miles of one another and had never met until now but unfortunately, neither of them go to speedway anymore.

There was another, even closer 'encounter' but not so much of the 'speedway kind', but something that I had handled rather badly at the time. Back in my early days at Edinburgh, I had a girlfriend and when she fell pregnant I took off to race in Australia. I wanted to concentrate on my speedway career and not be tied down with a family so we lost touch. Many years later, when I had met Edith and before we got married, I told her that there is a little girl out there somewhere, I did not know where, but she just may turn up one day.

It was not until 2010 that we met up. Before that I received an email in my office from a Karyn Jayne in Holland. This was my long-lost daughter. Between my speedway and my BHR business, I was quite easy to track down. Her mother had taken her to Holland when she was a baby. She grew up there speaking Dutch and English and still lived in Holland. At first I guess I was pretty scared of what she may have to say about me abandoning her. Edith said "You must go to Holland to meet this girl. She wants to meet you, trace her roots and get things sorted out." It was eventually agreed that we would go over to Holland to meet Karyn and Edith would come with me. We arranged to meet at a hotel in Karyn's home town

of Breda, not far from the Belgian border. I was still all set to ask for a DNA test just to make sure that she was my daughter, but when she arrived, hiding behind a huge bunch of tulips she had brought for Edith, I realised that I could no longer deny it. The poor girl had inherited my hair, my chin and even the same hands, so I was hooked. There were no recriminations about my earlier conduct so all was well. Now we are in touch constantly and with Karyn's husband Ton and daughter, Danique, we now have an extra branch of the clan as Karyn was born in Edinburgh so that makes her Scottish.

Bert and Karyn

239

Freddie Williams' granddaughter, Joanna is a top ice skater. In 2016 she was living in America where she was touring with the *Disney on Ice* show. Fred's wife Pat was also an Olympic ice skater when they met and Joanna even won the same ice skating trophy which her grandmother had won almost 50 years earlier.

Joanna has settled in America and was getting married to her American fiancée, Nick Anthony in Ann Arbor in Michigan. To my great surprise, they asked me to marry them. It was a great honour to be asked but I am not a Minister even although I went to the Church of Scotland Sunday School as a kid and I was worried that I would all be arrested in Michigan for impersonating a vicar. Fortunately, they got married earlier in secret legally, but did not tell their wedding guests so we went ahead with the ceremony. There were over 80 guests which included about eight of us from Britain. I had to speak clearly for the Americans.

The wedding was held outdoors at Misty Farm in the countryside. There were chairs on the grass beside the lake and bottles of water supplied to each guest to combat the heat. We had a Wedding Arch covered in flowers and I had a microphone, but not much shade.

The six Bridesmaids and Groomsmen and most of the guests were from Joanna's ice skating world, so the reception afterwards, which was held in the huge barns on the farm, produced lots of wonderful dancing, but not on ice skates. One dancer, with biceps the size of my thighs, got Edith to run towards him and jump. He then lifted her right over his head, John Travolta style, so that made her day, and week.

Everything went very well and the Americans even understood my Scottish accent – I think. I carried out my duties like a true minister, so watch out Reverend Michael Whawell, I may become the new World Speedway Riders' Association Chaplain.

Sponsoring events and riders was another way of keeping involved with speedway.

Left: Bert and Mark Lewisohn.
(Photo courtesy Mark Lewisohn)

Middle: Family holiday at Inverary Castle: Ton, Danique, Karyn and Bert.

Bottom right; Bert presiding at the Wedding with Joanna and Nick.

Bottom left: Harriet (Freddie Williams's granddaughter), Edith, Joanna, Bert, Nick, Jayne (Freddie's daughter and Joanna's mother).

Left: Jimmy McMillan, Jimmy Tannock and Bert at the VSRA Dinner Dance 2001.

Below: Bert receiving the WSRA Presidential Chain of Office from Ivan Mauger in 2008.

40. The World Speedway Riders' Association

In my racing days, I was aware of what was then called The Veteran Speedway Riders' Association, but it wasn't until I was invited by Freddie Williams to attend one of the VSRA Dinner Dances at the Rembrandt Hotel in London that I realised what this elite group was all about. It was quite a formal affair in those days with all the guests wearing dinner suits and bow ties. However, by being formal, that did not prevent it from being a very fun-filled evening. All around were former riders, many of whom I had only read about in the speedway history books. There were pre-war riders such as Jack Barnet, Bob Lovell and Tiger Stevenson up to the more modern riders of the day.

Founded in 1957 by journalist and broadcaster, Peter Arnold, the Association was originally called 'The Veteran Dirt Track Riders' Association'. There were still a few pioneer members who had ridden in the 1930s, but the 'Dirt Track' part of the title was soon dropped and replaced by the word 'Speedway' because the sport no longer used the Dirt Track name.

Unfortunately, Peter Arnold lost his life in a car crash on his way home from Reading Speedway so fellow journalist, Ron Hoare took over as secretary. Following on from Ron was former rider and promoter, Vic White who, for many years, steered the Association forward with the help of a small committee of former riders. Vic was the Association secretary, treasurer, editor of the Newsletter and almost a one-man-band organising the various get-togethers and the annual Dinner & Dance. During that time, it was decided to drop the name 'Veteran' as it was thought to be putting the younger riders off from joining the Association so we became the WSRA, World Speedway Riders' Association with members throughout the speedway world.

When Vic White eventually retired from the Association after many years of solid service, finding a replacement was much harder than anticipated. One or two who volunteered got cold feet when they realised just how much work was involved, but the WSRA was saved when former rider Peter Sampson stepped in to take over. Peter, who rode for teams such as Rye House, Swindon and Hackney in the 1960s, owned Paradise Wildlife Park in Broxbourne in Hertfordshire, not far from Rye House. He agreed to head the committee to run and expand the Association and his input and assistance has proved invaluable.

Peter and his family-run Wildlife Park gave us land on which to build a National Speedway Museum. There are plenty of private motorcycle collections around the country, but this was to be the only one dedicated to speedway and to be open to the public all year round. Former West Ham rider, George Barclay and Linda Christie were in charge of the fund raising for the building project and visited almost every track in the country plus Mac and Elaine MacDonald, Terry Stone and others, also helped to raise funds. By 2007, the WSRA National Speedway Museum was open to the public. With bikes from Dirt Track, Speedway, Ice Speedway, Grass track and even Cycle Speedway, the museum covers the history of the sport from when it began at High Beech in 1928 up to the present day. It is a 'must see' attraction for every speedway fan. Housed inside Paradise Wildlife Park with its lions, tigers and snow leopards, the Museum is quite secure from any unwanted attention.

Left: Bert and Ove Fundin starting out on on their trip to Spain.

Middle: Bert and Ove before the rains came.

Bottom: Bert, Ove and Split Waterman.

The WSRA steadily grew and it now incorporates not just riders, but promoters, journalists, photographers and supporters, so there is a wide range of membership options. Every year a new WSRA President is elected and I was very honoured to become President in 2008. It was humbling to be voted into that position by my fellow speedway riders. A nice touch was that I was 'piped in' by bagpiper Lee-Ann Clarkson who came down from Aberdeen for the occasion. I was even more honoured when the chain of office was put around my neck by the out-going president, Ivan Mauger. Ivan and I go back a long way both on and off the track from the early days when he came up to Edinburgh with his Newcastle Diamonds to racing with him in various countries around the world and even having Ivan and Raye at our wedding in Abbots Langley.

Many great names from speedway have been president of the Association and there were so many famous names on this chain of office that I was the only one I had never heard of.

Events, lunches and get-togethers are held all over the country from Scotland to the south culminating in "The big one" at the end of the season, the WSRA Awards Night Dinner and Dance. This is when everyone gets together and the awards, the unique WSRA Steel Shoe trophies, are presented to the well-deserved winners.

The WSRA has had some interesting guest speakers over the years, from David Hamilton to Ronnie Moore, but one that sticks in the memory was when we had former England star and World Number 2, Squire Francis 'Split' Waterman as the honoured guest.

Now Split was renowned as being a very flamboyant character with a treasure chest of stories from his early days racing motorcycles when in the Army in Italy to his halcyon days with Wembley and Harringay, not to mention his occasional brushes with the forces of the law. When the time came, the guests eagerly awaited some words of wisdom from this legendary storyteller, but were left open mouthed when Split got up and said something along the lines of "Thank you for inviting me, it's great to see so many of my old speedway friends here. Have a nice evening" and then sat down again. All the way from his home in Spain for a few words that could have been written on a seaside postcard. Split was later seen holding court at the bar and regaling everyone with his great stories. Very entertaining, but just a little bit too late.

A couple of years ago, Ove Fundin rang me. He was living in the South of France and often rode from there to his other home in Tranas in Sweden, so still spent a lot of his time on two wheels. It was because of his love of long distance motorcycling that he was phoning me: "Hi, Bert, I have had a letter from Split Waterman in Spain and he says that as he is over 90, it is time for me to get on my bike and ride down to see him", Ove explained "and now I am asking you to get onto your bike and come down to see me and we can ride to Spain together to see Split."

Ove told me that it would be an adventure, but even he didn't realise just how much of an adventure this would turn out to be. The idea appealed to me, I had ridden speedway with Ove with the Wembley Lions but also in various countries around the world including Australia, America and even Israel, but this would be the first road trip with my former team mate, but there was a small problem. Ove lives in La Londe in the South of France near St Tropez and from the UK to Ove's house is 1,000 miles, a long way to ride solo from the UK if anything went wrong, add another 2,000 mile round trip to Spain, and that is a lot of riding.

We then came up with 'Plan B'. I would load my KTM 990cc motorcycle into my Mercedes van and with my wife, Edith, we would drive down to the South of France and do some sightseeing on the way and that worked pretty well despite the cloud and rain all the way. Arriving at Ove's home we had dinner with Ove and Joanna, then were up at 6am next morning and on the road by 7am for the 1,000 mile trip to visit Squire 'Split' Waterman in Nerja, near Malaga in Spain.

We left in very cold sunshine, but after a few miles we ran into heavy rain which lasted all the way to Spain so it was on with the waterproofs and heading south. The weather worsened with grey skies, clouds and torrential rain and wind. Stopping only to fill up with petrol and to pay the fees on the French toll roads, by 6pm that evening, we had covered 600 miles in atrocious weather. We stopped overnight at a hotel in Valencia to dry out and refuel ourselves with food. I had spent the past 600 miles trying to dodge the spray from Ove's rear wheel, a real touch of déjà vu.

Next morning, on with the waterproofs again and heading south into yet more rain for the final 400 miles to see Split. We arrived in Nerja around 3pm, 1,001 miles from La Londe, checked into a hotel near to where Split lives and phoned him. Split, who still drove at 90 years old, and his wife Avril came round and picked us up. They showed us their home with speedway trophies and photos of Split in his racing days shaking hands with The Duke of Edinburgh at a Wembley World Final.

We then went on to Split's favourite restaurant and the evening passed very quickly as Ove and Split reminisced on their speedway careers. When Ove first came to England to ride for Norwich, Split was the big star in British speedway and probably the rider with the widest handlebars in the UK.

"I was just a kid from Sweden and too shy to talk to you", Fundin confessed, to which Split replied "You may have been a kid but you were hard to beat!"

"Yes", said Ove, "I hated losing and even now, my kids won't play games with me in case I lose!"

Despite living in Spain for 32 years, Split still had his London accent and had to walk with a stick, the legacy of a knee injury sustained at Bradford during his racing days with Harringay. Although he has suffered three heart attacks, plus being wounded in the battle for Monte Casino in the Second World War, Split was still very sharp. The evening passed all too quickly for me in the company of these two speedway legends and soon it was time to catch up on some well-earned sleep at the hotel.

Next morning, Split and Avril waved us off on our 1,000 mile return journey. Avril wanted to give us some sandwiches but as Ove never stops, it would have been difficult to lift my helmet visor and have a bite of sandwich while travelling at 80 to 90mph. Before reaching the motorway, we pulled across the road to fill up at a petrol station where two Spanish policemen were waiting in an unmarked car. They asked for our licences and papers for the bikes and then wrote us out a ticket for 200 Euros. It seems that we had crossed a single white line to get to the gas station, so they gave us a fine. They generously said that if we paid straight away by credit card, it would 'only' cost us 100 Euros each. I protested "But we know Split Waterman!" to which the Spanish policeman promptly doubled the fine.

The return journey was dry but cold, although our biggest problem this time were the gale force winds which blew us all over the motorways all the way "home" to France. We were leaning the bikes at a 45 degree angle just trying to stay on the road. At one stage, we had to ride at 45mph and try to shelter behind a coach. Anyway, after another overnight stop, we got back to Ove's place the following afternoon, 2002 miles in three days and atrocious weather. Not a bad adventure with Ove, but a very long way to go for dinner.

The World Speedway Riders' Association is going from strength to strength, but we need the younger riders to come and join us and keep the WSRA flag flying high in years to come. Now Speedway has reached its 90th anniversary, a far cry from the Dirt Track days at High Beech in 1928. It has had its ups and downs, but I have always enjoyed my time in the sport on both sides of the fence from schoolboy fan in Scotland to professional international speedway rider. It sure has been a roller coaster ride in my Crazy Speedway World. I will leave you with this poem which I originally saw in a Liverpool Speedway programme in Sydney, which many a racer should take to heart.

There are little eyes upon you,
And they're watching night and day,
There are little ears that quickly
Take in every word you say
There are little hands all eager
To do anything you do,
And a little boy who's dreaming
Of the day he'll be like you.
You're that little fellow's idol,
You're the wisest of the wise,
In his little mind about you
No suspicions ever rise
He believes in you devoutly,
Holds that all you say and do,
He will say and do in your way,
When he's grown up like you.
There's a wide-eyed little fellow,
Who believes you're always right,
And his ears are always open,
And he watches day and night,
You are setting an example
Every day in all you do,
For the little boy who's waiting,
To grow up to be like you.

Author unknown.

Appendix 1: Statistics and records

World Championship

1971 British / Nordic Final 3 pts
1971 British Final 4th 9 pts

International appearances

British Lions 1971–72

Sydney	Australia 60	Great Britain 48	3 pts
Brisbane	Australia 61	Great Britain 47	4 pts
Brisbane	Australia 46	Great Britain 61	7 pts
Adelaide	Australia 57	Great Britain 51	9 pts
Melbourne	Australia 44	Great Britain 64	4 pts
Perth	Australia 49	Great Britain 59	9 pts
Perth	Australia 31	Great Britain 77	17 pts
		Total	53 pts

Great Britain won the series 4–3.

Sydney	Great Britain 41	Australia 40	Sweden 26	2pts

Scotland

World Best Pairs
1970 Qualifying Round: Second with Jim McMillan (13 pts)
1970 Final: Fourth with Jim McMillan at Malmo (8 pts)

World Team Cup
1974: British Qualifying Round: 1pt

Internationals

Year	Venue	Home	Away	Points	Rides
1964	Glasgow	Scotland 50	New Zealand 57	1	4
1964	Newcastle	England 56	Scotland 52	0	2
1964	Glasgow	Scotland 47	Rest of World 61	0	1
1965	Edinburgh	Scotland 51	Russia 57	2+1	1
1966	Glasgow	Scotland 61	England 46	Reserve	DNR
1966	Edinburgh	Scotland 29	Poland 79	3+1	4
1966	Newcastle	England 74	Scotland 34	0	3
1968	Coatbridge	Great Britain 37	Sweden 71	0	2
1968	Coatbridge	Scotland 62	England 46	10	5
1969	Coatbridge	Scotland 47	Australia 61	18	6 max
1969	Glasgow	Scotland 50	England 58	7+2	6
1969	Glasgow	Scotland 62	Norway 46	16	6
1969	Coatbridge	Scotland 56	Norway 52	10+2	6
1970	Glasgow	Scotland 47	England 61	3+3	5
1970	Newcastle	England 49	Scotland 59	4	6

1971	Glasgow	Scotland 60	England 48	11	6
1972	Glasgow	Scotland 53	England 55	6+1	5
1971	Costa Mesa	USA 48	Great Britain 42	5+1	4
1971	Ascot Park	USA 43	Great Britain 47	7+2	4
1971	Costa Mesa	USA 49	Great Britain 40	4	5
1972	Halifax	England 66	Scotland 42	4+1	6
1973	Coatbridge	Scotland 57	England 51	13	6
1973	Halifax	England 68	Scotland 40	7+1	6
1975	Newcastle	England 59	Scotland 48	9	6
1979	Edinburgh	Scotland 60	England 48	8+1	6
1979	Glasgow	Scotland 60	England 48	1	4
1979	Workington	England 70	Scotland 38	1	6
1979	Middlesbrough	England 66	Scotland 42	1	6

1972 & 1973: Scotland rode as Scotland Select
1973: England rode as England Select

Clubs

Year	Team	Meet	Race	Pts	Bon	Ave	Max	Paid
1962	Edinburgh	1	2	0	0	0.00		
1963	Edinburgh	2	7	2	1	1.71		
1964	Edinburgh	9	34	29	4	3.67		
1965	Edinburgh	21	71	59	15	4.17		
1965	Cowdenbeath	5	20	35	4	7.80		
1966	Edinburgh	34	113	119	17	4.81		
1967	Edinburgh	34	110	121	25	5.31	1	
1968	Coatbridge	38	163	226	33	6.36		1
1969	Coatbridge	36	143	255	29	7.94	3	2
1970	Wembley	37	157	262	25	7.31	1	
1971	Wembley	30	130	238	31	8.28	1	3
1972	Sheffield	35	142	221	33	7.15		
1973	Wimbledon	35	137	217	21	6.95		1
1974	Wimbledon	32	122	144	34	5.84	1	1
1975	Wimbledon	18	72	103	7	6.11		
1976	Bakersfield Bandits (USA)*							
1977	Wolverhampton	2	7	6	3	5.14		
1977	Edinburgh	42	178	335	25	8.09	3	1
1978	Edinburgh	35	149	238	29	7.17	2	
1979	Edinburgh	31	116	178	17	6.72		2
1979	Wimbledon	1	4	8	0	8.00		
1980	Milton Keynes	37	153	203	21	5.86	1	

* Bakersfield Bandits won the league, but individual rider records are not available

Individual honours
1967–68: Victoria Champion
1969–70: Runner up in New South Wales Championship
1970–71: Runner-up in Victoria Championship
1977: Scottish Champion
1977–78: South African Champion

Appendix 2: Bakersfield Bandits 1976: American Speedway League results

Date	Opponents (Home fixtures in bold)	Result (Bakersfield score first)
16 April	Orange County	35–43
17 April	**Ventura**	**41-42**
22 April	Los Angeles	43–36
24 April	**San Bernadino**	**42–41**
28 April	San Bernadino	29–49
4 May	Ventura	42–36
14 May	Orange County	Bakersfield won
15 May	**Ventura**	**Bakersfield won**
20 May	Los Angeles	34–44
22 May	**San Bernadino**	**43–35**
26 May	San Bernadino	46–32
29 May	**Los Angeles**	**48–30**
1 June	Ventura	26–52
5 June	**Los Angeles**	**42–36**
11 June	Orange County	41–42
12 June	**Ventura**	**42–36**
19 June	**San Bernadino**	**47–31**
23 June	San Bernadino	44–34
26 June	**Los Angeles**	**46–32**
29 June	Ventura	40–38
3 July	**Orange County**	**52–26**
9 July	Orange County	41–37
10 July	**Ventura**	**43–35**
15 July	Los Angeles	35–43
17 July	**San Bernadino**	**53–25**
21 July	San Bernadino	48–30
24 July	**Los Angeles**	**40–38**
31 July	**Orange County**	**45–33**
6 August	Orange County	40–38
7 August	**Ventura**	**41–37**
12 August	Los Angeles	27–51
14 August	**San Bernadino**	**42–36**
21 August	**Los Angeles**	**46–32**
24 August	Ventura	35–43
28 August	**Orange County**	**47–31**
2 September	Los Angeles	38–40
7 September	Ventura	35–43

Bakersfield home meetings on 4 and 11 September were rained off. There were not enough dates left to complete the fixtures, so Bakersfield were declared the champions with the best record.

Final table:

Bakersfield	Won 26	Lost 11
Los Angeles	Won 26	Lost 13
Ventura	Won 18	Lost 20
San Bernadino	Won 13	Lost 24
Orange County	Won 10	Lost 25

The story of the famous Wembley Speedway team

When the Lions Roared

Peter Lush and John Chaplin

Foreword by Bert Harkins

Published in 2016 at £14.95, available post free in the UK from London League Publications Ltd at £14.50 via www.llpshop.co.uk
Also available from Amazon and Abe Books, or order through any bookshop.